Dalit Women's Autobiographies

Dalit Women's Autobiographies:

Convergences and Divergences

Edited by

Dr Bijender Singh

KALPAZ

First Published, 2021
Published by

Kalpaz Publications
C-30, Satyawati Nagar,
Delhi - 110052
Ph.: 011-47034999, 9811692060
www.kalpazpublications.com
E-mail: kalpaz@hotmail.com

Printed at: Gyan Press, Delhi.

Cataloging in Publication Data—DK
Courtesy: D.K. Agencies (P) Ltd. <docinfo@dkagencies.com>

Dalit women's autobiographies : convergences and divergences / edited by Dr Bijender Singh.
pages cm
Contributed articles.
ISBN 9789353246167

1. Indic literature—Dalit authors—History and criticism. 2. Indic literature—Women authors—History and criticism. 3. Women authors, Indic—Biography—History and criticism. 4. Autobiography. 5. Dalits in literature. 6. Women in literature.I. Singh, Bijender, editor.

LCC PK2907.U56D348 2021 | DDC 891.409920694 23

Contents

Introduction

The idea for this anthology was conceptualised in December 2019 when I personally felt that few other autobiographies and memoirs also have got promulgated and the previously published anthology *Dalit Women's Autobiographies: A Critical Appraisal* (2016) may seem to be a bit less copacetic and gratifying and the need of a fresh anthology of this theme was felt. The previous anthology received an overwhelming response from the readers worldwide and it is enlisted in many world-class library catalogues. As an editor, it became my responsibility to include the possible critical analysis of all the existing Dalit women's autobiographies published till date. To give equal pedestal to all the works and the feelings associated with them, a few reputed Dalit women's autobiographies written in regional languages also have been duly inducted in the present anthology. It has made the whole gamut of the anthology more engaging and appealing to its readers. Up to now, nobody has published any book on the theme of Dalit women's autobiographies to the best of my knowledge. This book, therefore, is again a scholarly attempt to bring out Dalit women's autobiographies to the forefront from a new perspective.

The word "Dalit" in Sanskrit means "the abused." James Massey writes in his book *Christian Dalits: A Historical Perspective*, "The term "dalit" has also its parallel in Hebrew with the root "dal" means low, weak, poor, helpless etc" (6). Dalits are known with several other besmirched names and they have been exploited by the upper-caste hierarchs of the society. Since the *Manusmriti* believed that unlike other upper-castes,

Shudras were born from the feet of Lord Vishnu, therefore, they were outcasted and exploited, and came to be recognised as inferior section of the society.

The situation became more critical when Dalits women were discombobulated predominantly by our patriarchal society. Male domination comes as naturally as water to the fish. The scenario worsened following the hierarchal pattern where the power to rule over the house and the females rested with the seniormost or the oldest man and later passed it to his sons. It eventually resulted in subjugation of women and man thought that it is his birthright to have dominance over women.

Being subjected to poverty and hunger along with sexual exploitation from the very beginning, Dalit women have become exponential of inferiority, insecurity and subjugation. They were circumstantially forced to eat the leftovers, were deprived of their right to cover their body with a decent cloth, and moreover, they were completely robbed of their equal existence also. Being born as a girl and that too in a Dalit family is like accepting to live life in a hell. A Dalit woman has to encounter humiliation, prejudice and the taunts of the man-dominated society because a Dalit woman is nothing more than an object to satisfy carnal desires of not only her husband, but also of the upper-class people. In the present time also, the poor Dalit women especially in rural areas remain at high risk of sexual exploitation.

In ancient time, girls were generally married in a very tender age. Their minds, bodies and souls were not yet ready for the nuptial ties. It resulted into having children also in a very young age and fetal mortality rate also became dangerously low due to malnutrition. Being bounded for domestic works and in most of the cases, they worked as labourers also and it made them socially insecured with a threat looming on their dignity and sanctity. When women were deprived of their right to get education, it toted up their woes further.

Thus, Dalit women were denied from their rights and were labelled and considered as voiceless creatures. It was literature which gave them voice and a new identity. Literature has always played a very pivotal role in evolving new ideas and ideologies in the society. In fact, it acts like a mirror, which connects both the worlds—inside and outside. History leaves a trail of events and unforgettable incidents behind and the same is picked by authors in literature with all sensitivity. A narrative is woven with the threads of such emotions and stories from the different time-periods. As individuals, we grow not only in height or stature, but intellectually and morally also with the timestamp of narratives. The power of words ignites a meaning, transforms a nation and creates actions while being completely eternal.

Amongst many other genres, Dalit autobiography has also emerged as a strong tool to leave an everlasting impact on human mind. Dalit women's autobiographies have acquired a place of recognition and acceptance. The prominent Dalit women like Urmila Pawar, Bama, P. Sivakami, Baby Kamble, Sushila Takbhoure, Muka Sarvagod, Kumud Pawde, C.K. Janu, Shilpa Raj, Sujata Gidla, Yashica Dutt and many more Dalit women writers have penned down their life narratives. Moreover, Dalit women have used autobiographies as a platform to narrate their sufferings, anguish and bitter experiences of their communities. They constantly struggled for their dignity and honour, and autobiographical narratives helped them a lot realise their dream to reach their voice to the maximum people.

The initial struggle for their rights and self-respect began with Dr Bhimrao Ambedkar, Jyotirao Phule, Jagjivan Ram, Ramaswami Naikar, Narayan Guru and Mahatma Gandhi. In Indian Freedom Movement and all other important social issues, Dalits and especially Dalit women were not given a proper recognition due to caste discrimination prevalent in Indian society. They were looked down upon incongruously and were juxtaposed with non-entity.

It was Dr Bhimrao Ambedkar who made education an inseparable part for the socio-political development of Dalit women at large with his reformative policies in the Indian Constitution. After the efforts of many social reformers, pen was used like a sword to claim justice, equality and socio-economic rights. Autobiographical form of writing helped many Dalit women to break free the shackles of inferior treatment. This came to be known as 'Stri Dalit Sahitya' in Marathi. The momentum started gaining its speed in 1960s when Dalit Marathi Literature appeared in different regional languages. Its initial representation started in the form of short poems, which gradually evolved in other form of narratives like prose, fiction and drama. These were both in autobiographical and non-autobiographical forms, but each piece of writing aimed at self-assertion of one's identity with a touch of protest against the injustice meted out to the community at large.

Dalit women have been long suppressed not only by their male counterparts at home, but also equally by the society at large. The suppression was largely found at three levels—class, caste and gender. They found the autobiographical form of expression a good tool for them. Their pain, distress and sorrow were voiced loudly in their works. There was a sudden upsurge in Dalit women's writings in 1980s. Urmila Pawar, Baby Kamble, Shantabai Kamble, P. Sivakami, Bama, and Kumud Pawde were some of the prominent writers. Some autobiographies were written by other persons such as *Viramma: The Life of an Untouchable*, *I, Phoolan Devi*, *Mother Forest*, etc. because the narrators concerned were not able to pen down themselves due to lack of education.

No matter whatever was the region, state and area, there was no difference in the intensity of plight and distress of Dalit women. They were trapped, lynched, raped, abused and insulted at both the domestic and societal front. This eventually became the key to express their experience of distress and agony. Geeta Nagabhushan's Dalit novels, Bama's *Sangati* and P. Shivakami's

The Grip of Change bear a testimony to such narratives. From religions, deities, marriages and other customs to the humiliation, insults and deplorable conditions of living, the patriarchal society was given back in the same coin through the power of the pen. Writers like Baby Kamble, Urmila Pawar, Kaushalya Baisantri, Kaveri, etc. were quite vocal about their life when the very birth of a girl-child in the house was doomed and the *chakra* for the discrimination began from there.

Urmila Pawar in her works brought forth the issues of devdasi, prostitution, wife dissertation, etc. It was a new trajectory covered through her writings. Her works bring forth the distress caused not only by the male counterparts but also by a woman on another woman. The matriarchal role of mother-in-laws in demeaning the existence of their daughter-in-laws gets represented in her works. There are women like Sujata Gidla and Yashica Dutt who belong to Dalit feminist diasporic writing.

In fact, all the Dalit feminists generally target their journey from rejection to resilience. The present anthology is a collection of twenty-six well-researched papers on the diverse themes of Indian Dalit women's autobiographies. This anthology took more than one year in its making and now it is in your hands after much setback.

The very first paper titled "Dignified Human Avatar as an Undignified One in a Caste Conscious Society: A Study of Bhaskaran's *Mother's Forest: An Unfinished Story of C.K. Janu*" of this anthology has been written by Prof. D. Amalraj. His paper deals with the predicament, subjugation, loss of landed properties and peaceful existence of the Dalit tribal communities, who are living in communion with the Mother Nature in the mountainous areas situated in the district of Wayanad of Kerala. Men, being ignorant and sensual addict, succumb without any semblance of resistance to the covetous acts of the migrant middle-class farmers. Being a woman warrior, Janu is also deceived by the government, which has followed the delayed tactics to set right the problems of the people of her community. During her fight for the rights, she is shot dead, resulting in the loss of their mother forests forever. Lack of unity among the Dalits leads her to unnatural death even before her heart's dream becomes a reality. Dignity for being a human avatar loses its value before undignified deeds of the migrant middle-class farmers. All this has been the core theme of Prof. D. Amalraj's paper.

Dr Shikha Saxena's paper "Dalit Women's Sufferings in Baby Kamble's *The Prison We Broke*" is a comprehensive analysis of Mahar community. A threadbare analysis of Baby Kamble's work has been done from different angles such as social, political and psychological. Her paper also gives us an insight for the brutal, obsolete and inhuman treatment of women in Mahar community of Maharashtra. The paper also exposes some heinous practices against Dalit women till the awakening by Baba Saheb.

Kalyani Thakur Charal, a Dalit writer from West Bengal strongly voices her opposition against the oppression of the so-called Bhadralok community who look down upon the lower castes whom they refuse to acknowledge as Dalits. In her autobiography, Kalyani traced her life from her childhood in Bagula to her life as a clerk with South Eastern Railways in Kolkata where she faced both ridicule and repression from the higher caste employees. Dr Somali Gupta's paper entitled "The Remonstrative Voice in Kalyani Thakur Charal's Autobiography *Ami Kano Charal Likhi*" explores the unique history of Bengal and why Dalit writing appeared so late in the scenario, the emergence of Chaturtha Duniya and Kalyani's association with it and the experiences that made her reclaim her caste name Charal (given up by the Namashudra community through a petition give to the British Government) in an act of defiance and protest against the upper caste atrocities.

Dr Gunjan Shushil and Dr Santosh Kumar Sonker's have written the fourth paper in this anthology. Through their joint paper entitled "Bama's *Karukku*: A New Dimension of Caste Hierarchy", the authors have examined the marginalised status of Bama in the convent. The problems of Dalit girls and women have been the main emphasis of their paper.

Dr Ashok Verma, in his paper entitled "Dalit Consciousness and Autobiography: Reading Sushila Takbhoure's *Shikanje ka Dard*," explores the concept of Dalit consciousness in an autobiography written by a Dalit woman. Drawing upon the major postulations of Dalit writings and the role of autobiography in articulating Dalit experience, he critiques the text and establishes the author's adherence to not only Dalit or feminist but the larger humanitarian tenets as well.

Dr Ruchi Raj Thakur in her sixth paper "Urmila Pawar's Voice of Dissent: An Attempt to Uphold Egalitarianism" has attempted to bring out the bitter truths of a Dalit woman. Men's dominance over women and Dalit women's problems are the main focus of her paper. She also brings to fore how Urmila Pawar's personal experience shaped her writing style and changed her outlook in life.

Dalit Literature is the outcome of growing Dalit consciousness. It is a part of the fourth world literature, which brings to light the marginal position of the so-called 'lower caste' society. Bama, a Tamil writer, could surmount the difficulties she faced as a Dalit, as a woman, and as a Tamil. She emerged as a successful writer and has made her mark in the field of literature. Her autobiography *Karukku* is the first autobiography of its kind in Tamil Dalit writing. Dr Justin James's paper titled "The Barriers She Had to Cross: The Struggle of a Dalit Woman through Hegemony as in Bama's *Karukku*" reveals the social, language-geological, and gender barriers she had to cross and it traces the ways she chose to cross these barriers of hegemony.

The main objective of Dr Meetu Bhatia Kapur's paper entitled "Journey of Reclaiming Identity in Kaushalya Baisantri's Autobiography *Dohra Abhishaap*" is to highlight the plight of the Dalits and in specific Dalit women. Dalit Writing emerges as an offshoot of Indian Literature and deals with economic and social exploitation for years. Kaushalya Baisantri's *Dohra Abhishaap* is a stepping stone towards reclaiming equality and dignity, after facing humiliation for three generations.

Dr C. Ramya's paper entitled "Women's Struggle from Marginality to Centrality: A Study of P. Sivakami's *The Grip of Change*" attempts to examine a Dalit woman's position in the society. Nobody comes to help Thangam who is exploited by the people of her community. Through the character of Gowri, Sivakami has given a message that a Dalit woman's life can be changed through education.

Dr Meenu Dudeja has written the tenth paper in this anthology. Her paper entitled "The Hierarchical Deliverance of Sanskrit and its Casteist Nuances: A Study of Marginalisation in Kumud Pawde's Autobiography *Antasphot*" makes an attempt to explore the narrow mentality and sickness of our so-called modern society towards Dalits. She tried to express the grief and sorrow of Dalits. They have to suffer a lot for their rights, identity, freedom, self-respect, justice, equality, fraternity and human existence. With a deep sense of pessimism and melancholia, Dr Meenu Dudeja has explored many such stimulating issues in her paper.

Dr Avinash Kumar's paper titled "A Sensitive Soul Writing out Its Fragmented Existence: A Study of Kaveri's Autobiography *Tukda-Tukda Jeevan*" explores the double jeopardy of being a Dalit and being a girl in Kaveri's autobiography *Tuka-Tukda Jeevan*. The work has been critically analysed from postmodern and post-feminist perspectives while demarcating the ruptures in the self of an individual who stands up against the patriarchal and caste-based discrimination within the society. Dr Avinash Kumar has attempted to explore this autobiography from a feminist perspective.

The twelfth paper entitled "The World of Dalit Women in Viramma's Autobiography *Viramma: The Life of an Untouchable*" by Dr Suruchi Sharma analyses Viramma's autobiography from a feminist perspective and it also further explores how Viramma had to face problems since her childhood both being a woman and a Dalit. Dr Suruchi attempts to explore how Dalit women are exploited in their own homes by the people of their own caste and outside by the people of the upper castes.

Dr Kusum Kanger's paper entitled "Triple Marginalisation of Women in Mukta Sarvagod's *Mitleli Kavaade: Closed Doors*" showcases the gendered marginalisation and subordination of women by the people of their own family and the upper caste people. The problems faced by Mahar women have been explored by Dr Kusum Kanger in her paper.

Guni Vat's paper entitled "A Memoir of Conflict: Reading Dichotomy in Shilpa Raj's *The Elephant Chaser's Daughter*" explores conflict in Shilpa Raj's memoir *The Elephant Chaser's Daughter*. The author's life is the dichotomy torn between her home in the village and the residential school. She was sent to Shanti Bhavan when she was merely four-year-old. Through this cleavage, she narrates her story of alienation and belongingness. Guni Vat's paper attempts to explore this conflict in author's words that guides the readers through a narrative of the first-generation Dalit who is educated in an institution vowed to break the chain of oppression. Amidst the outer and inner world, the New Dalit consciousness struggles to find her 'self'.

Anusha A. J.'s paper entitled "Modernity and Gender Negotiations: C.K. Janu's *Mother Forest* in Kerala Feminist Iconography" finds fifteenth place in this anthology and she attempts to read and analyse *Mother Forest: The Unfinished Story of C.K. Janu* (2003) as a foray into the definitions of indigenous feminist iconography. It also calls to fore its significance in the articulation of a historiography and sustained mediations with urban modernity in the larger concerns of the state.

N. Padmapriyadharshini's paper entitled "The Struggles and Empowerment of a Dalit Woman: A Study of Shilpa Raj's Memoir *The Elephant Chaser's Daughter*" is an attempt to present the struggles and discriminations faced by a young Dalit woman Shilpa Raj to gain education. Analysing her memoir *The Elephant Chaser's Daughter*, this paper picturises how a girl being born in a subaltern community was treated by the society and how she made use of the opportunity that hit her door. Overcoming the loss of her sister, mother and unmanageable poverty, Shilpa stands as the perfect example and inspiration for many women born in marginalised communities. Thus, N. Padmapriyadharshini's paper appreciates Shilpa Raj's courage and strength in bringing out her real-life incidents in the novel.

The seventeenth paper of this anthology has been penned down by Dr Vinod K. Chopra. His paper entitled *The Weave of My Life*: Urmila Pawar's Arduous and Harrowing Journey from Caste and Gender Discrimination to Resistance" has analysed how Urmila Pawar suffered caste discrimination right from her childhood days that has engraved a very serious and traumatic impact on her psyche. He analyses that *The Weave of My Life* does not merely record anecdotes from Urmila Pawar's personal life and her community, but she adopts a wider perspective of the serious issue of caste and its repercussions also.

Dalit fiction and its literary movement are based on the common ground of social oppression. Bama is one of the emerging powerful Dalit Feminist voices that articulate the oppression, violence and subjugation of Dalit women both by the men and those of upper caste. In her novel *Sangati*, Bama graphically portrays the lives of Dalits in general and women in particular not in the grey colours of misery, oppression and suffering but rather as lively and vibrant for life which urges them forward in spite of all kinds of denial and depravation. Dr Avinash Kumar's paper is a study of marginalisation, discrimination, isolation and humiliation from haves of social ethos of life especially the tragic condition of Dalit women through the eyes of Bama, a champion of Dalit writing in her community autobiography *Sangati*.

The nineteenth paper entitled "Re-reading Sujatha Gidla's *Ants among Elephants* as a Microcosm for the Indian Society," written by Devanshi Bhatnagar, tries to analyse the ill effects of untouchability as well as discrimination on the basis of class, gender and region present in the Indian society. Her paper draws attention to the politics of language present in India that further deepens the chasm between North and South India. It makes us question some of the age-old practices that we have been following blindly.

K. Sunitha Devi's has written the twentieth paper of this anthology. Her paper entitled "Dalit Women the Most Dalit among Dalits: Reinterpretation of Marathi Dalit Women's Testiminios" focuses on selected Marathi Dalit women's autobiographies which have been translated into English and a few well-known Dalit women's autobiographies which are available only in Marathi.

Dr Tamanna has written the next paper of this anthology. Her paper is based on a Dalit woman journalist Yashica Dutt who is also in hot news in media due to publication of her book *Coming Out as a Dalit: A Memoir*. In her paper, Dr Tamanna has analysed Yashica Dutt's life from her childhood to her adulthood, from a weak woman to a strong woman, and from an enervated person to an empowered one.

Dr S. R. Chaitra's paper entitled "From Rejection to Resistance: Self-Assertion in Select Dalit Women's Testimonios" concentrates on different recurring themes in select Dalit women testimonios. Dalit women's autobiographies narrate the trauma of Dalit women's existence including the socio-economic deprivation and traditional atrocities because of caste, class and gender. Such women's struggle to asstert their identity along with their desire for social and gender equality is voiced in Dr Chaitra's paper.

Dr B. Manivannan has enriched this anthology by writing his paper entitled "Cognitive Mind and Dalit Self in a Select Women's Personal Narratives." Using cognitive science, his paper analyses Dalit consciousness in Dalit women's personal narratives. The key phrases discussed in his paper are Dalit self, Dalit women personal narratives and Epistemic cognitive perspective.

Dr Aadil Amin Kak and Dr Deeba Sarmad's joint paper entitled "Convergences and Divergences of the Dalit Question in Literature: A Case Study of *The Bandit Queen of India: An Indian Woman's Amazing Journey from Peasant to International Legend*" explores the significance and impact of the complex caste stratification in Indian society at the religious, social, economic and political levels. It surveys the positionality of the Dalit and the non-Dalit, upper caste writers vis-à-vis the themes and contexts of the Dalit Question. Their paper investigates categories like class, caste, ethnicity, gender etc. as markers of social hierarchy and differentiation, and also traces how the practice of caste has strengthened over the years. The aim of their paper is to open readers' sensibilities to communicate the universality of human hopes, fears, triumphs and failures.

Father May Be an Elephant and Mother Only a Small Basket, But ...is a landmark in Telugu literature. Tracing Gogu Shyamala's childhood, Dr Suchitra Gupta has tried to bring out Shyamala's feminist approach. Despite all their labour, potential, resilience and the stoicism, women have no voice even in their homes. Dr Suchitra Gupta has tried to bring out the travails of these simple women who are thrice marginalised in her paper entitled "Celebrating Women: Gogu Shyamala Relives Her Childhood in *Father May Be an Elephant and Mother Only a Small Basket, But ....*"

Dr S. Chelliah has penned down the last paper of this anthology. In his paper Dr Chelliah has taken a less explored autobiography *Amchya Jalmachi Chittarkatha* which is less known in the academic circles because it has not been translated into English up to now. Dr S. Chelliah has explored the patriarchal as well as upper-caste pressures on a Dalit woman in his paper entitled "Pangs of Patriarchy and Casteism in Shantabai Kamble's *Amchya Jalmachi Chittarkatha: The Kaleidoscopic Story of My Life.*"

Thus, all possible Dalit women's autobiographies available in English and some important autobiographies available in regional languages also have been taken for analysis so that this anthology may become unique and complete in all aspect. Like my previous anthologies, it has been my effort to offer a critical, analytical and narrative analysis of all the existing Dalit women's autobiographies published from national and international publishers so that like previous anthology on this topic, this anthology may also reach to the maximum readers in India and abroad.

I am whole-hearted indebted to the pedantic and erudite contributors of this anthology who vested their trust in me and submitted their papers on time. Without their complete devotion and sky-high efforts, this anthology would have remained merely a dream for me. I am whole-heartedly thankful to all the research scholars and faculty members. I owe my gratitude to the members of our reviewing panel who suggested defensible and justified modifications on the papers to enhance the quality of the manuscripts. I am thankful to my family members, friends, colleagues and many other people who helped me, more or less, on any aspect of this manuscript.

Last but not least, I am thankful to Mr Amit Garg, the Managing Director, Kalpaz Publications, New Delhi for accepting the book for publication and his entire editorial and production team for publishing this book timely, dexterously and impeccably.

Dr Bijender Singh
Editor

Contributors

Prof. D. Amalraj began his teaching career in October 1969 in Kandasamy Kandar College and retired from his service on 31 May 2004. After his retirement, he has worked as the Head and Research Supervisor in Vivekananda College of Arts and Science, a self financing Women's College at Tiruchengode from June 2004 to 31 December 2011. He again worked as a Part-Time Professor in Bishop Appasamy College, a Self-Financing College at Coimbatore for one year from 2012 to 2013. He is a writer of literature oriented Study Aid Series on five plays of Shakespeare. He is the author of a reference text titled *Research Methodology for Literary Research*. His sixth and revised edition 2020 with an ISBN has been published by Omkareswar Press, NOIDA. This reference text is purely meant for the students and scholars pursuing MA, MPhil, and PhD in English Literature. It contains all the prescribed guidelines of three prescribed reference Texts such as Assignment and Thesis Writing 4th edition by Anderson and Poole, and MLA 7th and 8th editions. It is a prescribed reference text in Periyar University at Salem and PSG Arts and Science College at Coimbatore. He has published his memoir *My Life My Flight* recently.

Dr Shikha Saxena presently works as Professor and Head of the Department of Humanities in Maharaja Agrasen Institute of Technology, Delhi (Affiliated to GGSIPU, Delhi). She is having more than 20 years of teaching experience. She is a poet, a short-story writer and ELT expert. She has 27 papers to her credits in reputed national and international journals and edited anthologies. Her poems have been published in reputed international journals. She has also attended various workshops.

Dr Somali Gupta presently works as a Professor in the Department of English in VYT PG Autonomous College, Durg, Chhattisgarh. She is actively engaged in research and is the recipient of the Research Award by UGC in which she studied Youth Stress and Anxiety in the Students of Chhattisgarh with Reference to Studying English. She has delivered a number of keynote addresses both within India and outside (England, Serbia, Bosnia). She is a professional member of ISABS (Indian Society for Applied Behavioural Sciences www.isabs.org). She is the member of the editorial board in few international journals. Her publications include one book on Nirad C. Chaudhuri entitled *Confluences of Cultures* and several research papers. She is also actively involved in training and consultancy with various NGOs and other Government and non-Government organizations.

Dr Gunjan Sushil is a Professor in the Department of English at the University of Allahabad. She has supervised 20 PhD scholars. She has 27 papers to her credit in reputed national and international journals and edited anthologies. She has also attended various workshops. She has contributed numerous scholarly articles in reputed journals and has participated and presented papers in several national and international seminars and conferences.

Dr Santosh Kumar Sonker is an Assistant Professor in the Department of English and Foreign Languages, Indira Gandhi National Tribal University, Amarkantak (Madhya Pradesh). He completed his PhD on "The Plays of Mahesh Dattani: A Study of Theme and Technique" from University of Allahabad, Prayagraj, Uttar Pradesh. He has edited two books *Dalit Assertion and Its Space in Literature*, and *Situating Tribals of India: Language, Culture and Self*. He has translated a collection of poems by Mahadev Toppo with title "Lessons from Forest and Mountain." His area of interest lies in Drama, Theatre, Dalit Literature, Tribal Literature, Translation and Indian Literature. He has published 16 papers and attended 25 Seminars and

Conferences. He has been member of editorial board of three journals. He has staged, directed and written plays in Hindi. At present he is translating *Suardaan*, a novel by Roopnarayn Sonker.

Dr Ashok Verma is an Associate Professor in the Department of English, Bhagat Phool Singh Mahila Vishwavidyalaya, Khanpur Kalan (Haryana). His areas of interest include Translation Studies and Marginal Writings. He has published sixteen research papers and presented papers in more than twenty seminars/conferences including one in Germany and another in Norway.

Dr Ruchi Raj Thakur presently works as an Assistant Professor of English at Himachal Pradesh National Law University, Shimla since October 2016. She has a teaching experience of nine years. Her PhD from Himachal Pradesh University is on "History, Culture and Social Commitment in Yashpal's Selected Works". Diaspora, Expatriate Writings and social issues pertaining to the underprivileged, disregarded and oppressed sections of society have been her area of research. She has published many research papers in national online and offline journals. She has also presented papers in several national and international seminars/conferences organised in India. She has worked as Assistant Professor in the School of Basic Sciences and Language, Department of Communications Skills at Bahra University where she taught at both undergraduate and postgraduate level for five years. She has also worked as the Counsellor at IGNOU for FEG and MEG programmes offered by from September 2010 to June 2012.

Dr Justin James (MA, MPhil, Cert. ICT, TESOL, PhD) is currently teaching at the University of Technology and Applied Sciences, Sultanate of Oman. He is an experienced English Language and Literature Teacher, ELT Consultant and a skilled EFL, ESL & ICT Teacher Trainer with a demonstrated history of working in the Education and Education Management

Industries. He is proficient in English as a Second Language, Teaching English as a Foreign Language, Classroom Management, Lecturing, and Lesson Planning. He is an international resource person for many accredited colleges and universities in India. He has many international publications to his credit. He is an efficient education professional with a Commission from Officers Training Academy, Kamptee, Ministry of Defence, Government of India.

Dr Meetu Bhatia Kapur presently works as an Assistant Professor of English in Vivekananda Institute of Professional Studies affiliated to IP University, New Delhi. She has completed her Doctorate from Rajasthan University, Jaipur, Rajasthan on the novels of Amitav Ghosh. With a teaching experience of more than 20 years, she has many national and international presentations and publications to her credit along with translation of Jain Scriptures. Her areas of interest are Women's Writings and Contemporary Indian English Writings.

Dr C. Ramya (MBA, MA, MPhil, PhD) presently works as an Assistant Professor of English in E.M.G. Yadava Women's College, Madurai, Tamil Nadu, India. She has completed her master's degree in English, master's degree in Business Administration, Master of Philosophy and doctorate degree in English. She has five years of teaching experience. She has authored four books and has published more than 95 research papers in peer-reviewed international journals and several edited anthologies. Her areas of interest are Psychoanalysis, Spiritual Studies, Dalit Literature and Comparative Literature.

Dr Meenu Dudeja is working as an Assistant Professor in Maharaja Agrasen Institute of Technology, New Delhi. She is having more than 17 years of teaching experience. She is having more than 12 papers to her credit in reputed national and international journals. She has attended various workshops. She has authored three books entitled *Communication Skills for Professionals*, *Communication Skill Part 2* and *Lab Manual for*

Professionals. Her areas of interest are American Literature, Indian Writing in English, Gender Studies and Communication Skills.

Dr Avinash Kumar is Assistant Professor and Head, Department of English, DAV Post Graduate College, Siwan, a constituent unit of Jai Prakash University, Chapra, Bihar. He teaches Literary Theory, New Literatures, Indian Aesthetics and Canonical British Literature to students at under-graduate and post-graduate levels. He completed his PhD from JNU, New Delhi in 2014. The topic of his PhD thesis was "Bridging Dichotomies: A Study of Iris Murdoch's Literary Oeuvre." He has taught in colleges in Delhi University before joining JP University, Chapra. He has also offered optional courses on African Literature, American Literature, Australian Literature, etc to undergraduate students of JNU doing courses in foreign languages. Dr Avinash Kumar has got many publications in refereed journals. He was a member of the editorial team of Prof. Kapil Kapoor in *Encyclopedia of Hinduism* published in 11 volumes by Rupa Publications as well as *Encylopedia of Indian Poetics* being published by Sahitya Akademi, New Delhi.

Dr Suruchi Sharma (MA, PhD, UGC-NET) is an Assistant Professor in RKSD College, Kaithal, Haryana. She has done her PG from KMV Autonomous College, Jalandhar, Punjab. She has been awarded PhD in English on Khaled Hosseini. Her areas of interest are Diaspora Studies, Critical Theories and Cultural Studies. She has presented her papers in many national and international seminars and conferences. Her papers have been published in many national and international journals and seminar/conference proceedings and several edited anthologies.

Dr Kusum Kanger (MA, MPhil, PhD) is an Assistant Professor in BAR Janta College, Kaul, Kaithal, Haryana. She has earned her MPhil from Kurukshetra University, Kurukshetra. She has been awarded her doctoral degree on Angela Carter and Bapsi Sidhwa from NIMS University, Jaipur. She has presented and published her papers in many national and international seminars and conferences. She has published her papers in many national and international journals and edited anthologies.

K. Sunitha Devi (MA, MPhil) is an Assistant Professor in the Department of English in Govt. Degree College, Sindhanur, Karnataka. She is doing her PhD on the topic "Shakespeare: Theme and Technique". Her areas of interest include Shakespeare Studies, Dalit Literature, Kannada Literature, and Indian Writing in English.

Guni Vats is a PhD Scholar in the Department of English at the University of Lucknow, Lucknow. She has completed her Master's degree in English Literature from Central University of Rajasthan and she has earned the Bachelor's degree (Honours in English Literature) from the University of Delhi. She is a keen reader, budding researcher and an enthusiastic writer who takes immense pleasure in looking at diverse aspects of life from a psychoanalytical bent. She loves to experiment with themes, subject and writing styles. She is keen to research on the Indian women writers and carves a niche for them in the predominantly masculine world. She is currently attempting a thesis tracing the feminist waves in Indian literature and analyzing them through translations. She has many publications in reputed journals and literary anthologies to her credit. She is also a poet-in-making.

Anusha A.J. is a PhD Research Scholar in English, University of Kerala. She has eighteen research papers, five articles and two book chapters to her credit. She was a Guest Faculty at Women's College and All Saints' College, Trivandrum. She is a University Rank holder in MA English Language and Literature from the University of Kerala. Her areas of interest include Digital Humanities, Marginality, Cultural Studies, British Drama, Film Studies, etc.

N. Padmapriyadhshini (MA, MPhil) is pursuing her PhD from Department of English, Madurai Kamaraj University, Madurai. Her research work focuses on complexities in human relationships and identity crisis. She has attended four international conferences and presented four papers out of which three are published. She has published one article in an international journal of peer review with impact factor. She participated in two workshops—one on the social evils in literatures and another regarding the usage of online materials for research.

Devanshi Bhatnagar is presently pursuing her PhD in English from the University of Lucknow. She has done MA in English from Isabella Thoburn College, Lucknow. She qualified UGC-NET for JRF in June, 2014. The title of her PhD thesis is "Language, History and the Politics of Identity in Gayatri Chakravorty Spivak's Literary Theory". Her areas of interest are Cultural Studies, Contemporary Literary Theories, Poetry, Asian Literature, Indian Writing in English, Gender Studies and Dalit Literature.

Dr Vinod K. Chopra earned his PhD from Himachal Pradesh University, Shimla in 2002 on the topic "Community, Communalism and Gender: A Study of Short Stories on Partition". He is an honorary faculty member at Career Point University, Kota, Rajasthan. He has guided thirteen MPhil scholars and at present he is supervising four PhD scholars. He has published a book *Partition Stories: Mapping Community, Communalism and Gender* in 2009 and he has translated a monograph *Saga of a Revolutionary Hero: Pt Inderpal, a Freedom Fighter* into English. He has published ten research papers in national and international literary journals and five papers in different anthologies. He has also presented eight research papers on literature and education in national and international seminars. He is a permanent member of Indian Association for the Study of Australia (IASA), The English Language

Teachers' Association of India (ELTAI) and English Teachers' Forum (ETF).

Dr Avinash Kumar [MA (Gold Medalist), PhD) is PhD holder from Patna University who has a penchant for Afro-American Literature and Indo-English Poetry. He has a wonderful command of Feminist Discourse and Dalit Literature. He has contributed immensely to esteemed journals and edited books from reputed publication houses. He evinces keen interest in publication of insightful research articles on Post-colonial and Feminist Literature in journals of home and abroad and edited anthologies. His books on Literary Theory and Literary Terms are under print.

Dr Tamanna [MSc (Mathematics), MA, MPhil, PhD (English)] is serving as an Assistant Professor in the Department of English at Mahila Mahavidyalaya, Jhojhu Kalan affiliated to Chaudhary Bansi Lal University, Bhiwani. She has attended quite a few seminar and international conferences. She has already published many articles on R.K. Narayan and Mulk Raj Anand in reputed journals. In addition to Narayan and Anand, her area of interest is chiefly related to Indian writing in English, post-colonial studies and diasporic literature.

Dr S.R. Chaitra works as an Assistant Professor in English in Maharaja's College which is a constituent college of University of Mysore, Mysuru, Karnataka. Her areas of interest are Stylistics, Indian Feminism, Marginal Literature, Black Feminism, Dalit Feminism, Diasporic Literature and Post-colonial Literature. She has presented papers at various national/ international seminars and conferences. Her research papers have been published in different national and international journals.

Dr B. Manivannan (MA, MPhil, BEd, PhD) has been retired as an Associate Professor from the Department of English in VO Chidambaram College, Thoothukudi. He is a Tamil poet, author, translator, soft-skill trainer and environmentalist.

He has edited a book titled *Studies in Indian English Poetry: From Aurobindo to Laksmi Kanna.* He has published his articles in many national and international journals and edited anthologies. He is one of the Preliminary Panel Advisers, Award Committee, Sahitya Akademi, Govt. of India. He has been the Chairman, PG English Examination Board, MS University, Tirunelveli, University nominee, PG Board of Studies, Sadakatullah Appa College, Tirunelveli, Member, PG Board of Studies, MS University, Tirunelveli, Member of Editorial Board in *Outreach: Multidisciplinary Research Journal.* His poems and short stories have been published in Tamil magazines. He has received Loyola Literary Media Award (2014) and Kavi Venthar Award (2015) for being the best poet among more than 300 poets in Tamil Nadu in 2014, conferred by Anantha Jothy Literary Circle and Meera Publishers.

Dr Deeba Sarmad is an Associate Professor of English, and has taught for over 20 years both at the UG and PG levels. She specializes in Diaspora Studies and under the general rubric of diaspora, she engages with the themes of migration, minorities, displacement, homelessness, exilic perspectives and identity questions. Her present position as Dean, Humanities and Liberal Arts, Cluster University, Srinagar, involves developing academic programmes and performing other administrative functions. She also supervises various aspects of the faculty and student body and participates in university long-term planning and policy setting.

Dr Aadil Amin Kak is a Professor of Linguistics at the Department of Linguistics in the University of Kashmir. His areas of specialisation include Language and Society, Language Teaching, Language Maintenance and Shift, Phonology, Language Documentation and Translation. He has a number of publications and books to his credit, and has presented papers in a number of national and international conferences and seminars. His current focus is on the use of language in technology and the impact of languages on one another in a multilingual context.

Dr Suchitra Gupta is a Professor of English at Govt. VYT PG Autonomous College, Durg (Chhattisgarh). She has 35 years of teaching experience. Her area of specialisation is Indian Writing in English. Her areas of interest are Classical Criticism, Indian Writing in English and Colonial and Postcolonial Literature.

Dr S. Chelliah is the Dean of Arts, Humanities & Languages, and Professor, Head, and Chairperson of School of English and Foreign Languages, and Special Officer for Planning & Development at Madurai Kamaraj University, Madurai (Tamil Nadu). He did his MA in English Literature from Madurai Kamaraj University, Madurai and got his PhD degree in English from the same university. He has produced 19 PhD scholars, more than 209 MPhil scholars and 196 MA projects. He has published 11 books and 317 papers in various national and international journals and edited anthologies. He has served as the Dean for Curriculum Development of Madurai Kamaraj University, Director for Board of Studies Section, Director for Spoken English Institute of Madurai Kamaraj University, Co-ordinator for CBCS Wing, Liaison Officer for SC/ST Cell of Madurai Kamaraj University and Member of Board of Studies of both UG/PG of Pondicherry University, Manonmaniam Sundaranar University, Bharathidhasan University, Trichy, Bharathiar University, Coimbatore and Gandhigrahm University and an Examiner of various colleges and universities at both PG and MPhil levels and also Co-ordinator for UGC remedial coaching scheme for SC/ST/OBC and minority categories. He has been awarded the Best Research Publisher Award (Highest Profile) and DLitt for excellent contribution in English Literature and Language by International Economics University (SAARC Countries).

1

Dignified Human Avatar as an Undignified One in a Caste Conscious Society: A Study of Bhaskaran's *Mother's Forest: An Unfinished Story of C.K. Janu*

Prof. D. Amalraj

Men and women have been created only by one God and not by too many Gods having joined together for the act of creation. Yet "It is this one God, [the creator], whom no [human] eye has seen, about whom no [human] ear has heard and of whom no [human] mind has conceived" (*Family Devotional Study Bible,* 1 Cor. 2.9). Christians have identified their creator in God, the Father of Jesus Christ. The Muslims always believe in their Allah as the creator of human beings. The Hindus have recognised their creator in Brahma. The Christians and the Muslims except the Hindus worship their respective one and the same God. But the Hindus, besides their Brahma, worship innumerable number of Gods and Goddesses. However, the people of all religions know that as men and women, they are only God's creations. This belief is still being common among all the sensible and religious human beings. As per God's will, the first man and woman became the creators of their own posterity and from their respective posterity all other descendents have come and occupied this earth. Besides, the creation of future human beings by the living posterity will continue and it will go on unchecked till the last day of the extinction of all the living things on earth. Every such thing does happen only with the blessings of unseen God.

As God's creations, all human beings are the most dignified ones, irrespective of the differences in castes and religions. Differences in caste are more dominant among human beings and it can be seen among the groups such as higher class, higher-middle class, middle class, lower class and the Dalits. The creation of human beings as men and women is by God alone but the creation of caste disparity among the human beings is mainly because of the attitudes of the human beings. All those who are caste-wise higher only think of themselves as Godlike on earth, and they also feel that they are beyond the reach of the people born in lower and isolated classes. In doing so, they belittle the dignity of the human avatar in other caste. Just like the assassination of Julius Caesar lay in the hands of Brutus, Caesar's friend, dividing the human beings into upper class, upper-middle class, middle class, and discriminated class such as the Dalits lies in the dirtiest mind of the human beings. All types of castes other than the Dalits join together and mindlessly discriminate and oppress the fellow beings just because they are born as the Dalits. They also make all out efforts to keep themselves placed in dignified posts in all fields of human endeavour. Moreover, they never fail to display discriminatory attitudes and behaviour as and when they meet the socially inferior Dalits.

All deadly and infectious viruses like Corona will have certainly their own end one day or other, but the disparity of one group by other groups will last till the last day of the existence of the earth. The deadly viruses do not differentiate one social group from other social group when it spreads among human beings. Neither do they spare a group among human beings from the infection just because such a group belongs to superior social status. They infect all without minding the differences in their social statuses. Only when all human beings feel that they are only the children of one and the same God, the life on earth will be heavenly. Such a world cannot be a reality nor can such a world take any shape even in human imagination. All religious groups think that each group has been created only by its respective God and not by one and the same God. The world of the reality is the one where all higher social groups discriminate, suppress, and isolate the entire Dalit group on various grounds. If a higher caste is a dominant in one area, the Dalits are to be always at the mercy of it for their peaceful coexistence. If one religion is dominant in one particular state or nation, other religious groups are to meet with all types of disparity and humiliation at the hands of those people of the dominant religious group. However, among all types of discrimination, only the caste discrimination, in particular about Dalit group, is the bane of Indian society.

The present study has been pursued to highlight the humiliation of the Dalits. This is not the group, which is isolated and discriminated, while living along with the higher caste groups in one and the same city or village. This is the group, which is known as Dalit tribal communities and these people have their own lands and houses in the mountainous areas and who have been living independently from time immemorial. Though these tribal communities are far from the civilised areas, yet they cannot also escape from humiliation and discrimination as and when the middle class migrants invade their areas and covet the fertile lands belonging to the tribal communities. As usurpers, the middle-class migrants take possession of the lands and houses of the Dalit tribal communities as if they were their own, and then drive them to the waste lands so that they can mend for themselves. To drive home this truth that the lowest social class usually known as Dalits, wherever they are living, whether they are in the civilised areas or in the hilly regions far from the civilised towns, are meant only for being discriminated, oppressed, suppressed, and deprived of their own avenues of livelihood. The writer of this article has taken the autobiography of C.K. Janu, the member of the Dalit tribal community, written in Malayalam by Baskaran and translated in English by N. Ravi Shankar with the title *Mother's Forest: An Unfinished Story of C. K. Janu*. It is about the real life events, which Janu, a Dalit woman, has experienced. Janu has fought for her people living in the hilly regions quite far away from the other castes who are living in the towns at the foot of the mountains. It conveys a bitter truth that the Dalits are unfit to live in this world along with the higher caste people. This type of attitude in the minds of the higher caste people is an incurable disease.

Most of the states of India have hilly areas far from the dwelling places of the human beings. Even in some hilly areas, tribal communities have their own houses and fertile and dry lands, and they eke out their living by cultivating their fertile lands without being a nuisance to the city dwellers. They have had their habitation for as long as if anyone can remember. There is one such hilly area in the state of Kerala and it is in the district of Wayanad. The Dalit tribal communities have their own lands, which are very fertile and such lands cater to all their needs for thriving without much ado and without depending on the people of the towns at the foot of their hills. They consider their entire mountainous fields as the mother's forest as they have been living there for many generations. Since all such places are very fertile round the years, the middle class farmers from the mainstream civilised Kerala towns situated at the foot of the mountain have driven these voiceless tribal communities away from their homes and fertile and vacant lands towards the wastelands. As they are illiterate and socially inferior, they do not have any courage to resist from being driven away from their mother's forest. They have no individuality of their own and so they are not able to establish their rights over the lands in the mountainous areas against occupations of the migrants. They simply reconcile themselves to their fate for being born as Adivasi Dalits.

C. K. Janu is an Adivasi Dalit woman from the wastelands in the mountainous areas of Wayanad district. Her family is living with all other fifty three families in the hills. She is illiterate but she is practically wiser than all her people. Besides being a Dalit, she is a social activist and she lives only to protect her community from having been discriminated and exploited by others belonging to the middle-class migrant farmers. Her main aim for the people of her community is to ensure their rights to live in dignity with their own lands in the mountain areas as their mother's forest. She is of the strong belief that the God who has created middle and middle-higher class farmers has also created them without any disparity as His children. But the people of the middle and higher middle-class farmers of the plains treat them as if Adivasi Dalits were not their equal. Moreover, the Dalit Adivasis have no right to coexist with the migrant middle-class farmers. Their act of claiming the rights to the lands of the Dalits is like a thief claiming his rights over his stolen things. Janu knows well that just like the people of middle and higher middle-class having lands of their own in the plains, her Dalit people have their own places and lands in the mountainous areas. Her people follow their own cultural habits quite different from those of the people in the plains. They have their own Gods to worship and own rituals to practice. As a fighter for the sake of her own people, she has to face physical tortures from the civilised society and the police. She has brought to light her first hand experiences of the unbearable hardship of her entire neglected and belittled community including her sufferings in this translated autobiography.

The loss of cultivable lands to the migrants leads to fragmenting the lands and the total absence of any kind of cultivation. The migrant middle-class farmers who have usurped the fertile lands of the Dalits do not keep quiet. As and when the Dalit men convert their wastelands into cultivable one, the migrant farmers make all out efforts to get even such lands transferred to them by tempting the Dalits with the offer of alcohol. Becoming addict, the Dalit men cannot but succumb to the temptation and thereby they get exploited. Janu looks helpless at the vulnerability of her men to such kinds of exploitation. She thinks of the weak-mindedness of her men. Instead of standing with her fight as a kind of moral support, they let her down when she needs them most. She simply thinks of the inherent frailty of her men and their exploitation:

> There are still some of her men who own their lands. Besides, there also Dalit men who have cleared the woods, burnt the undergrowth, [converted the land into a cultivable one] sowed thina, the jenmi and the migrants [have appeared] before such men. They befriend our men, give them arrack or a small sum of money and transfer the land in their names. (31-32)

The rightful Dalits have to depend on the usurper of their lands for their livelihood since they have nothing to fall back now. The Dalit women become the labourers in their own usurped lands and as such they become literally the slaves of the migrant middle-class farmers. As and when the Dalit women begin working in the fields like the bonded labourers, they have to bend down their heads and do their works silently. But on seeing a migrant man standing and watching them with his eyes rooted at their back, they look always frightened of him and his presence. While they are working, his presence creates some kind of unknown fears in their hearts. Janu has highlighted this fear of her women in the following words:

> When our people [are working] in their own [grabbed] fields, there [is] a man dressed in a sleeveless shirt standing on the ridge, supervising our work. We [are] quite frightened of him. In those days we were afraid of almost everything. The backs of our people seem to be so bent because they have been terrified of so many [imagined] things for generations. When our people speak [to him] they don't raise their eyes and that must be because they are so scared. (13)

Moreover, the cultivable lands become converted into vacant sites for carrying out other works other than agriculture. It results in reducing the Dalits to the state of pennilessness. Even with whatever money they have, they are forced to spend it to buy things in the shops at the foot of the hills. Those who do not have sufficient money at hand open their accounts in the shops and settle it periodically as and when they have money. This kind of living after losing everything has made them indebted to the shop owners who are selling essential commodities. As the days and nights pass, their needs rise up and so they are in need of more money to make both ends meet. When the entire hilly region has been their mother's forests, they have never visited any doctor for any ailment. The forests themselves have acted as the provider of natural medicines to them. They do not also belong to any religious group but they have to change themselves according to the life seen in the Hindu society at the bottom of their mother's forests. Yet they are not treated on far with other people of the society. Their human avatar is belittled to a greater extent by all and sundry belonging to the migrant farmers from the plain.

Mother's forests have lost their grip when the children of the Adivasi Dalits have started pursuing education for their advancement in the schools in the plains. Those who have had no work in the mother's forests have resorted to using sensual drugs and remain inactive and intoxicated. Even women have given themselves to be sexually enjoyed by men as and when these men have offered tobacco or food or some kind of stones these women are after. This kind of immoral activity on the part of Dalit women has resulted in their violation of their cultural habits and in their earning bad name. The migrant middle-class farmers always keep the Dalits poor, starved, and helpless. Only when these migrants like the Dalits become homeless and landless, and stand at the mercy of the higher castes, they will realise the bitterness of the life of discrimination. The Dalits are not at all considered as human beings and their movement to different places is decided with restrictions. Their burial places have been separated with fences. Thus, Janu's entire Dalit community has experienced poverty, starvation, and powerlessness. They become feelingless mute beings. The places, which they have occupied in the hilly regions, have gradually become unlivable ones and yet they have their own huts built for their living in the wastelands with the help of women under Janu's leadership. However, some middle-class migrants have made all out efforts with the help of the police to drive them away even from their present places but they have resisted attempts strongly under Janu's leadership.

The politicians for the sake of getting votes from their middle-class migrants have even gone to the court against the occupation of the lands in the hills by the Dalits. Even before the court takes their cases, these politicians have adopted various inhuman methods such as denying water and electricity supply to them. They have even stopped issuing ration cards. If issued, they fear that these ration cards with the residential addresses of the Dalits in the hills will ensure them that this is only their own mother's forest and none can deny it. All politicians and middle class immigrants have looked not only indecent but also their deeds against the voiceless Dalits are devilish. Adding fuel to the fire, the politicians and the illegal migrants have started defacing the walls of their houses of the Dalits with the pictures of different gods, actors and actresses. There has been no decency and decorum in the behaviour of the illegal occupants of the mother's forest of the Dalits. The pastness of the happy gathering of the Dalits in front of their houses, and of spending their time by narrating stories of great interest among themselves, of enjoying cool and fragrant breeze and sun shine, and of hearing the lullaby of the smooth flowing streams have become the past now. Besides, they have also become quarrelsome over petty things among themselves at present. Moreover, disharmony among them reigns supreme because of their addiction to sensual drugs. The innocent and peaceful life in their mother's forest has gone into oblivion.

However, Janu has to digest all these unavoidable happenings in the life of her Dalit people, knowing full well that she cannot alone bring unity among her people. She becomes a teacher and instructs her women how they should live in unity so that they can establish their individual identity and independence and claim their rights over their usurped lands through legal fight. She has also become a member in the Communist party to stabilise her place as someone important in her Dalit community and to give them hope of getting back what they have lost. When she has come to know that the communists are also not real as they appear, she has started a separate group for the welfare of the natives of the mother's forests. She is not all alone in her fight against the oppressors and usurpers of their rightful lands. She has Lakshimi Devi and Valli as her close companions wherever she goes and whatever she does. Both are a great help to her in time of need. Janu confesses to her close relationship with them. She also gets boost to her spirit to fight against any kind of discrimination of her people.

Janu has staged dharnas along with her tribal people to get back what they have lost to the illegal migrant farmers. She has not stopped with fighting through agitations only for her tribal community. Her fight has been for all the tribal communities spread over entire Kerala. She has experienced physical torture at the hands of the police for having led an agitation and undergone imprisonment. Yet, she has not lost her spirit of fighting for the sake of her tribal people. For her yeoman service to her tribal people, she has been honoured and recognised as the greatest tribal leader all over the world. But before her dream of achieving the lands for all the landless tribal people of Kerala, she has lost her life by being shot dead at the hands of an assassin. Though her work has remained unfinished, her name has been inscribed indelibly in the heart of every tribal of Kerala. The government too has flattered her to deceive by siding with the other superior classes. Prof. P. Malathy in her article "Tribal Education: A Case Study with Reference to C. K. Janu of Wayanad" has exposed the bitter reality behind the seemingly good nature of the Kerala government.

> The tribal people, the original inhabitants, indigenous people are always subjugated by the illegal encroachers. Having lost their land to outsiders, the tribal communities worked for meager wages. Their population, which exceeds 40 million, looks forward to the solution from the government. Both their isolation and minority status prevent them from moving with the mainstream society, which has majority higher and middle higher class. Though the government takes steps to mingle the minority groups into the mainstream society, it is doubtful whether these tribal people will enter the mainstream society with their social and cultural beliefs intact. (28)

All human beings belonging to different castes and following different faiths are neither completely good nor completely bad. The good outnumber the bad in every community but many have the tendency to exaggerate the reality by talking and writing about only bad exceptions. There are good and bad officers but people always talk about the bad as if there were no good among them. There are teachers both exemplary and ordinary but the students find fault only with the teachers who work for the sake. There are both sincere and time passing students in the class but the teachers always blame the students who attend the classes for the sake. There are more people belonging to all social classes who consider the highly educated and professionally well placed Dalit men and women as their equal and respectful one. Whatever might be the social status of one, one can establish one's individuality by being exemplary from all others. Just like the character being destiny, it is the behaviour of the people outside that may invite respect or hatred whatever might be his social status. Something good is to happen in the lifestyle of the Dalits so that they can establish their respectful personalities in the society.

Works Cited

"I Corinthians -1:9." New Testament. *The Family Devotional Study Bible,* The Bible Society of India, 2002.

Malathy, P. "Tribal Education: A Case Study with Reference to C. K. Janu of Wayanad." *Journal of Humanities and Social Science*, n.d., pp. 28-30.

Shanker, N. Ravi, translator. *Mother Forest: The Unfinished Story of C. K. Janu,* by C. K. Baskaran, Kali for Women, 2004.

2

Dalit Women's Sufferings in Baby Kamble's *The Prison We Broke*

Dr Shikha Saxena

Dalit movement in Indo-political history is quite significant as it has its roots from Indian social scenario. The caste divide in India was originally based on the deliberate selection of 'Karma or duty' that an individual or a family may adopt as a profession or duty to the society. But this *Varna-Vyavastha* emerged as the lifelong curse for certain sections of the society particularly for Dalit community. Dalits were treated as untouchable and could not keep pace with the progress of society. Women were the worst affected sections of the society and family. Due to lack of education, crippled social and family structures, they were compelled to live a life of morbid absurdities. They could not even raise their voice against their mental, emotional, physical and financial servitude.

Baby Kamble's *The Prison We Broke* is a heart-cry of a woman from Mahar society who accounted the incessant ordeal of a woman in the family, society and even at the mainstream of nation which extends equal rights to all genders and all citizens of India. Kamble's autobiography is a valid account of an oppressed, socially marginalised, so-called low-caste woman who is subjected to incessant exploitation at all stages of her life and our crippled social structures legitimize it. Social taboos for a girl-child education muffle her voice forever.

The Prison We Broke is a pioneer move in accounting the histories of Dalit women's status in India and Baby Kamble registered her agony and suffering in the form of the current autobiography. It was originally written in Marathi titled as *Jina Amucha* in 1986 and was later translated by Maya Pandit. Her autobiography has been received as a valid documentation of caste based discrimination, exploitation and oppression of Mahar community by upper caste people; inhuman living conditions of women; illiteracy and untouchability prevalent in the society and above all subjugation and exploitation of women in Mahar community. In this autobiography, Kamble has given a threadbare account of their community and it served a window to the entire literary world. To quote the words of Maya Pandit:

> *The Prison We Broke* is in this tradition of direct self-assertion. But it also went two steps ahead; it was a head-on confrontation with Brahminical hegemony on the one hand and with patriarchal domination on the other. In one sense it is more of a socio-biography rather than an autobiography. (Pandit xiii)

Baby Kamble's *The Prison We Broke* is considered as an autobiography as a literary genre, but her vivid depiction of Mahar community made her writings the chronicle of Mahar's sufferings. It is Kamble's honest attempt to represent the unheard voice of Mahar community and the plight of oppressed women in that society. She admits the fact that she is writing for the Mahar community. To quote from her Preface to the original 1986 Marathi autobiography:

> Today our young and educated and so-called 'progressive' people are ashamed of using this word 'Mahar'. But what is there to be ashamed of? It tells us that we are the great Mahars of this Maharashtra...***the true, original sons of this soil ...Even the*** name 'Maharashtra' derives from my name, and though you may feel awkward using the name, I do not.

> I love the word 'Mahar', it flows into my veins, in my blood, and it makes me aware to the core of my being of the tremendous struggle for truth that we have waged. (Pandit xvii)

Since childhood Mahar community is subjected to untouchability. Their touch will pollute all strata of society. To quote from the text:

> ...the lady of the house would go to the village shop. Standing in the courtyard, keeping a distance from the shopkeeper, she would pull her pallav over her face and then, using the most reverential and polite terms of address, she would beg him with utmost humility to sell her the things she wanted, "Appasab, could you please give this despicable Mahar woman some shikakai for one paisa and half a shell of dry coconut with black skin?"... "Chabu hey you can't you see the dirty Mahar woman standing there? Do not you touch her? Keep your distance. Immediately our Mahar woman gathering her rags around her tightly so as not to pollute the child" ... "Take care little master! Please keep distance. Do not come too close. You might touch me and get polluted." (Kamble 14)

The so-called upper caste people also follow double standards. They do not touch the people of Mahar Community, but they accept the currency notes given by Mahar community.

The girls after Baba Saheb's awakening started going to school but they experienced another ordeal. Their classmates do not sit with them. Their school belonged to higher caste. For the first time Mahar girls were admitted to school. So "they treated us like lepers, as if our bodies dripped with dirty blood or as if pus oozed out of our rotten flesh. If they had to pass by us they would cover their nose, mutter 'chee chee' and run as if their life is in mortal danger. The teacher had allotted a place in the corner near the door from where we will not move till the school is over for the day" (Kamble 108).

Above quote clearly exhibits the inhuman practices and prevailing system of subjugation and above all the worst part of it is the Mahar woman's humble submission to all these inhuman practices. From generation to generation they are subjected to this kind of treatment and their mute acceptance to it clearly exhibits their mental servitude.

The discrimination of Mahar community by upper-caste people is so deep delved that they forget to oppose or revolt against it. Mahars pray Hindu gods and goddesses, follow Hindu rituals but always subjected to hate and neglect. To present this irony of their life Baby Kamble used sarcastic remarks to express the heart-cry of her community. To quote her words:

> Hindu philosophy had discarded us as dirt and thrown us into their garbage pits on the outskirts of the village. We lived in the filthiest conditions possible. Yet Hindu rites and rituals were dearest to our hearts. (Kamble 18)

Deprived of education, exposure to modern thinking and scientific knowledge, they easily fall prey of superstitions. It became a vicious cycle of their life that they are unable to come out of it. Baby Kamble lamented on this situation in the following words:

> The entire community had sunk deep in the mire of such dreadful superstitions. The upper caste had never allowed this lowly caste of ours to acquire knowledge. Generations after generations, our people rotted and perished by following such a rotten way of life. (Kamble 37)

In such a social scenario as depicted by Kamble, women come at the bottom in social hierarchy and the worst was the condition of a daughter-in-law. They do not have access to medical care, not enough to satiate their appetite and they were wrapped in rags. To quote from the text:

> Once five suwasinis gathered in the house, the woman of the house kept a wooden plate in front of them...One girl

> would be asked to mix the jaggery and water well. Then seven to eight chapatis were crushed to crumbs...and kneaded well with the jaggery mixture...the poor daughter-in-law would sit quietly, their eyes fixed on the plate. Hordes of flies hovered over the plate and many fell into mixture. Several kids related to them in different ways, accompanied the daughter-in-law and they would attack the plate...The daughters-in-law, worried whether any food would be left for them at all, stared anxiously at the quickly depleting mixture on the plate. Since they were daughter-in-law, decorum demanded that they eat only after the children had finished. The poor souls could do nothing but just stare at the plate, licking their lips, hoping against hope that some food remained for them. (Kamble 27)

In the social hierarchy women and daughter-in-law are at the bottom. When karbhari distributes the food in equal portions children started to snatch food from their parents' hands.

> However, without saying a single word with their eyes glued on the food, the poor daughter-in-law would helplessly wait for their turn to eat. Just in case a *sasu* noticed this, she would contemptuously throw a morsel on her daughter-in-law, saying. 'Push that down your throat, your shameless hussy...Your evil eye, will make the child choke. Don't you know how to behave like a good daughter-in-law? (Kamble 30)

The above description clearly exhibits that a daughters-in-law's share in Mahar community is leftovers. They must thrive on leftover meals. It was the only succour for them.

Another ritual that require special mention that in almost all religious processions, rituals and religious congregation women get possessed in Mahar community. Women yell as they are giving voice to their subdued tones. They demand for their wish-fulfilment as they cannot even dare to demand normally.

They are adorned with Kumkum and turmeric powder and after repeated appeasement by menfolk of the community they are pacified. Psychological analysis of all such incidents clearly exhibits the alteration of their identity by so called 'spirit' and whatever subdued emotions and feelings they express, they can shun away the responsibility for that. Many Mahar women get possessed during religious processions. Such mass hysteria can be interpreted as the expression or revolt against their inhuman plight. They can be an outcome of sexual assault or chronic depression. Such oppressive conditions clearly exhibit the social maladies of society. To quote the text:

> Some woman would become possessed and the spirit of some goddess would speak out...Many young girls on the threshold of life succumbed to death. One in every ten lost their lives during childbirth. (Kamble 6)

New mothers had to go hungry. They must undergo a brutal behaviour during their 'confinement' after childbirth. Kamble points out:

> Labour pains, mishandling by the midwives, wounds inflicted by onlooker's nails, ever-gnawing hunger, infected wounds with pus oozing out, hot water baths, hot coals, profuse sweating-everything caused the new mother's condition to worsen and she would end up getting a burning fever...There would be neither food nor money! Only unlimited grief and suffering. (Kamble 60)

The entire text is divided into various chapters and every chapter unveils the inhuman condition of women and heinous attitude towards them. Their character assassination was rampant in the society. To chop off the nose of a married woman was also a common practice, "It is because of the *sasu* who would poison their son's mind" (Kamble 98).

There are incidents of corporal punishments to the wives. Husbands used to flog off the wives till the sticks broke away. The following quotation reveals a gruesome incident, "Everyday

Maharwada would resound with the cries of helpless women in some house or the other" (Kamble 98).

The worst exposure of their social systems was that Mahar women were tortured by their in-laws and were not protected by their maternal family. If they would try to run away from such incessant tortures, they would be followed by her in-laws and "nobody, neither her in-laws nor any of the others, had any sympathy for the poor tortured girl. The husband ...would beat her to a pulp. Even her brother and father would flog her mercilessly and ask the in-laws to take her back. The poor girl numb with pain and hunger, was forced to return to her husband's family" (Kamble 99).

Another ordeal she must face when *sasu* pours venom in her son's head. To quote the incident from the text,

> Dhondya, what good is such a runaway wife to you? ...She must be having an affair. You are her husband but obviously bitch prefers someone else...No, no! I do not want such a slut in my house. She wants to ruin your life. Don't let her off so easily. Dhondya cut off the tip of her nose; only then will my mother's heart breathe easy! (Kamble 100)

Thus, it becomes a chain reaction from one generation to another. One day the nose of the girl would be severed and she would be thrown out of the house with a profusely bleeding nose and she would be called 'mudy' and her entry will be banned in so called 'good houses' (Kamble 101).

On all such inhuman episodes, Kamble wants to analyse the deep-rooted psychology behind that. She came to conclude that the vengeance of *sasu* is behind all such crimes. "She would feel elated that the harassment she had suffered was being finally compensated for. An innocent girl would thus be sacrificed to atone for the *sasu's* sufferings" (Kamble 101).

The entire text is full of all such stories of oppression and the reason behind all this is that Dalit man has been traumatised by the Brahminical patriarchy and they transfer their agony to the person who is weaker to them. Women are the weakest chain in this link. Dalit men receive slave like behaviour from their masters and they started enslaving the woman-folk of their community. They think that "woman was not a human-being for her in-laws but another piece of wood" (Kamble 99).

To imitate the behaviour of high-caste Hindus, they started misbehaving their woman-folk in the Mahar community. To quote from the text:

> The other world had bound us with chains of slavery. But we too were human beings. And we too desired to dominate, to wield power. But who would let us do that? So, we made our own arrangements to find slaves-our very own daughters-in-law! If nobody else, then we could at least enslave them. (Kamble 87)

Throughout the text, we find the references to Baba Saheb Ambedkar and some new awakening in the society due to it. When the Mahar girls face ill-treatment by upper-caste girls, they 'never listened to them' as they 'have greatly emboldened by Baba's brave spirit' (Kamble 108).

Baba Saheb's teaching and guidance was a great force in changing the condition of Mahar community. To quote his words:

> From now onwards you have to follow a different path. You must educate your children. Divorce your children from god. Teach them good things. Send them to schools. The result will be there for you to see. When your children begin to be educated, your condition will start improving. Your family your life will improve. (Kamble 64)

Baby Kamble as the representative of entire Mahar community laments that till the new beginning given by Baba, "We were imprisoned in dark cells, our hands and feet bound by the chain of slavery. Our reason was gagged" (Kamble 49).

The entire narration in Baby Kamble's *The Prison We Broke* is a journey from the dark era to the new awakening of Mahar's community. How the preaching of Baba Saheb helped them to come out of dark prisons to see the new light in Post-Independent India. To quote the words of Baby Kamble, "I made a firm resolve...to lead my life according to the path sketched by Dr Babasaheb Ambedkar, the light of my life" (Kamble 115).

Baby Kamble's explained in an interview how her subjective experiences became the voice of every women of Mahar Community. She shares, "Well I wrote about what my community experienced. The suffering of my people became my own suffering. Their experiences became mine" (Pandit 136).

Thus, in this autobiography, dalit women's sufferings have been narrated. They are exploited not only by the upper caste people but also the men and the *sasus* of their own family. Due to this poignant theme of this autobiography, Baby Kamble's literary creation got acclamation from all literary spheres. We can summarise its importance in the words of Gopal Guru:

> First, Baby Kamble's autobiography *The Prison We Broke* is an important text which offers us an insight into the possibility of understanding the tension between modernity and tradition. (Guru 163)

Works Cited

Kamble, Baby. 'Jina Amucha'. Translated by Maya Pandit as *The Prisons We Broke*. New Delhi: Orient Blackswan, 2009.

Kumar, Amit. "Caste and Patriarchy Dominate the Lives of Dalit Women in Baby Kamble's *The Prisons We Broke.*" *Research Scholar*. Vol. 3 No. 3. August 2015. pp. 174-180.

Limbale, Sharankumar. *Towards an Aesthetic of Dalit Literature: History, Controversies and Considerations*. New Delhi: Orient BlackSwan, 2014.

Rajinkar, Ashwin. "*The Prisons We Broke*: Saga of Dalit Women's Pathetic Condition." Retrieved from http://ashwinranjanikar.blogspot.in/

2013/11/dalit-women-autobiography-baby-kamble.html?m=1 Accessed 10 December 2017.

Rajput, Deepa. "Dalit among Dalits: Dalit Women with Special Reference to Baby Kamble's *The Prisons We Broke.*" *Galaxy: International. Inter-Disciplinary Research Journal.* Vol. 2, Feb. 2014 pp. 139-143.

Shaily. "Trauma of Dalit Women as Thrice-Suppressed in Baby Kamble's *The Prisons We Broke.*" *Literary Herald.* Vol. 3, No 2, 2017. pp. 306-310.

Guru, Gopal. "Afterword". *The Prisons We Broke.* New Delhi: Orient Blackswan, 2009.

3

The Remonstrative Voice in Kalyani Thakur Charal's Autobiography *Ami Kano Charal Likhi*

Dr Somali Gupta

What makes Dalit writing in Bengal different? The state, known to have brought forth many reformative movements involving women, like widow marriage and abolishing Sati, was late in giving voice to its Dalit writers. The Renaissance and the humanistic impulse that reached the shores of India with the advent of the British rule influenced Bengali writers like Rabindranath Tagore, Sarat Chandra Chattopadhya, Bibhuti Bhushan Bandopadhaya, Shankar, Sunil Gangopadhaya and more recently Mahasweta Devi and Amitav Ghosh. These writers included the plight of the marginalised in their works and addressed issues that were never raised before. But these were not writings that emerged out of experience of an empty gut and the blood and sweat of generations forming a collective memory of the oppressed. The reformist Brahmo Samaj was joined by the elite and well to do Bengalis and while they looked into the plight of the women, there is no record of any dalit woman ever becoming a Brahmo. Dalit existence remained largely unrecognised in Bengal, so much so that when the dalit movement started in here it was difficult for the Bengalis to acknowledge their presence in the society. But a language that was strewn with class differences, there had to be someone with a strong voice of remonstration to bring it up and fight for their right.

Born in 1965 in a small village called Bagula, of Nadia district, West Bengal, Kalyani Thakur Charal has been the most vocal Dalit Feminist writer from Bengal. Four books of poetry, a collection of short stories, a collection of essays, a Journal 'Nir' and her autobiography *Ami Kano Charal Likhi* published in 2016, constitute her bulk of work so far. Out of these, her autobiography grabs special attention because of its defiant title *Ami Kano Charal Likhi*. Kalyani Thakur makes it clear to her readers that she has chosen to add Charal to her name as a protest against the casteist mindset and will not be shamed for it. She proudly owns it and tells us in her autobiography how stunned it left her oppressors in the railway office, when she loudly proclaimed it. But her autobiography is not just a tale of Dalit oppression and suffering. It is the story of a dalit woman who faced discrimination not only because of her caste but also because of her colour and gender. Dalit discrimination in India is far more entrenched in our society since the last 2000 years and cannot be compared with the black discrimination in the West.

Kalyani Thakur begins her autobiography by describing her childhood spent in Bagula, then her transition in life when she travelled to Kolkata at the age of fifteen, life in the hostels of Kolkata and her experience as an employee of the railways. Small incidents make up her story and they are neatly built-up to call out to the deep-seated bias that still continues to be ingrained in the Bengali society. The terms Bhadrolok (elite) and Chotolok (low caste) so often used during speaking, don't just emphasise the economic divide between the rich and the poor but are a testament to structural oppression which the people of Bengal refuse to acknowledge.

There aren't many women Dalit writers in Bengal. It is only in recent times that women writers both from the dalit

(Namashudra) and tribal communities have started expressing themselves through their writings. Women writers like Sushma Moitra Sarkar's compilation of essays about her work and movement is entitled Monmukure (Mirror of the Mind), Bina Ray Sarkar's book of essays is "Jago Nari Jago" (Arise Women, Awake). Other writers like Kiran Talukdar, Lily Halder, Manju Bala, Smritikana Hawlader, Sujata Biswas, etc. have written poetry, fiction and essays. While none of them have written autobiography, they have written about their experiences and their plights and are slowly forming a legacy of their own. In her interview with me recorded over the phone she said that during a literary meet few years ago she was told that there are autobiographies from the women dalit writers of Bengal and no information available on the internet either. She was requested to write her autobiography so that it could be a record of the present era of women writers and could be taken up in future for reference.

In Bengal, writing was the prerogative of the upper caste Brahmins, Baidyas and Kayasthas just as formal education was. Yet there were dalit voices rising in the form of biographies of Harichand Thakur (1812), written by Tarak Chandra Sarkar (1853-1913) and the biography of Guru Chand Thakur (1946) written by Mahananda Halder (1899-1972). Kalyani was deeply influenced by both. The Matua dharma formed by Harishchandra Thakur, a sect Vaishnavite Hinduism adopted by the Namashudra community (Chandals) further inspired her towards writing. In her autobiography she credits her rebelliousness to the influences of Harichand Thakur, Guru Chand Thakur and Babasaheb Ambedkar.

What makes Kalyani Thankur Charal's autobiography important is the history of dalit movement in Bengal? Why is Dalit writing in Bengal different from the rest of India? The reasons are many. In his article "Is there Dalit Writing in Bangla" published in *Economic and Political Weekly* Oct 13, 2007, Manoranjan Byapari says:

> In West Bengal, Dalit writing began 20 years after Maharashtra although the central figure of the dalit movement Babasaheb Ambedkar had a close relationship with this eastern region. The Bengalis are a politically conscious people, but to understand the late emergence of the dalit movement here one has to examine closely a certain sequence of socio-political movement. (Byapari 2)

Tracing the history of the Namashrudas of Bengal (who were earlier known as Chandals) he says that their dislocation from East Bengal where 90 percent of them lived, to West Bengal during partition was a major cause. They were rehabilitated in different parts of India from Dandakaranya in Madhya Pradesh to the uninhabited islands of Andaman, due to which they were constantly struggling to find a livelihood and survive. He writes:

> For decades after independence the dalit community in Bengal was so completely demoralised and scattered (some of them stayed on in East Pakistan) that there was no collective life to speak of. In their unrelenting struggle for survival and security, creative activities like writing were unaffordable luxuries. Dalits in other states did not have to lead such a precarious existence and they could organise themselves to initiate social and literary movements. (Byapari 2)

Yet there is no doubt that finally the voices have emerged. Stall number 22 in College Street called Chaturtha Duniya (Fourth World) is run passionately by Kalyani Thakur and Manohar Mouli Biswas. It exclusively holds the collection of books by only Dalit writers. Opening only once a week for a few hours it is a struggle to keep it going just like the struggle to keep up their identity is, in the world which is still dominated by non-dalit writings. With no support from any publisher, Kalyani Thakur had to publish all her books on her own.

'*Why do I Write Charal*?' is the story of a little dalit girl, brought up by parents who in spite of being uneducated themselves, believed in educating their children. With two elder brothers and two elder sisters, Kalyani Thakur was youngest of the five siblings. Her book opens with her earliest memories as a child in Bagula, spent like any other child in a village, roaming, playing and frolicking with her brothers and sisters. Like any normal child of her age, her main concern was not to get caught for playing too long and being scolded and spanked by her mother. More than the school the playgrounds and ponds were her favourite places. Her maternal uncle's place which was close by provided a safe hideout from her mother's wrath. She recalls going to school with books and her own mat she yet doesn't recall much discrimination during her childhood. Life was hard and she and her sister had to sell vegetables in the nearby markets and railway station. Her father who was also the caretaker of the school ensured that his children studied. When her elder brother got a job in merchant navy raising the family's economic condition, her father decided to send her to Kolkata to study further. At the age of 15, she travelled to Kolkata then Calcutta, and stayed in a hostel to finish her 12th in 1980 from Ramkrishna Ananda Ashram. She then also completed her BCom Honours degree in accountancy. She realised early on that education was the only way to beat the tirades of casteism and she continued her studies in Calcutta University to do her M.Com taking classes that were in the evening. All this while, she stayed in a working women's hostel which had appalling conditions. During this period, she was also in a lookout for a job to support herself. She writes in her autobiography:

> I was taking several exams for a government job as I knew in order to continue my education I have to earn money. In the second year itself I got through Indian Railways Group C's clerical post. My office was in Sealdah and I stayed at the working women's hostel. The initial few years were a trying time for me as I could hardly get some food and was working in the day and studying in the night. This was between 1987 and 1990. (Ghosh 3)

The poor conditions of the hostel brought out the rebel in her and she raised her voice against her landlord. It was not an easy task to convince the other girls too as they were afraid of losing the only abode they had and in those days there weren't many working women's hostels in Kolkata. But Kalyani continued her protest forcing her landlord to make repairs of the dilapidated building and that was just the beginning. She started a wall magazine 'Nir' during this period of living in the hostel, which is now a full-fledged magazine and has contributions from eminent dalit and tribal writers of Bengal.

During my interview with Kalyani Thakur Charal she revealed why she chose the name 'Nir'. In spite of having deep affection for a gentleman who ran a magazine called 'Nest', she decided not to get involved when he asked her to join his magazine. She withdrew from it with a deep sense of hurt as it made her feel that she was being manipulated. But the impact of the relationship was so strong that she named her wall magazine *Nir*.

Kalyani's real encounter with discrimination happened when she was employed with the railways. In an interview given to Scroll on March 8th 2018, International Women's Day, Kalyani said:

> First, I was not given any table or chair and was only allowed to sit on a bench lying in a corner of the office. Later, I was given a chair and a small table and was pushed to the furthest corner of the room, where there were no fans. Kolkata's humid weather did not affect me as much as my so-called colleagues who plagued my sense of existence. I soon started taking medicines to fall asleep as soon as office got over each day. (Ghosh 3)

In her autobiography she compared her time working in a traditional government office with Sita's *agnipariksha*. She had to prove her worth to people who looked down upon her because of her caste. When there were too many questions regarding her surname and her caste in her workplace she decided to keep her community name as her surname and started to call herself Kalyani Thakur Charal. To adopt the Caste (Chandal) that was revoked by the community itself in 1911 by a petition given to the British government was her way of confronting the casteist mindset of the society. But the story of any woman does not and cannot end with caste.

She writes about how she was asked not to wear orange saree as the colour wouldn't suit her. She admits that this is also when she realised that there was a gendered exploitation too that was happening with her. The way people looked at her and commented on her skin colour was not just because she was a dalit, but because she was a woman and a dalit. In her autobiography she explicitly speaks of these experiences of body politics while she was working in the railways. It is ironical that the experiences of such extreme patriarchy eluded her in the small village Bagula where her parents, especially her father ensured equal opportunities for his children and the City of Joy made her realise that there is also a gendered perspective to the comments made to her.

Changes came in to her life only after she shifted to Kolkata. She was an adolescent when she left Bagula and spent her formative years in Kolkata. Tragedy hit her family when her mother passed away and she has to return to Bagula to take care of her father. But she never stopped writing. She has written both poems of love and revolt.

Martin Luther King who visited in India February in 1959 called it his pilgrimage to pay respects to the land of the man who fought for the rights of Untouchables, was deeply impressed by the steps taken by the then political leaders like Ambedkar to redress the oppression of the scheduled castes and tribes. The Indian constitution officially abolished discrimination based on caste and untouchability in 1950. King went back to his country with praises for the newly formed government which resolved to weaken the caste system by ensuring education for low caste people to schools and universities and creating space in Government jobs. But Charal's autobiography tells us that while changes have happened and a certain section of the Dalit community has been able to rise up with the benefits, (they now are termed as the 'creamy layer') most of the Dalits continue to be identified as people meant to serve the society as maids and cleaners, and that the struggle to create a respectable niche is still on.

The ossified model of caste system was based on birth, a heritable hierarchy, but the castes Charal, Chamar, Dom etc. continue to be used to call out names, as an abuse. Kalyani's fight is against this social reality, which has to change for the sake of the country's growth. Gayatri Chakravarthy Spivak's question, "Can the Subaltern Speak?" (Spivak) will continue to remain because even today their voices are struggling to gain recognition in the academic syllabus.

Works Cited

Byapari, Manoranjan, and Meenakshi Mukherjee. "Is There Dalit Writing in Bangla?" *Economic and Political Weekly*, Vol. 42, No. 41, 2007, pp. 4116-4120. *JSTOR*, www.jstor.org/stable/40276544. Accessed 10 Aug. 2020.

Charal, Kalyani. *Thakur Kano Ami Charal Boli.* Chaturtha Duniya, 2016.

Ghosh, Amita. Scroll March 18, 2018 Interview) "Meet the Writer Why Bengali Dalit Feminist Poet and Writer Kalyani Thakur Added Charal (For Chandal) to Her Name?" www.scroll.in/tag/Amitav-Ghosh. Accessed 10 Aug. 2020

Spivak, Gayatri Chakravorty. "Can the Subaltern Speak?" *Marxism and the Interpretation of Culture.* Ed. Cary Nelson and Lawrence Grossberge. London: Macmillan, 1988, pp. 271-313.

4

Bama's *Karukku*: A New Dimension of Caste Hierarchy

Dr Gunjan Shushil and Dr Santosh Kumar Sonker

> The emergence of Dalit personal narratives is a historic breakthrough because Dalits in India, till very recently, were voiceless.... [It] is an act of resistance because Dalits are using this opportunity to assert their identities through their writings. The growing number of Dalit autobiographies today is a clear instance of how Dalits have been breaking down an age-old barrier of silence. (Kumar 2012: 259)

Dr B. R. Ambedkar has articulated that "Caste is the natural outcome of certain religious beliefs which have the sanction of the *Sashtras*, which are believed to contain the command of divinely inspired sages who were endowed with a supernatural wisdom and whose commands, therefore, cannot be disobeyed without committing sin" (291). It clearly establishes that the caste has intrinsic relationship with religion. If we go back into the origin of the caste, we have to cite 'Purush Shukta' of the *Rigveda* which talks about the origin of four *Varnas*. In the age of *Smrities* and subsequent periods, the caste turned into hereditary system. "Caste in India means an artificial chopping off of the population into fixed and definite units, each one prevented from fusing into another through the custom of endogamy" (Ambedkar 254). Gandhi was of the view that

"...if Hindu society has been able to stand it is because it is founded on the caste system.... Different castes are like different sections of military division. Each division is working for the good of the whole" (qtd Ambedkar 151). Gandhi's observation about the caste is that—"The spirit behind caste is not one of the arrogant superiority; it is the classification of different systems of self-culture. It is the best possible adjustment of social stability and progress.... Caste does not connote superiority or inferiority. It simply recognizes different outlooks and corresponding modes of life...." (qtd. in Kumar 2012: 135). An American Sociologist, Harold Gould opined on the issue of caste system:

> By modelling ritual behaviour on the division of labour and ranking all occupational behaviour on a pollution scale, Hinduism provided the basis for virtually unlimited permutation of Indian society into hereditary compartments ordained to perform their separate but interdependent religious and economic functions. The caste system was the result. (qtd. in Kumar 2012: 120).

Jodhka has articulated that "Sociologists have often described caste as a "closed system" of stratification where social groups, often divided on the basis of their occupation, strictly follow the code of behaviour prescribed by tradition regarding marriage and kinship alliances". Further he states: "Caste groups are unequal, ranked on a scale of hierarchy based on their ritual status, from pure to impure. Their 'status' or position in the system determines with whom they can interact and with whom they cannot. The idea and practice of untouchability is an integral part of the caste system" (xi). Thus, caste system is a unique phenomenon of Indian society believing in a religion termed as Hinduism. It is very rigid even in present society. Its rigidity has compelled Girish Karnad to create one speech in his play, *Tale Danda*: "One's caste is like the skin on one's body. You can peel it off top to toe, but when the new skin forms, there you are again: a barber—a shepherd—a scavenger!" (21 qtd. in Sonker 53).

In Indian society ridden with caste system based on purity and pollution supplemented with religious texts, those who are socially recognised as low castes have to live a wretched life wrapped in deprivation of basic human rights. To get rid of this caste based identity and untouchability, socially low castes preferred religious conversion. "During British rule, and particularly in the nineteenth century, Christian Missionaries were important agent of change in the lives of the untouchables.... They gave the untouchables only such things which would immediately grant them social status and self-esteem. They built as many churches as they built schools and hospitals..." (Kumar 2019: 26). A well-known authority on conversion opines: "New educational opportunities gradually came available to converts, and changes in life-style became accepted. Converts ...were encouraged to show their greater cleanliness, and soon found it possible to enter a variety of occupations which had hitherto been closed to them, such as school teaching, or work in one of the mission industries" (Forrester 78; qtd. in Kumar 2019: 26). Thus, Christianity provided them a hope for a better life. Many low castes adopted new religion. But they could not get what they expected. They had to experience: "Heard melodies are sweet but those unheard are more sweet" (Keats). This is what Bama's *Karukku* presents. It reveals caste hegemony in various aspects of Christianity. What Hindu converts expected of Christian missionaries and what the latter claimed in India and to which extent they could fulfill their promise constitute thematic crux of the autobiography. Aim of the paper is to reveal problem of caste prejudices within and beyond Hindu religion.

"Dalit (auto)biographical narratives and fictional narratives ...neither hide nor romanticize anything. The people that inhibit these texts are not objects of pity. Their life is often miserable, humiliating, and filled with daily reminders of their impurity and pollutedness.... But these are presented in Dalit literature without romanticisation or glib defensiveness" (Limbale 13). But Dalit women autobiographies add one more feature to the Dalit autobiographies i.e. influence of patriarchy on their life, thus, thrice subjugation forms the crux of themes. Bama's *Karruku* transcends religious boundary and presents an account of perpetuation of caste discrimination even after conversion into a different religious order. Bama tries to create a new identity and new space for her community people through this autobiography. Possibly this is the reason that she negates her original name and moves from personal to public.

Pramod Kumar Nayar recognizes *Karukku* more as a *testimonio* than mere an autobiography. He observes: "*Karukku* as testimonial life-writing enables Bama to share her tale of pain, so that personal testimony becomes accurate historical witnessing of a social structure of traumatic oppression" (85). S. B. Biradar comments that "*Karukku* explores a new horizon for the marginalised and subjugated.... it explores many accounts of 'unspeakable' horrors and horrendous degree of exploitation" (218). Raj Gautaman opines: ".... Bama's *Karukku* explores a changing Dalit Identity. It exhibits a very powerful sense of the self and community as a Dalit.... She proposes a new identity of her own and tries to change hearts and minds of the readers. It explores altogether a different world of experience" (qtd. in Biradar 217). Amala Dasarathi opines:

> Unlike most autobiographies, Bama's narrative is not linear. She does not describe events only in terms of the impact they had on her later life, but writes of the experiences she had as moments of oppression that composed her daily lived reality. In the book, one sees Bama's quest to understand and present how her multiple identities as Dalit, Christian and woman have impacted her oppression. (n. pag.)

Bama wrote the book in Tamil after leaving the convent on 08th November 1992. In *Karukku*, translated by Lakshmi

Holmstrom in 2000, Bama observed about the book: "That book was written as a means of healing my inward wounds.... *Karukku* made me realise potent a book can be" (ix). Further she opined: "*Karukku*, written by a wounded self, has not been dissolved in the stream of time. On the contrary, it has been of comfort to many who have been brought low, and who suffer the pain of caste discrimination, untouchability, poverty, and destitution; it has given them courage and helped them to love life once more" (x). She added that "Karukku stands a means of strength to the multitudes whose identities have been destroyed and denied.... [it] has enabled many to raise their voices and proclaim, 'My language, my culture, my life is praiseworthy, it is excellent'. [it] insists only on a humanism which crosses all boundaries; the truth it tells may be bitter to some, to some they may be ridiculous" (x-xi).

Lakshmi Holmstrom stated in "Translator's Note to the Second Edition" that "*Karukku* was written out of specific experience, the experience of a Tamil Dalit Christian woman" (xiv). Further, Lakshmi Holmstrom articulated in 'Introduction' to *Karukku*: "[*Karukku*] grows out of a particular moment: a personal crisis and watershed in the author's life which drives her to make sense of her life as a woman, a Christian, and a Dalit.... It is her driving quest for integrity as a Dalit and a Christian that shapes the book and gives it its polemic" (xv-xvi). Preface to the first edition of *Karukku* Bama describes the issues which have been discussed in the book:

> The driving force that shaped this book are many: events that occurred during many stages of my life, cutting me life, cutting like karukku and making me bleed; unjust social structures that plunged me into ignorance and left me trapped and suffocating; my own desperate urge to break, throw away, and destroy these bonds; and when the chains into fragments, the blood that was split—all these taken together. (xxiii)

Bama foregrounds her story in the social setting of her own community. She describes that plight of the people constituting of her community share the same fate as she has. In *Karukku* she narrates in this way:

> The story told in *Karukku* was not my story alone. It was the depiction of a collective trauma—of my community—whose length cannot be measured in time. I just tried to freeze it forever in one book so that there will be something physical to remind people of the atrocities committed on a section of the society for ages.

At this aspect, Pramod Kumar Nayar has remarked: "...[*Karukku*] is not a personal autobiography alone, but a collective archive of suffering. Bama is the narrative voice through which the sufferings and atrocities of two communities, Dalit and Christian, are addressed to us" (85). Thus, the book covers three dimension—personal, social, and religious. Atulkumar Parmar writes about this book:

> *Karukku* is a part of the body of Dalit writing that has exposed the dominant versions of history and society that has been invoked through the centuries of legitimizing the caste system. *Karukku* also exposes the hypocrisy of the Catholic Church, which while claiming to care for the Dalit convert, exploits them, as much as the rest of society. (Parmar 222)

Personal accounts of Bama's childhood are embedded in a Hindu social setup which has fourfold caste system. The Hindu society propounded a village settlement plan according to which there was a clear-cut divide between habitats of upper castes and lower castes in a village. Habitats of lower castes were often allocated at the outskirts of the village near pond which was used as the defecation area. In this autobiography also the author describes the village settlement. The autobiography starts with description of the geographical location and division of the village of its author like *Joothan* by Omprakash Valmiki.

However, the present autobiography incepts with the positive and soothing geographical description. Situating amidst the beautiful mountains range, the village has a bus-stand at its entry and a stream which overflows if it rains and if not, "it is nothing but a stinking shit-field" (Bama 7). Left part of the village known as Odapatti was populated by Nadars, right by Koravars, then Chakkiliyar, some distance away were Kushavar, then Palla settlement; next to it was the Paraya settlement where the writer was living next to the cemetery. Apart from the writer's settlement, there were the streets of Thevar, Chettiyar, Aasaari, and Naikar. Beyond that were Naikar and Udiyar streets. The point of attention is what the writer narrates: "I don't know how it came about that the upper-caste communities and the lower caste-communities were separated like this into different parts of the village. But they kept themselves to their part of the village, and we stayed in ours. We only went to their side if we had worked to do there. But they never, ever, came to our parts" (Bama 7). This division of settlements pronounced the division of men as per their castes.

Castes are infested with purity and pollution concept having religious sanction. Those who are categorised the lowest in the caste ladder, they are treated not only inferior but also impure and thus, untouchable. The writer goes back to her childhood to describe untouchability. One day she was returning from her school and saw an elder man coming from the direction of market holding a small packet. The writer wanted to "shriek with laughter at the sight of such a big man carrying a small packet in that fashion" (Bama 15). But her laughter vanishes as her brother tells her the reason for holding the packet in the special manner. She expresses: "Annan told me the man wasn't being funny when he carried the package like that. He said everybody believed that Naickars were upper caste, and therefore must not touch Parayas. If they did, they would be polluted. That's why he had to carry the package by its string" (Bama 15). She is enraged after listening that the Naickars treat them as untouchables. She raises very apt and basic questions: "Because they had scraped four coins together, did that mean they muse lose all human feelings?" (Bama 16).

Caste works in day-to-day mannerism also. Upper castes claim to be very civilised and mannered but their behaviour is very shameful with socially created low castes. Even kids of uppers do not talk with older Dalits respectfully. It is the height of ill manner which questions the very 'meaning' of cultured and civilised. Bama narrates such a scene:

> Both my grandmothers worked as servants for Naickar families. In the case of one of them, when she was working in the fields, even tiny children, born the other day, would call her by her name and order her about, just because they belonged to the Naickar caste. And this grandmother, like all the other labourers, would call the little boy Ayya, Master, and run about to do his biddings. (Bama 16)

Not only this, a Naickar woman poured water from a height of four feet in the cupped hand of a Patti woman. Castes are observed in the schools also. Dalit students were humiliated and tortured without rhyme and reason. Annan was insulted by the Headmaster of the Chaaliyar caste just because a coconut fell from his touch while he was playing a game of touching the coconut with others after the school as usual. He was not allowed to enter the school. He was suggested to get a letter from the priest by one of his master who came from his street. What priest said after listening to whole from his mouth is very shocking and reflects the traditional image of Dalits in the minds of the Sawarnas: "After all, you are from the Cheri. You might have done it. You must have done it" (Bama 19). It aggrieved him much and tears rolled down his eyes. Anyhow, the priest gave a paper with note to allow him into the school. After receiving the letter, the Headmaster again abused with bad words that came to his mouth before allowing him to enter. After finishing his eighth standard in his village, he got admission in the neighbouring town. He had to suffer humiliation there also. The Warden-Sister remarked ill about him and other low caste students: "Look at the Cheri children! When they stay here, they eat their fill and look as round as potatoes. But look at the state in which they come back from home—just skin and bone!" (Bama 20). While he was returning from school in vacation by bus, as soon as a Naikar woman came to know that he is from the Cheri street, she got up immediately and sat on another seat or asked him to do the same.

Education is only tool to bring honour to the socially marginalised sections of society. Once Annan was given stool and addressed as 'Sir' when entered M.A. in the register in library. Annan told this to his sister: "Because we are born into the Paraya jati, we are never given any honour or dignity or respect. We are stripped off all that. But if we study and make progress, we can throw away these indignities.... Work hard and learn" (Bama 18). Though in the later part of autobiography and life of the author as well, Annan's suggestion stands futile in some aspects because every class of society has its own face of untouchability, however, it gives you some relief in one aspect and more grief in the other. After getting education, you acquire conscience and observe discrimination based on your social origin which trouble you every minute. Schools have its own mechanism to observe caste. Students of low castes were badly treated. "If anything bad happened, they would say immediately, and without hesitation, 'It must be one of the Cheri children who did it'" (Bama 18). Harijan children in schools were seen with contempt but were always preferred to engage in the low work. "...they [upper castes] didn't hesitate to use us for cheap labour. So we carried water to the teacher's house; we watered the plants. We did all the chores that were needed about the school" (Bama 18). When Bama scored first in SSLC exam, and her name was called out, she stood up with pride without feeling ashamed of her caste, Harijan. After finishing her school, Bama started her college studies. There also she faced caste discrimination against her idea that her caste would not be bothered in such a big college away from her village among so many students. After college, she finished BEd also facing and resisting caste differences. She joined a school as a teacher after finishing B.Ed. And there, she frankly disclosed her Paraya identity being asked by a nun who was a Telugu girl and cared less for the Dalits. She was happy there teaching students who were mostly Dalits. Because of education only, she managed to "survive among those who spoke the language of caste-difference and discrimination" (Bama 22).

As Hindu caste structure humiliated her due to her birth in a socially recognised low caste, she decided to be a nun to end oppression of Dalit children and teachers. Her decision to accept religious conversion speaks her desire to reject Hindu caste identity and adopt a new religious identity with hope of equality and respect. She did not pay any heed to the suggestions by his family members and outside person about not being a nun: "They said that caste-difference counted for a great deal within convents" (Bama 23). But the situation was just opposite to what she hoped for. It had no connection with the poor and downtrodden.

Religion establishes mental phobia. It is ingrained in the mind of a person that if you do not do this, something bad will happen. Being afraid of mis-happening, he continues to do illogical things. The writer reveals her childhood training in the church. She had to attend "morning Pusai" and "catechism classes" in the evening after school classes were over. If she was absent for any reason even in the rainy season when lake was swollen with water, she was beaten brutally with a cane by the priest or by the teacher. As a child, she had good memory and she was only student who could read prayers. When she was in the second class, she made her first communion which was confirmed by Bishop of Madurai. In her primary schools, run by nun, she was entrusted to lock up and open the parish church.

She felt fear whenever she was alone in the church because the stories told by the sisters haunted her. She remembers:

> They had told us that if we kept on committing sins, the Devil would put them all down in a long list written into a big notebook, which he would show to God. Sister said, in the Scriptures lesson, that if we committed so many sins that the notebook actually filled up then he would peel the skin off our backs and write our sins there.... The Sisters never seemed to tell us any cheerful stories. It was always stories of the Davil. (Bama 83)

Besides, she was warned repeatedly that Jesus was inside the host and we should neither bite Him nor should touch with our sinful hands because if it was touched, blood would flow down my hand. One day she tested it but nothing happened. Another lie told to her was that the Spiritus Sanctus would descend upon her the moment the Bishop would slap on her cheek during the confirmation service, but it also did not happen. During college time, she realised that "...they are all hypocrites and frauds" (Bama 102). Gradually, influences of all the rituals and religious lessons vanished. After getting B. Ed. degree, she got a job in the school run by nuns. After some times she experienced, "...they were truly like whited sepulchres, as Jesus said" (Bama 102). She was happy to some extent working for the poor and Dalits but atrocities inflicted on them blazed her with anger. In the boarding school run for the destitute, she witnessed that the menial jobs were done by the children of low castes and caste, class and language division was very much in practice among nuns also. The way the Dalit children were treated brought in them hopelessness for any change which strengthened in her a desire to become a nun "to treat these [Dalit] children as all children ought to be treated, to look after them rather than torment and exploit them" (Bama 104). Her experience about the lessons on God is very shocking. Everybody taught that "...God is loving, kind, gentle, one who forgives sinners, patient, tender, humble, obedient. Nobody had ever insisted that God is just, righteous, is angered by injustices, opposes falsehood, never countenances inequality" (Bama 104). "The oppressed are not taught about him, but rather, are taught in an empty and meaningless about humility, obedience, patience, gentleness" (Bama 104). The behaviour of nuns and priests lost her interest in Church. A time came when she felt that the Church is made up of priests and nuns and their kith and kin belonging to the upper castes and holding positions of power while most of the Christians are Dalits. Living a comfortable life, they possessed all the powers and robbed of the poor and low castes by thrusting in them blind beliefs and devotion and turning them into slaves in the name of God.

After entering into the order, she expected that she would get an equal status and her Dalit identity would not follow her there. But she experienced just a contrary situation in training centre. There also, she faced discrimination in every aspect of life. She couldn't believe that poor Dalits do not get admission in the convent. She encountered a very odd situation one day, when she was enquired about her different dates of birth on marks sheet and christening certificate. Her reply that her date of birth on the marks sheets depended on what dates school teacher wrote could not satisfy the Sister and she complained: "You Tamil people want to get admission into schools under false pretences, changing the dates on your birth certificates" (Bama 24). Thus, a Tamil is looked down up as a lower caste in the order. Every candidate who was taking training with her was curious to know her caste which she revealed when she was asked one day. When her training was about to over, a Sister spoke that they would not accept Harijan women in some orders as nuns and there would be even a different order for them which came to her as a thunderstruck. It made her to cry inwardly: "I lamented inwardly that there was no place free of caste" (Bama 25). After finishing her training for nunnery, she was sent to a convent elsewhere. She was baffled to find out that "...this convent too was not without its caste divisions"

(Bama 25). The convent employed low castes for menial jobs such as "sweeping the premises, swabbing and washing the classrooms, and cleaning out lavatories" and maltreated them (Bama 25). They didn't consider low-castes as "human beings" which infuriated her but she did not have courage to retort as she was also "a low-caste woman" (Bama 25). The writer described attitude of the Convent towards low-castes: ".... low-caste people are all degraded in every way. They think we have no moral discipline nor cleanliness nor culture. They think that this can never be changed. To aid us is like aiding cobras" (Bama 26). This is what the writer had to listen continuously as a deaf and dumb having no sensibility and "dying several deaths within" (Bama 26). The idea that what would happen if they came to know about her caste, trembled her. She gave vent to her feeling translating the real situation of the low castes: "In this society, if you are born into a low caste, you are forced to live a life of humiliation and degradation until your death. Even after death, caste-difference does not disappear. Wherever you look, however much you study, whatever you take up, caste discriminations stalk us in every nook and corner and drives us into a frenzy" (Bama 26). Even caste of Dalits problematises life of Dalits every moment. As soon as upper castes come to know about caste of a Dalit, they "screw up their faces" and look at him with disgust which causes ineffable anguish in him. Bama questions why Dalits are not treated as human beings. No conspiracy is left for keeping them in pitiable situations where no progress could be made. Due to enslavement of generations of Dalits, there is no way for their redemption. She feels that "We must not accept injustice of our enslavement by telling ourselves it is our fate, as if we have no true feelings; we must dare to stand up for the change" (Bama 28). After finishing her training, she was sent to a convent as a nun. She found that the convent had value for rich students only. Each class was full with children from wealthy upper castes. As a token of gestures they admitted four to five students from the Dalit castes. "These wretches usually shunned the rich ones and lurked in corners, trembling" (Bama 112). The rich children denied to sit next to these black skinned and play with them. The three vows of poverty, chastity and obedience taken by nuns to liberate them from prejudices to live life among ordinary people were turned into tools of "control and enslavement" (Bama 113). Before entering this order, the writer was living a life of poverty among poor people which she got rid of after she reached convent, however, her life was like one trapped in comfort within luxurious cage. In the convent, there was no freedom even to think differently. One has to fit in the framework established there. One's self was destroyed completely to create a new one as per requirement of the convent. Almost no one in the convent knew who Dalits were and whoever knew its meaning had a poor opinion of them. Some of them say: "How can we allow these people to come into our houses? In any case, even if we were to allow them, they would not enter our homes.... There is nothing we can do for these creatures.... Because to do so would be like helping cobras" (Bama 115). They had readymade answer for any question that the whole school run from the income made out of rich students. If she wanted to do real service, she might go elsewhere. Thus, she left the convent within six months and came back home. After leaving convent, she did not get job because the village had a school run by Nadar where a Dalit was not given a job. Dalits had no school to get admission and to work in. Even the schools run by Catholic nuns marginalised Dalits addressing them as of poor quality. She faced difficulty in means of earning survival and saving her body as a woman. Her painful realisation about Dalit community is true even today sometimes: "We think so many thoughts. We hope so much. We study so many things. But in real life everything turns out to differently. We are compelled to wander about, stricken and unprotected" (Bama 119). Here, Dr Ambedkar's view seems to be very pertinent: "Caste has killed public spirit. Caste has destroyed the sense of public charity. Caste has made public opinion impossible.... Virtue has become caste oriented and morality has become caste bound" (Ambedkar 275).

The writer narrates that life in convent is very strange because there one cannot realise the other's pain. She accepts that renunciation of convent life has landed her into problems but she does not regret for it because it was a 'counterfeit existence' for her. She explains her situation after leaving convent: "I am like a bird whose wings are broken. After wings are broken, it is protected only if it stays in its cage. But it comes out, it can only flap wings uselessly, unable to fly. And that is the state in which I am now" (Bama 121). In her bad days, she loses most of the people associated with her in prosperous days. Some of those who come to heal her wounds actually itch it. But she feels satisfied with her present state:

> ...with all pain, there still is a certain happiness in the depths of my mind. I have courage, I have a certain pride. I do indeed have a belief that I can live, a desire that I should live.... For the time being, I cannot see my way ahead. Yet I believe it is possible to live a meaning life, a life that is useful to a few others. I comfort myself with the thought that rather than live with a fraudulent smile, it is better to lead a life weeping real tears. (Bama 122)

In her "Afterword" Bama reveals what she has experienced: "each day brings new wounds ...I have seen the brutal, frenzied and ugly face of society" (105).

Thus, Bama's journey of searching for a new identity as a converted Dalit Christian from a rural mooring in an Indian social system ends up in leaving convent and retreating to her roots which provides her with a new space of writing to express and assert her "Self" enthusiastically. Her wilful decision to adopt a pseudonym for her writings reflects her reaction to the patriarchal and caste based social structure. It also explicates rejection of Shudra identity imposed on her in a Hindu social setup. It is a unique autobiography because it travels through two worlds—Hindu and Christian—and creates a new world 'self' assertion. She gets a "resounding standing ovation", recognition and becomes motivation for the thousands of the oppressed.

Bama treadles between two worlds and takes shelter into the third world i.e. writing to create a space for expression of her 'self'. No religion, neither Hindu nor Christianity gives her equality as a Dalit woman. The story of the autobiography continuously takes reference of the community feeling which reflects that this problem of caste is an archetype for Dalits. Thus, Dr B. R. Abmedkar's view seems to be very pertinent and relevant, "Caste is not a physical object like wall of bricks or a line barbed wire which prevents the Hindus from co-mingling and which has, therefore, to be pulled down. Caste is a notion, it is a state of mind" (289).

Works Cited

Ambedkar, Dr B. R. "Annihilation of Caste." *The Essential Writings of B. R. Ambedkar*. Ed. Valerian Rodrigues. New Delhi: OUP, 2002. Print.

—. "Castes in India." *The Essential Writings of B. R. Ambedkar*. Ed. Valerian Rodrigues. New Delhi: Oxford UP, 2002. Print.

Bama. *Karukku*. Tran. Lakshmi Holmstrom. Third Impression 2013. Macmillan India, 2000. New Delhi: OUP, 2011.

Biradar, S. B. "Exploring the Issues of Caste, Gender and Identity in Bama's *Karukku*." *Dalit Assertion and its Space in Literature*. Ed. Santosh Kumar Sonker. New Delhi: Yash, 2018. pp. 216-222.

Dasarathi, Amala. "'Karukku': An Autobiography by Bama Exploring her Tamil, Dalit and Christian Identity." *Feminism in India*. Feb 20, 2017. <https://feminisminindia.com/2017/02/20/karukku-bama-book-review/> Accessed on 16 July, 2020.

Forrester, Ducan B. *Caste and Christianity: Attitudes and Policies on Caste of Anglo-Saxon Protestant Missions in India*. London: Clarion Press, 1980. Qtd. in *Dalit Literature and Criticism* by Raj Kumar. Hyderabad: Orient BlackSwan, 2019. Print.

Jodhka, Surinder S. "Preface." *Oxford Indian Short Introductions Caste*. New Delhi: Oxford UP, 2012.

Kumar, Raj. *Dalit Personal Narratives: Reading Caste, National and Identity*. Hyderabad: Orient BlackSwan, 2012. Print.

—. *Dalit Literature and Criticism*. Hyderabad: Orient Blackswan, 2019. Print.

Limbale, Sharankumar. *Towards an Aesthetic of Dalit Literature: History, Controversies, and Considerations*. Trans. from the Marathi by Alok Mukherjee. New Delhi: Orient BlackSwan, 2004; Reprint 2012. Print.

Nayar, Pramod Kumar. "Bama's *Karukku*: Dalit Autobiography as Testimonio." *Journal of Commonwealth Literature*, 41.2 (2006): 83-100.

<https://www.researchgate.net/publication/240713501_Bama's_Karukku_Dalit_Autobiography_as_Testimonio/link/55697cf408aec22683033940/download> Accessed on 02.07.2020 time 20:59

Parmar, Atulkumar. "Caste and Its Penetration: A Study of Bama's *Karukku* and *Sangati*." *Research Guru: Online Journal of Multidisplinary Subjects*. 13.1 (2019): 220-224. < file:///C:/Users/Santosh%20Sonkar/Downloads/Caste_and_Its_Penetration_A_Study_of_Bamas_Karukk.pdf>

5

Dalit Consciousness and Autobiography: Reading Sushila Takbhoure's *Shikanje ka Dard*

Dr Ashok Verma

The basic postulation of Dalit writings has been to challenge and subvert the traditional *brahmanical* hegemony and seek a rightful position for those sections of society that have remained marginalised throughout history. There is no denying the fact that the Indian society has cherished and nourished the *varna* system and as a result, one section, down at the lowest rung, has been exploited thoroughly in the name of socio-religious practices. Using the rhetoric of propriety and superiority, the 'upper' castes have awarded sub-human treatment to the 'lower' castes that form "a quarter of the country's people" (Mukherjee, "Translator's Introduction" viii).

In order to understand the dyadic relationship between the dalits and caste-Hindus, a diachronic study of history is required which explicitly shows that the relationship between history on one hand and society and culture on the other hand has never been unidirectional. It has been a two-way process. If history shapes and conditions the social, cultural milieu, at the same time, it itself gets influenced and wrought by that particular milieu. That means the social, cultural, religious and economic factors do determine and constitute the concept of history.

It should not come as a surprise then that history and the representation of various social groups has never been objective to the extent of being in seamless perfection.

The above postulation holds true in the Indian context where writing of history has always been the prerogative of the Brahmins—the so-called learned class. In fact, the *varna* (caste) system as mentioned in the scriptures provisions for four basic *varnas*—Brahmin, Kshatriya, Vaishya and Shudra in the order of hierarchy. The Brahmins, being the learned ones, thus become the supreme. It is they who have got the power of knowledge. As such, their perspective, being the only perspective available, becomes valid and attains finality. In this set up, the *Shudra* being at the very bottom of the hierarchy, the first three *varnas* exercise the religious (or what they call the power of knowledge), political and money power respectively on those who are absolutely devoid of any power whatsoever. It is a vicious nexus that leaves no scope for the people at the lowest stratum to lead a respectable life. As such, the Dalits and Tribals have ever been denied a proper 'voice' in history.

Here it is important to note that the word "dalit" encompasses all such oppressed and powerless who have ever been denied share in power. It is an umbrella term encompassing those who are oppressed at any of the levels i.e. class, caste or gender etc. No doubt, in the Indian society, certain castes have remained at the lowest rung according to the Varna system, and as such, they are Dalits, but to use it as a mere caste marker would be limiting its scope and denying access to power to those who are facing oppression at any level other than caste.

The oppression of the Dalits continues at various levels making their day-to-day life dreary and monotonous. Any attempt at breaking free from oppression and towards progression in terms of knowledge or material progress would be termed a breach against the prescription and thus would be viewed seriously and attract severe punishment from the 'custodians' of the social behaviour. That means the prevailing power structures would never allow a change and all loci of power would come together to deprive the have-nots of their just rights and to propagate the prevailing power structures.

With the growing consciousness, particularly in the 20th century, however, things have started changing for the better. Exhibiting the awareness that Dalits gained over the years through the persistent efforts made by reformers like Jotirao Phule and Ambedkar, they now want equal share in power. They reject the inhuman treatment on the basis of *varna* and seek to revisit history and redefine the social order in favour of the egalitarian principles of liberty, equality and fraternity. In this process, their 'radical' ideas are coming to be in clash with the age-old ideas that have been prevailing in the society for hundreds of years; hence the dichotomy as the present power structures would not accede to their demands in mere subservience.

Today, there is a whole corpus of vibrant Dalit literature challenging the stereotypical, upper caste mindset and its resultant practices. In fact, writers like Omprakash Valmiki, Suraj Pal Chauhan, Daya Pawar, Namdev Dhasal, to name a few, have potently challenged the brahmanical, caste-Hinduistic hegemony. The focal concern of these writers is assertion of their Dalit identity rather than feeling ashamed of it. This is a phase of political awareness and to use Mukherjee's words, it is a journey from "Erasure to Assertion". These authors successfully project Dalits as upper caste Hindu's other and reject the subservient place for the Dalits in the self-other binary.

Ambedkar, in his seminal essay, "Untouchability and Caste System" relates the plight of the untouchables with the institution of caste system and talks about three kinds of sanctions i.e. legal, religious and social which provide life force to any institution. While either of these sanctions can sustain an institution, the *varna* system has got all the three sanctions;

religious—since religion promotes caste divisions thus making an average Hindu consider his caste sacred; social—as the society recognizes the caste and finally, up to some extent, legal—as the government has also made provisions in the Constitution for particular castes.

Akkarmashi fame Sharankumar Limbale, like Ambedkar, maintains that in the present system, Dalit subalternity is eternal, unalterable as against colonial subalternity. It's inherited from birth and sanctioned by sacred authority. Taking a historical view of dalit subalternity, Limbale exposes the inherent injustice meted out to dalits under the pretext of religious and social inferiority and impurity. *In Towards an Aesthetic of Dalit Literature* (2004), he questions the concept of *satyam, shivam* and *sundaram* which forms the foundation of traditional Hindu aesthetics; and turns it, on its head in terms of its applicability to Dalit literature. He declares:

> Satyam, Shivam, Sundaram—these are fabrications used to divide and exploit ordinary people. In fact, the aesthetic concept of satyam, shivam, sundaram is the selfish mechanism of upper caste Hindu society. It is necessary to replace this conception of aesthetics with one that is material and social. (21)

Limbale further goes a step forward to subvert the notion of *satyam, shivam*, *sundaram* and calls for the portrayal of the untruth, unholy, unbeauty by Dalit writers in their works. This subversion shows the intensity of the radical element in his work. He feels that it is highly inappropriate "to expect pleasure or beauty, instead of inspiration for social transformation, from a literature that has been written primarily to raise awareness" (21). To Limbale, Dalit literature must be seen from the socio-historical perspective rather than evaluating it from the 'pure', aesthetic lens. The rejection of the traditional, mainstream aesthetics is, in fact, one of the basic postulations of Dalit writings as it is inappropriate and insufficient for judging the 'literary' value of a Dalit text. Hence, the need for a "new and distinct aesthetic" that is "life affirming and realistic" (19).

This brings in the age-old debate as to what should be the parameters for judging literature. The famous Art for art sake school maintains that a work of art is primarily a work of art which has its own intrinsic, aesthetic beauty and therefore it should be judged from the aesthetic perspective only—devoid of any social, moral, cultural role that it may have to perform. On the other hand, there is a parallel school that believes that literature is the by-product of its social, cultural, ethnic and religious milieu. No literature is produced in vacuum. As such, literature has a role to perform. This approach is called Art of Society Sake. Obviously, Dalit literature falls strictly under the second category. Dalit authors cannot think of any other aesthetics beyond their sordid experiences. It is quite natural and understandable as well. To them, the concept of literary aesthetics is also drastically different from the traditional notion of literature and its role in society. Dalit writers maintain that because the genesis and the purpose of Dalit literature is different, it should not be judged on the yardsticks of mainstream aesthetics. Since Dalit literature comes as a reaction, it needs to be understood from an altogether different perspective. Some Dalit writers further believe that only writers who themselves are Dalits can express this perspective and simply reject writers like Mulk Raj Anand and Premchand on the grounds that these upper-caste writers can at the most sympathize but never acquire a sensibility to feel the anguish and deprivation that are the essential ingredients of a Dalit experience.

In this struggle, autobiography has emerged as the specific genre to allow the emotional anguish of the Dalits to flow through the written word. In fact, autobiography forms the major chunk of the entire corpus of Dalit oeuvre. Autobiography becomes the natural choice of the Dalit authors to give vent to their pent-up emotions. They use autobiography as a potent medium for conveying to the mainstream their perspective—

their anguish, their emotions, their helplessness, their haplessness, etc. which otherwise remain unexpressed and therefore, unrepresented. For mainstream people, it comes as something natural and as such they simply do not understand the trials and tribulations that the Dalits are doomed to experience. It appears that they have unwittingly internalised the ideologically promoted hegemonic image of caste hierarchy and continue to suffer.

Dalit autobiographies differ from the genre of autobiography as such. First and foremost, they are narratives of a life of pain and suffering—the wretched experiences of Dalits as pariahs and outcastes. Second, Dalit autobiographies serve as a potent medium of identity assertion for the author. Then, through that assertion and complete defiance of the mainstream structures of oppression, Dalit autobiographies help mobilise resistance at a broader level, thus paving the way for reconstruction of Dalit socio-cultural historiography. Raj Kumar, a noted Dalit scholar, while referring to the act rightly observes that "writing an autobiography is a special act for the members of this group who use the genre to achieve a sense of identity and mobilise resistance against different forms of oppression" (5).

Sushila Takbhoure's *Shikanje ka Dard* (2009) is another significant text in the now-not-so-new tradition of Dalit autobiographies. Written in Hindi by a Dalit woman who passes through the extremely challenging circumstances of her life to acquire a 'respectable' status in society, it underscores the pangs of Dalit life in the states of Madhya Pradesh and Maharashtra. The way the text rips apart the veneer of social hypocrisy to expose the sordid reality in all its nakedness is what renders it a uniqueness of its own. The use of the word "Shikanja" itself speaks volumes of the suffocation and uneasiness of Dalit experience. The expression becomes all-the-more poignant when it deals with the life of a Dalit woman i.e. a multiply oppressed being—at the levels of caste, gender, class, etc. The author herself defines the term thus: "*Shikanja* means trap that leaves no scope for any movement. It means snare that won't allow an escape. According to dictionary, it means clasp. It also refers to rack—an old instrument of torture in which pain is inflicted by stretching the culprit's body...." ("Preface" 4). Clearly then, the title which literally means "Anguish of the Trap" has been used in multiplicity of shades to underscore the agony of being Dalit in a highly casteist society. The pain, the suffering, the humiliation at every step brings to the fore the essentially discriminatory Indian social order nourished by the age-old caste system.

Takbhoure's description of her childhood experiences, the sub-human conditions that she lived in, the work conditions of her grandmother, the volatile ambience of the family largely due to non-fulfillment of basic needs—all have been portrayed with an authentic touch in consonance with Limbale's postulation. The day-to-day life experiences have turned her grandmother and parents skeptical and dry. And yet, they cannot come out of the vicious circle of superstitions and rituals propagated by the casteist society. Takbhoure recounts the observation of rituals by her mother and grandmother despite their sordid living. It's only her father who exhibits some spine in rejecting the celebration of Diwali that again emanates from his own experiences: "These festivals are not meant for us. Do we have Lakshmi (money) that we should worship?" (36). This question clearly shows the redundancy of such festivals for the have-nots.

Takbhoure further narrates how her brother Shankar had to succumb to the octopus-like stranglehold of the oppressive forces and he had to leave college and discontinue his studies because he had beaten up some upper-caste boys who continuously teased him for his low caste. The irony-soaked observation of the author takes the incessant suffering of the Dalits to an altogether level: "It was normal to deprive a promising boy, born in a family of untouchables, of a better future" (75-76). Such accounts leave the reader in no doubt about the pitiable plight of the Dalits in Indian society.

The author stoically undergoes the suffering and it is only through her persistence and, up to a great extent, stubbornness, that she is able to continue her studies. She has come to imbibe her grandmother's advice that education is the key to counter the caste-based oppression. Ironically, however, despite being highly educated and qualified, Takbhoure is primarily known by her caste only. She is referred to as *jharuwali* and *jamadarni* by her neighbours who cannot see things beyond the lens of caste, religion, etc. She lets out her disgust through the following poem:

A PhD holder
College Lecturer
Is called *Jharuwali*
In the name of her caste. (223)

This particular experience establishes that in Indian society, caste identity is permanent and impervious. It cannot be come over either through education or any other means. Apart from the direct, unhesitant expression of caste superiority displayed by the neighbouring women, Takbhoure experiences the affected behaviour of the so-called liberal, upper caste friends who would proclaim to be open-minded and preach equality but would practice exactly opposite of what they preach. By and by, the author comes to understand the duality of behaviour of her friends and writes: "I came to realise the bitterness beneath the sugarcoated geniality of the upper-caste Brahmins" (228).

Another rhetoric that Takbhoure encounters is the rhetoric of aestheticism. Now that she is already equally qualified and has become a writer, thus cannot be avoided, the 'custodians' of the mainstream literature try to convince her to join them in the name of the aesthetic function of literature. "Madam, whosoever you are by caste, we consider you a *brahmin*. Why do you talk of contestations on the pattern of the Ambedkarites?

You create aesthetic literature, and be with us. We will bring you laurels. Leave this Dalit literature thing, paint on the bigger canvas" (226). By this time, however, Sushila Takbhoure has grown mature enough to see through their manipulations and machinations and notes thus: "But I know these rhetorics do not emerge out of true compassion (226).

While Takbhoure brings to the fore the hypocrisy of the upper caste people, she successfully highlights the ignorance and pigheadedness of her 'own' people who would not come out of their ignorance. To her, this is the biggest challenge to pull out the people from the darkness of ignorance as they have internalised their ideologically promoted hegemonic image and would resist any change in status-quo. Takbhoure narrates an interesting account in this regard:

> I always told my people: 'Stop running after religion, and try to understand the notion of social awareness and revolution. Embrace development and change. Maharishi Valmiki was a Brahmin; he is neither our forefather nor our preceptor. Dr Ambedkar is our only leader and well-wisher. Embrace his teachings and thought.' My own people then stopped inviting me to Valmiki Jayanti celebrations. (246)

Sushila Takbhoure also questions the legitimacy of the Hindu scriptures by testing them on basic human parameters. "These Hindu scriptures preach *varnashram dharma* and uphold casteist society and still are venerable. They are the foundational texts for our oppression. At that time, it was difficult to think beyond them as the insight and perspective to analyse them and read them with logic was missing" (109).

Without mincing of words, Takbhoure advocates resistance against oppression. "Now the problems must be addressed. The phase of questioning must be over. No more questions but answer—precise answers. The problem is centuries old. We have been suffering since. No more talks of suffering and pain, now we must talk of resistance and rebellion too....we will not succumb, we will force them down, caste must be eradicated—this is the new message to the society" (279).

Thus, Sushila Takbhoure's autobiography is a saga: of suffering, pain and anguish; and at the same time, of struggle, perseverance and rebellion. Through this saga, she poses some disturbing questions to the mainstream Indian society and seeks unambiguous answers to them. Though some of the author's averments may sound radical, they are the by-products of her personal experiences and call for a solution using basic human parameters. As a Dalit woman—a being oppressed at multiple levels, she calls for her rights that any society based on egalitarian principles must accord to its members. The healthy amalgam of her views both as a dalit and a woman, is presented in a poised manner in the following lines: "The society moves in the right direction; fatalism and bigotry is eradicated, my people [dalits] get to know their constitutional rights and be able to get them though education and struggle, women get liberated from oppression and injustice and become really empowered, get respect and equality in the society—it should be the duty and aim of every enlightened being" (292).

Hence, Takbhoure envisions a social order that is founded on the humanitarian principles of liberty, equality, fraternity and justice; it's an order where there is no oppression on the basis of class, caste or gender. While addressing key Dalit issues, she successfully induces the reader to perspectivise Dalit experience in the right spirit rather than brushing it aside by terming it divisive and fatal for the Indian society. This is a significant contribution to Dalit cause. Rather than perceiving things from a narrow position—either that of a Dalit or a woman, she is essentially humanistic and liberal. Her understanding of the concept of woman emancipation and empowerment also holds testimony to this aspect of her writings:

> Woman Emancipation and Empowerment actually mean that women do not remain confined to their home and hearth only; they should move ahead in every walk of life. They should get their rights along with their duties and attain a respectful life and personality. Only when the present generation and the generations to come understand this basic fact, the path of their growth and prosperity will open. Man and woman are two wheels of the chariot of life; both should get equal status and opportunities. (292)

Works Cited

Ambedkar, B.R. "Untouchability and the Caste System." *Ideas Aglow*. Ed. Dinesh Kumar & V.B. Abrol. Kurukshetra: Kurukshetra University Press, 2004. 38-41.

Limbale, Sharankumar. *Towards an Aesthetic of Dalit Literature: History Controversies and Considerations.* Alok Mukherjee, translator. New Delhi: Orient Blackswan, 2004.

Kumar, Raj. *Dalit Personal Narratives: Reading Caste, Nation and Identity*. New Delhi: Orient BlackSwan, 2011.

Mukherjee, Alok. "Reading Sharankumar Limbale's *Towards an Aesthetic of Dalit Literature:* From Erasure to Assertion." Limbale, 1-18.

Takbhoure, Sushila. *Shikanje ka Dard*. New Delhi: Vani Prakashan, 2009. Print. (English Translations mine).

6

Urmila Pawar's Voice of Dissent: An Attempt to Uphold Egalitarianism

Dr Ruchi Raj Thakur

The subjugated masses are expected to be tongue tied due to numerous social, political, economic and cultural issues. Certainly, in the course of time, the oppressed find themselves in a better position due to announcements and implementation of new policies aiming at their elevation and welfare. A lot has been done and a lot more needs to be done in the future years to coin parity in all the arenas of life. Literature, which started its journey from imagination, mythology, etc., seems to have changed its focus of attention. Since nineteenth century, literature has become purposive and real. It delves deep into the real world and exhumes the frivolities and harsh truths of life. So to say, such truths are furnishing the writers with the idea to write. Consciousness for the oppressed and subjugated too results from the same observations of the writers. This does not mean that writings are only based on observations because they result from one's experiences too. Dalit writings or voicing the concerns of subalterns, projection of the inhuman experiences of transgender or any minor section of population emerges from this consciousness. Literature is earnestly shouldering the task of informing the readers about such dark realities of oppression, humiliation and subjugation by narrating the stories of those who have been denied the right of a respectable living.

The predicaments of Dalits, which have usually been brushed under the carpet for long, are now acquiring recognition in the literary society. The silence of Dalit has started bothering literary minds and so they have started writing. Dalit writings may come from upper, middle or lower strata. They may have been shaped by Dalit themselves as a mark of retaliation against what is believed and practised in our society. Dalit writings mainly examine the adverse affects of Caste and gender on the lives of Dalits.

Sometimes writings revolve around the first aspect or may revolve around the latter or both become reasons of their plight. One may notice that male Dalits fight for human treatment and equality while Dalit women are fighting because they are subjected to communal violence and gender disparity. It is pertinent to mention that it is a well-acknowledged notion that Dalit men and Dalit women write with a different perspective shaped by their experiences. It is believed that because Dalit men's struggles are different from men so this becomes conspicuous through their writings too. It is said, "This selective amnesia by Dalit males shows that men are not ready to acknowledge Dalit women's contribution to the family, the community and the Dalit movement at large. The absence of these women in the men's narratives is not only deliberate but also calculated. These men refuse to accord their women equality even in literary representation. The silencing and stereotyping of the women has hence led to an alternative voice from the women themselves" (4). Dalit men are also accused of being neutral to the woeful state of Dalit women. It is remarked, "Dalit women's personal narratives not only challenge their absence in Dalit men's narratives but also voice the concerns shared by women across all strata. These alternative accounts openly criticize the patriarchal structure in their society thus reflecting on women's problems with specific issues in a Dalit society" (4).

Education and various awareness programmes have imbued consciousness, sense of dignity and self-pride in the community and so many have started protesting the age-old divisions responsible for their degradation and unacceptability as human beings. Many Dalit women writers use autobiographical expressions to show utter detest for the insensitiveness and shenanigans which are deeply rooted in our social setup. Such writings aim to voice the everyday violence Dalit women experience and endure due to their lowest categorisation in the lowest strata of social hierarchy. The narrative of women and Dalit women does not differ much but their inheritance with lower caste and the way they deal with such brutalities make their battles for recognition distinct. To put it in other words, the woes of women as a whole are universally similar but sometimes the existence of other factors make their experiences a little different from each other. Writers have directed their attention to such peculiar stories where women are struggling at each step to make their existence noticeable. Many Dalit writers have challenged the notion that compels Dalit women to accept exploitation as their fate.

Autobiographies of various Dalit women writers became a new fashion of writing because they felt that none expect the real sufferer could express the pain truly and purely. They also opine that though they are obligated to all the writers who have shifted their attention to the deprived Dalit women community, yet they feel that the miniscule details can only be justly share by the original mouthpieces. Dr Tejaswini aptly says:

> Autobiographies by the upper caste women were not in direct speech. On the contrary, they were in the indirect speech form. Caste rarely appeared in these autobiographies but, it did appear in Dalit women's autobiographies. They probed into the evil practices of Dalit community, and writer gave criticism of the community from within. The life of Brahmin women, in fact, was different from that of Dalit women as their life was filled with rituals, customs and so. (89)

In support of the argument, Shweta says, "While men choose to remember their humiliation and clamour for self-respect in society, women vocalise their concerns over the double exploitation. Representation itself raises questions of authenticity or alleged authenticity; imagination or perception; and reality or actuality. An autobiography with its claim of genuine remembrance and retelling can also have a counter-claim of genuine forgetting and omission as is evident from the treatment of women in male autobiographies" (45).

A peculiar feature that strengthened their strife for recognition was that they raised voice for the whole Dalit women community and not in the individual drive. Sharmila Rege has a similar take on this. She argues, "Dalit life narratives are in fact testimonies, which forge a right to speak both for and beyond the individual and provide the context explicit or implicit for the official forgetting of histories of caste oppression, caste struggle and resistance" (Rege 2006: 13).

It is pertinent to mention that the voyage to gain recognition was set long back. It started with Phule and Ambedkar. Babytai Kamble, Shantabai Kamble, Mukta Sarvagod, Kumud Pawde and Urmila Pawar are a few names who have emerged to underline the double exploitation faced by women. Various Dalit women writers are using their pens to the hilt so as to record the stories of humiliation and subservience to the so-called savarans. They also write to inform the readers about their deplorability in the social, political and economic peripheries. Another aim which compels them to write is to bring to surface their narratives so that they may not only understand their negligible position in the society but also work for their own upliftment.

Speaking about Gayatri Spivak, Clara Nubile writes, "the voice of the subalterns cannot be heard properly: It is not so much that subaltern women did not speak, but rather that others did not speak, but rather that others did not know how to listen, how to enter into a transaction between speaker and listener. The subaltern cannot be heard because of their words cannot properly interpreted. Hence, the silence of the female as subaltern is the result of failure of interpretation and not a failure of articulation" (35).

Dalit Autobiographical expression is a diverse ways of challenging the social mores and the rigid approach of the society towards them. Urmila Pawar brings to fore how her personal experience shaped her writing style and changed her outlook in life. It also traces her journey from a Dalit girl of Konkan to a bride of Ratnagiri and then a Mumbaite. She could not endure the injustices and humiliation of her community and so decided to retaliate against the same with a special mention directed to Ambedkarite movement and its influence. She became an activist and promoted her aim through her role playing in theatre, awareness camps and her writing predilection. Deshpande writes, "In *Aaydan*, Urmila dedicatedly navigates her readers through her long journey from the harsh landscape of the Konkan region to Mumbai—first as a Mahar and later as a woman—as she challenged the conventions of both caste and gender to emerge as an activist and a strong literary voice".

Urmila Pawar's *The Weave of My Life: A Dalit Woman's Memoir* is an attempt to unveil the harsh realities experienced by Dalit women. These narratives are not mere fictions but they are the stories which Pawar or almost every Dalit woman has lived, seen and questioned all through her life. She has attempted to unfold the stories of struggle, exploitation, and suppression vis-à-vis caste, gender and class. Pawar has also attempted to give voice to the frightened Dalit women who have been unheard or unspoken. Pawar's attempt will be fruitious only if the woes of these women are heard.

Urmila weaves variegated forms of subjugation in her autobiography. She highlights the stories of powerlessness, apathy and dispassion as inseparable part of Dalit women's existence. She sketches a detailed picture of her community by sensitively and consciously highlighting gender prejudices and the lowest and demeaning social status women of her community are placed on. She recounts many instances of her experience in her autobiography. *The Weave of My Life,* which originally is *Aaydaan*, has used the concept of weaving to depict the low status of Dalits and extreme poverty they are compelled to live in. Urmila's mother weaves bamboo baskets to earn and sustain. She declares, "My mother used to weave *aaydans*. I find that her act of weaving and my act of writing are originally linked. The weave is similar. It is the weave of pain, suffering and agony that links us" (9).

Her mother had been a great inspiration for her because from her she had learned that the biggest folly of any human being would be to tolerate unnecessary oppression and injustice. The childhood learning impacted her life so much that she never compromised in her life to please any one. She stood against all odds fearlessly and fought her battles fiercely. In her school too she did not feel intimidated from her teacher who once told her to clean school verandah. She was slapped by him "Because I refused to clean the school veranda" (56). This infuriated her mother and quoted a proverb! "When it is the widow's son's turn to receive alms, the giver gets a boil on his palms!" Everybody else can get education, but when it's the turn of my child, it turns out to be a big problem" (56).

Her mother had managed her life all alone because her father had died in her early years of childhood. Pawar had lamented the condition of her mother who used to toil day and night to feed her children. No matter how much she worked, life was not easy for them. This has been underscored categorically in the writer's autobiography. She writes, "Therefore food was always scarce in our house" (79).

Urmila has recounted all forms of exploitation, her people had endured due to the caste and social structure, in her autobiography but she directed her special attention to her women community as they had accepted their vulnerability as their fortune. She voices the doleful condition of her women so as to empower the women of this community. She writes to the hilt to represent their unending sufferings within the patriarchal set up where they are pushed to the wall to be placed at the relegated position. Urmila Pawar also questions this unfair treatment experienced by Dalit women. She champions the cause of these women by challenging the stereotypes and inculcating much needed self-respect by enabling them to value their existence and negating the unbalanced standards of society and the upper caste dwellers. She remarks:

> The women were commodified and exploited as they were considered not to be at par with men; the lack of representation despite a general sense of injustice harbours a despondent narration. While domestic abuse, be it mental, physical, psychological or verbal, was finally recognised there is still a lack of fair representation of Dalit women. The contribution of women to the household economy is also overlooked. It was not in the writings of the upper caste or Dalit women but in the writings of the upper caste men that the upper caste women had been valorised, the middle class marginalised and the Dalits victimized. (45-46)

To depict Dalit women's woes, Urmila has illustrated all incidents, acts and deeds of the upper caste living around her community so as to remind the readers of the deep patriarchy. Despite, these women's more than equal involvement in making the family economically sustainable, domestic violence remains a darker chapter of their existence. They are beaten and thrashed but they still discharge their duties sincerely with a hope that someday their contribution will be acknowledged.

The writer remembers it clearly that many women would get back to their domestic chores even in excruciating pain inflicted on them by their husbands for a simple reason of not sponsoring their husbands liquor expenses. Her eyes pained to see the state of these unfortunate women who would walk painfully by somehow managing to drag their aching bodies to work. These women would hurl abuses at their husbands when alone and would pray for their deaths too. They would say, "Let his drinking mouth be burned off forever. Let his hands rot" (23).

In our patriarchal social structure, men would flaunt their supremacy for being men. If this is so, then why are family and economic obligations trounced on women. They would have to cater to men's needs. They would look into household affairs, feed children, raise them, earn for family as a whole and some for the husband because the husbands have urge to booze in the evening and then of course they have to satisfy their husbands' sexual desires too. The writer adds more to the already scornful and pathetic conditions of Dalit women by saying that these women would toil day in and day out by developing endurance for starvation. With a sense of duty and responsibility, they would not eat anything all day so that they could return to their kids a little early or may be on time. Pawar narrates the plight of these women through her writings and she writes:

> The walk back home would be quite different. Their baskets would be light. Some of the women, before they started their journey back, would first sit in our yard, draw water from the well, quench their thirst, roast cheap tiny fish on dry twigs and eat them with some dry bread. But some, who did not have any time even for this meagre refreshment, would start walking the long way. They would just take some morsels of dry bread and fish in their hand and nibble on them while walking. (25)

Urmila Pawar grew up witnessing all such social evils closely. Her family environment also conditioned her consciousness and she decided to raise a voice of dissent so as to purge the society off such disparaging traditions. Her mind resisted to see her sister's condition who was also a victim of domestic violence. She was tortured to all limits to which she ultimately succumbed and lost her life. Pawar cannot forget the untimely death because of her husband's brutal patriarchal mind set. She writes agonizingly:

> Tai tried hard to cope with the problems: space, crowding, people, heaps of dirt, spit covered walls, hoards of flies hovering all over, and the rats and mice. But soon she was at her wits' end. Besides, she had a morning job. She had to get up at the crack of dawn, make chapatis and vegetables for all the people in the house, and reach her office in time to sign the register. She returned to a house in which soiled clothes and dirty utensils would be kept so that she might wash them. Once she had cleaned them, she had to cook the evening dinner! Her mother-in-law ... got angry all too easily—when Tai was late in doing something, when she took help from her sisters-in-law, when she did not like what Tai did. Any of these would make her get mad at Tai. She thought that work in the office was nothing but just sitting in a chair and relaxing. She complained, "How much more work will I do?" The outbursts invariably ended in a threat to commit suicide under the train. Sometimes she really pretended to walk out of the house for that express purpose. That's when Tai's father-in-law and husband vented their fury on Tai. Poor Tai poured her heart out to us when she came on a visit, and my brother would say, "Here she comes with her tales of woe!" (99)

Urmila laments that subjugation was ingrained in the life of Mahars from the beginning. Girls and boys were taught how to behave as per the requirement of the social concept of 'gender'. Boys were told to command while girls to remain subservient to any male figure in their respective families. Urmila detests such a practice and so whenever she used to notice her brother intimidating his wife, her sister-in-law, she would interfere and tell her brother not to. She tells that there was a ritual in Mahar community that was to be observed at the time of marriage ceremony. She narrates:

> There was a game that taught the groom how to deal with his wife. The bride would be given a pot to carry water on her head and also a small jug and sent away with four or five karavalis or girl attendants to some distance. Then the groom would be made to sit on the threshold at the back door of the house, with a stick in his hand. They would teach him the lines he would have to tell the wife when she returned. When the bride came back with the water, he would strike the ground with the stick and demand an explanation, "Why are you so late?" The women would help the bride to come up with answers such as, "I was late because the cows muddied the water, so I had to wait till the water cleared," or "The rope fell into the well and I had to wait till it could be brought out," and so on. Then they would make her swear that she would never be late again." (76)

Urmila never found any rational in such rituals but she knew it was not easy for her to make her people comprehend that such rituals were only desolating the lives of Mahar women.

She herself became prey to gender discrimination. An incident from her life filled her heart with hatred for such oppression which shook her out of wits. She recalls, "I was an unwanted child because I was a girl, when I was born, my cousin Govindadada wanted to throw me away on the dung heap. When I grew a little older, many would beat me" (54). Her heart still misses a beat to remember that she could have trapped in the evil designs of her uncle who tried to molest her and took advantage of her innocence. She writes, "My maternal uncle plays dolls with me and pretends to be my husband drags me into an alcove and presses me hard" (125). She had also tried to speak against the duality of Brahmins who had always stopped lower caste from entering the temple but she her childhood memories had never stopped chasing her. What she could mutely see in her child was protested in her writings. In her autobiography she retaliates against the hypocrite society which calls Dalits 'untouchables' but does not mind making out with the lower caste women or girls. She herself had noticed a priest raping a lower caste girl in the temple but could not react to it at that moment.

Urmila writes that almost every day her village would witness a strange incident of male supremacy. When she was in class nine or ten, she witnessed the most horrific incident of her life. A widow of her village was reported to be pregnant and she had refused to abort her baby. The so called wise men 'sarpanches' of the village pronounces the abortion to be done by kicking the woman till the baby finally gets aborted. It would not be incorrect to say that it was indeed a valiant act of bravery because they managed to protect the false honour of the village. She adds:

> In another incident, when an eight-month-pregnant woman openly accused her husband of having illicit relations with another woman, the villagers gave her the same punishment. Women, mad with excitement, kicked her till the baby died inside her, and the woman died in pain in a week's time. Why should this so-called honour, this murderer of humanity, this tool of self-destruction, be so deeply rooted in women's blood? (103)

As a woman, Pawar herself had witnessed a lot of dominance. Life as a bride was not simple for her. She had to make various adjustments in her new family so as to assimilate in her husband's world. Of course, assimilation and adaptation are not easy for anyone and so was hard for Urmila too. On getting married to Harishchandra, she had to change herself completely. She could never imagine that her husband would also value her virginity on top of everything. After making love with her on the first night, her husband proclaimed with pride that his wife was a virgin. She narrates her private experience:

> I got up in the morning and was horrified to discover that I was bleeding. My periods were regular. So I was quite confused as to how this had happened...I asked my husband, who was loitering behind me in the verandah, said, "Aho, how did this happen?" He gave me a sharp tap on the head and said, "You idiot, don't you understand? Let us go in; I'll tell Aai. The first time is always like this." But he was not really scolding me; he was laughing. He had yet another proof of my virginity! Of course, this may not happen with all women. (118)

Our society measures a woman's character with the virginity report that her husband announces after making love with her for the first time. If female's hymn breaks and she bleeds, she is declared 'pure' and if it does not then she is looked with suspicion for she could have slept with many men and that certifies her 'impurity'. Using this yardstick to weigh one's strong character or weak would have been still acceptable if men too undergo the same examination. But our society does not mind being dual faced. In an article published in *The Times of India*, Dr Mahindra Vatsa, a gynaecologist and sex counsellor, "It's just the man's and his family's inflated ego that results in such unrealistic demands". Rachel Fernandas opines, "Remember, virginity and chastity are not the only measures to base a happy marriage on, honesty and trust are far more important traits that both should possess" (*TOI* n.pag.).

Urmila feels agonised to recall that on the very first night she was told about her frigidity in the bed. She broods over women's pathetic condition who cannot express their desire openly because if they do so then their husbands might suspect their moral conduct and if they do not then they earn the title of being frigid. She writes, "Had I taken any initiative, he would have suspected my virginity! I was not at all frigid! I understood every move very well. However, these were being done to me against my wishes...(118). Urmila did not wish to spoil her relations with her husband, so mechanically kept nodding at every demand her husband made. She kept listening to her mother-in-laws advices for quiet good years of her married life. Few of her words were engraved on Urmila's mind. She writes, "Yet a sentence Aai once said had made a deep impression on my mind. "If the husband calls you a whore, the whole world is ready to sleep with you." So I was absolutely sure that I wanted to have good relations with my husband. At any cost!" (124).

Initial days of her marriage were not smooth. She was insulted by her husband for her mother's extreme poverty too. On her first visit to her Aai's house after her marriage, her Aai could never welcome Urmila's husband with pomp and show. This offended Harishchandra and so he insulted her in return. She narrates, "He pinched my arm hard and exploded, "Ugh ... what a house! And what a mother-in-law! Miser of the first order! What a gift she bestows on her son-in-law! A bag of shellfish! To hell with your mother and your family!" (118).

As a writer, she is also heard of talking about menstruating cycle as a natural phenomenon. Not only as a child she was humiliated for menstruating but after her marriage too it became a big problem. She says, "When she got her first period, she started to cry. Her mother handed her a piece of cloth and asked her to sit in one corner lest she make things in the house "impure" by touching them...as if I wasn't discriminated enough by others outside, now family too, has set rules for me". (87) After her marriage too, she faced the same because her mother-in-law religiously observed the restrictive measure to maintain purity of the house. But the observance of those details during the menstruating days was very difficult for Urmila because she was too new for the environment. She recalls her initial days in her in-law's house. She writes, "During those days, washing the pads was a great problem. I had to hide them. When I went to wash, Mai would accompany me and draw water from the well. Again my *sasu* asked, "Haven't you washed clothes just now? What are you washing again? And why are both of you going at the same time?" She would watch me like a policeman" (120). As a child and as a grown up too, she could never understand the practice of making her sit in a corner and reminding her off to refrain from touching anything because that could defile the environment. This is a way she has resisted against the society's mention of 'purity' and 'impurity'. Her fearless approach to life and the audacious writing makes her a very popular Dalit feminist writer and wins her a lot of readership.

Urmila raised her voice by writing about these social mores responsible for the subdued condition of women in Mahar community. Her writing penchant also became a victim of society's patriarchal mind set. Though Urmila's husband ridiculed her for various reasons but did not stop her from completing her graduation, though a few conditions were pronounced. When I asked for Harishchandra's consent, he said, "Look, you can do what you like only after finishing your daily chores in the house. Cooking, looking after children, and all that stuff. If you think you can do this and get more education, fine!" This was actually his way of saying "No," but I took it up as a challenge" (153).

Urmila was comfortable with her husband because he stood with her whenever she needed him. She recalls how her procurement of graduation degree was celebrated by him. He would flaunt that she was a graduate. Harish never stopped her from working outside the house. She was also very determined of earning and not depending on her husband. She shares:

> When I got my first salary, I could not believe that all that money was mine; that I could spend it the way I liked. Before my marriage, I used to hand over my salary to my mother. Now I started handing it over to my husband. If this is not like deliberately offering your head for the butcher's knife, what else is it? (139)

Urmila was comfortable with her husband because he stood with her whenever she needed him. He was more than delighted to have an educated wife but Urmila's desire to do post graduation infuriated him to the extent of destroying the close marital bond they once shared. Harishchandra would always question her about the need to do post graduation. He would tell her to focus on her family and children which Urmila was already doing splendiferously. She retorted:

> Look, I am paying enough attention to the house and the children. I take good care of their food, studies, and all the household work. Besides, I work in the office as well. My children are quite healthy. And if they ever fall ill with some minor ailment, I take leave and nurse them without sleeping a wink at night. I am looking after them very well, thank you! It is you who needs to pay more attention to the house now. Instead of going to the bar, why don't you come home early and pay some attention to their studies? That would be far better. Besides, whatever I study, I do it in my spare time! Why should you object to it? (155-156)

Explaining things to Harishchandra was not easy because right from the beginning men are taught that looking after the house is the sole responsibility of the women. Men have the freedom to behave the way they wish. Life could not again be simple for Urmila because she has set on to the journey to live her dreams and do something for the well being of Dalit women. Before joining Maitrini group, she tried numerous times to reconcile with her husband but all her attempts were dashed to smithereens. After a long and tiring working day, Urmila would still press her husband's feet to make him happy. She says, "I was ready to die for a smile, a glance from him". But he accused me, "Let alone an ideal wife, you are not even a good one!" (159) Men seem to have taken Manusmriti's saying rather seriously who propagated that:

> The wife should even treat the husband as God though he is characterless, sensual and devoid of good qualities.... If the wife disobeys the husband when he is given to bad habits or

> becomes a drunkard or is suffering from physical ailment, then for three months she should be deprived of her valuable clothes and jewels and kept away...Day and night women must be kept in dependence by the males of their families... her father protects her in childhood, her husband protects her in youth and her sons protect her in old age; a woman is never fit for independence. (qtd. in Ambedkar 429)

Urmila endured the pain of her husband's hostility because she loved him dearly. Her heart would often miss a beat when he would accuse her of being a bad mother. All her painful experiences and endurances made her a strong headed woman who wanted to discover herself. She decides to write but becoming writer was not very easy for her. She writes, "my writing, which was getting published, my education, my participation in public programmes—irritated Mr Pawar no end. Gradually, he began to be full of resentment" (159). She faced numerous discouragements and de-motivating moments but nothing could stop her from becoming a writer. Her penchant for writing was never treasured in her family. The same resentment for her writing dexterity and predilection was shown to Urmila by her children about which she says, "...and my son and my two girls misunderstood me because they could not understand my need to have a life beyond home. It's as if our lives had been juxtaposed" (*The Theatre Times* n.pag.).

Urmila also brings to the notice of her readers that nothing but only writing would give her a sense of satisfaction. She would complete her household chores and at night would sit down to write without any disturbance. Her husband would often tell her take rest lest she would fall ill but Urmila would tell herself not to stop until her goal, to reform the society, is attained. Extensive hard work and lack of sleep would result in severe headaches. But she could not gather the courage to tell her husband to press her head. She writes:

> How can a wife ask her husband to do such things! I also avoided asking him to do such things. Not because I wanted to save him that bother, but because if I asked for something, he would demand something else! Many a time, I would write in the dark. I would keep a pen and papers near the pillow and write whatever came to my mind, even in the dark. I did not want to forget and forego. Thus, I continued to write. (149)

Urmila wrote and worked for destitute women. In her activism, she sensed the futility of her attempts to reconcile with her husband. She even found wearing mangalsutra meaningless. She could only see it as a symbol of subservience. She does not conceal her feelings in her writings about the meaninglessness of the string. She tells that she had mustered the courage to go to the women's programmes without wearing the mangalsutra, but for marriages or naming ceremonies I would customarily wear it. She narrates it categorically:

> Sometimes my troubled conscience made me go to the office and elsewhere with a bare neck. If somebody asked my why, I would deliver a lecture on women's liberation. And sometimes, when my heart overflowed with love for me husband, I found myself wearing it again. In the beginning, my husband would throw a fit if he found me without the mangalsutra. But, later on, even he vacillated between...! (163)

Urmila has faced a lot at every front and every day became posed a threat to her new found identity. She stood all odds and made a mark for herself in her world and in the literary world too. She has inspired many Dalit women to protest social fetters to discover themselves. She was combating against all the odds not only in her outer world but inner world too. She decides not to merely lament the social mores but to deal with them sternly. She fought audaciously against these detrimental forces to discover herself after triumph over her sense of humiliation and inferiority which have been inextricable to her existence ever since her childhood. She was determined to make women to acknowledge that all of them were individuals and certainly have entitlement to all rights of an individual. She questioned the social notion that man has muscle strength which is not a big deal because then the fact to appreciate and consider is that she is the creator of the universe. All human beings have distinct capacities and should neither be compared. Urmila wishes the society to live with a new vision and a new perspective which does not uphold gender disparity. She also envisions seeing an unafraid world which purges off subordination and authority completely. She promulgates a world in which every man and woman is equal individuals. Her efforts will bore fruit only if the world sets itself free from all prejudices and biases on the basis of caste and gender.

Works Cited

Pawar, Urmila. *The Weave of My Life: A Dalit Woman's Memoirs*. Columbia University Press, September 2015.

Hemangi. "Aaydaan"—Urmila Pawar's Drama about Dalit Women in India. India, Review, Theatre and Gender. *The Theatre Times*, July 17, 2016.

Narayankar, Dr Tejaswini P. "Dalit Autobiography: An Evaluation of Individual Self." *Research Front* 2.2 (2014).

Nagpaul, Dipti. "Notes from the Margins: Dalit writer Urmila Pawar's Autobiography Inspires a Marathi Play. *The Indian Express*. July 20, 2014. https://indianexpress.com/article/lifestyle/notes-from-the-margins-dalit-writer-urmila-pawars-autobiography-inspires-a-marathi-play/

Nubile, Clara. *The Danger of Gender: Caste, Class and Gender in Contemporary Indian Women's Writing*. Sarup & Sons Publishers, 2003.

Rege, Sharmila. *Against the Madness of Manu*. Delhi: Navayana, 2013.

—. *Writing Caste, Writing Gender: Reading Dalit Women's Testimonios*. New Delhi: Zubaan, 2006.

Singh, Shweta. "Representation of Dalit Women in Dalit Men's and Women's Autobiographies." *The Delhi University Journal of The Humanities & The Social Sciences*. Volume 1: 2014. pp. 39-47.

Mahurkar, Vaishnavi. "The Truth about Fiction: Looking at Caste, Gender and Dissent in Urmila Pawar's Short Stories". February 10, 2017.

7

The Barriers She Had to Cross: The Struggle of a Dalit Woman through Hegemony as in Bama's *Karukku*

Dr Justin James

I

Dalit literature came into existence comparatively recently, but it has carved its indisputable place in Indian literature in particular and world literature in general with its unique identity as one of the compelling genres of literature. It is the outcome of growing Dalit consciousness. It is a part of the fourth world literature, which brings to light the marginal position of the so-called 'lower caste' society. The emergence and growth of the fourth world literature are about the economic, social, political, and cultural scenario of the marginalised. Dalit literature chants not only of the sufferings and agonies of Dalits but also of how they have made their way through the antagonism that surrounds and suppresses them. There are not many Dalit writers and among them a very few are women writers. Dalit women's autobiographies are a rare phenomenon, especially in Tamil. Bama's *Karukku* is one such exceptional creation, and it is translated into English by Lakshmi Holmstrom. Though it talks about the life of its author, it can be taken as the biography of the Dalit community as a whole; it is the voice of Dalit consciousness. This article analyses *Karukku* from social and gender perspectives. To understand the plight of the Dalits, the chapter employs the theories of two great Indian personae who waged war against the caste system and patriarchy—B.R. Ambedkar and E.V. R. Periyar. The application of Western feminist and subaltern theories is consciously and deliberately avoided in this study, as there is always a question lurking in my mind as to whether the Occidental minds can voice out the agony of the Oriental Dalits.

Bama, also known as Faustina Mary Fatima Rani and Bama Faustina Soosairaj, a contemporary Dalit writer and a dedicated teacher, was born into a Tamil Christian Dalit family in the year 1958. She has experienced all the afflictions that a Dalit woman is destined to undergo. Her family converted into Christianity with the hope that they would relish better living conditions. Her father was serving in the military. She had an average life of a Dalit family in her childhood until she reached her adulthood. She had a collegiate education, which was not readily available for the women of the Dalit community. She completed her BEd too. She was posted as a teacher in a school. She resigned from her post and entered into a nunnery as she thought that she would be able to serve the poorest of the poor through the religious order. But there she found that things were not as she imagined them to be. So, she came out of the nunnery and came back into society to live a life of ordinary men. Bama could surmount the difficulties she faced as a Dalit, as a woman, and as a Tamil, emerged as a successful writer and has made her mark in the field of literature. Her books are translated into English. Her success as a writer can also be attributed to the fact that she does not entirely blame society for the subjugation of Dalits. She also recognizes the drawbacks and flaws inherent among the Dalit community itself.

II

Bama rose to prominence as a writer with her autobiography *Karukku* (1992). She can be termed as a feminist, as she touches upon the feminist issues too in her works. Her *Sangati* (1994) is another novel that tells the readers of the everyday life of Dalits. Her story *Vanmam* (2002) reveals how inter-caste rivalry becomes an impediment in the uprising of Dalits. *Kusumbukkaran* (1996), *Oru Tattavum Erumaiyum* (2003), and *Kondattam* (2009) are three collections of her short stories. *Just One Word* is another of her short story collections in which she has depicted the people she lived with and has placed them in their social context. Her novels and short stories centre on the life and position of Dalits and Dalit women in the patriarchal, caste-conscious society. Her style is powerful with the employment of the real day-to-day language of Dalits.

III

Karukku is the first autobiography of its kind in Tamil Dalit writing. As every autobiography tells the readers the story of its subject, *Karukku* also portrays the life of the writer, Bama. But, what is unique about it is the genuineness and simplicity with which it is told and its evolution into a genre as a social discourse in addition to being self-introspective in tone. It is a story not only of the life of the author, but also of her community as a whole and, appropriately, the protagonist is not named in the story. It is a Dalit discourse of discontentment. The lives of the author and her community are intertwined as one. It is an expression of the silenced subaltern experience, anguish, and agony. What Dhawan and Sumita Puri have said in their "Introduction" to *Bama: A Dalit Feminist* is appropriate for *Karukku*.

> Writings by Dalit women have emerged as a counter-movement to mainstream Indian feminism, becoming a 'site of resistance.' The journey for a non-upper caste/class Dalit woman like Bama becomes all the more arduous in the construction of the Dalit self. The confessional mode of the autobiography transcends the form of the personal narrative

> to embrace the pain and suffering of the entire community. (19-20)

Karukku portrays the barriers the Dalit women have to cross—social barrier, economic barrier, linguistic barrier, and gender barrier—generalising what Bama has experienced. A careful and concentrated reading would tell the readers how Bama tries to overcome these barriers and emerge successfully. Bama says in *Karukku*:

> *Karukku*, written by a wounded self, has not been dissolved in the stream of time. On the contrary, it has been a means of relieving the pain of others who were wounded. *Karukku* has been of comfort to many who have been brought low, and suffer the pain of caste discrimination, untouchability, poverty, and destitution; it has given them courage and helped them to love life once more. *Karukku* stands as a means of strength to the multitudes whose identities have been destroyed and denied. (x)

The translator Lakshmi Holmstrom says:

> *Karukku* was written out of a specific experience, the experience of a Tamil Dalit Christian woman. Yet it has a universality at its core which questions all oppressions, disturbs all complacencies, and, reaching out, empowers all those who have suffered different oppressions. It is precisely because it tells the story of Bama's personal struggle to find her identity that *Karukku* also argues so powerfully against patriarchy and caste oppression. (xiv)

There is not only patriarchal hegemony and caste hegemony, but the basis for these is also economic hegemony. There are social barrier, economic barrier, language barrier, and gender barrier that a Tamil Dalit woman has to cross.

IV

Dalits are treated as untouchables in the caste-ridden society. In earlier times, caste just denoted the familial profession. But, as time went by, people have begun considering some professions lowly, and even today, the people in these professions are being ill-treated and considered as 'lower caste.' These 'lower caste' people are treated as slaves by the 'upper caste' people. In *Karukku,* the area in which they live is in the centre of the village because the 'upper caste' people find it convenient to have the Dalits at their beck and call. All the government offices, big shops, the church, and schools are in the streets where the Naikers, Thevars, Chettiyars, Aasaaris and the Nadars live. These people use the Dalits for menial works and as labourers in their agricultural fields. They give them meagre wages and treat them almost like slaves. The Dalits are aware of what they are, but they take it as their destiny.

Even as a child of eight years, the protagonist has experienced the humiliation as a Dalit. She has accompanied her grandfather, grandmother, and mother, who have been working for Naiker families. She has witnessed how they have been disgraced and affronted. As she grows and gains knowledge and awareness, she becomes skeptical. She reflects:

> Because Dalits have been enslaved for generation upon generation, and been told again and again of their degradation, they have come to believe that they are degraded, lacking honour and self-worth, untouchable; they have reached a stage where they themselves, voluntarily, hold themselves apart. This is the worst injustice. ... The consequence of all this is that there is no way for Dalits to find freedom or redemption. (28)

Once, she was accused of stealing a coconut just because she was a Dalit and from Cheri. In her hostel, "The Warden-Sister ... get hold of us and scold us for no rhyme or reason. If a girl tended to be on the plump side, she'd get it even more" (20). The same plight continues in her college life too. There too, she is treated with contempt for her caste.

Karukku narrates the spiritual growth of the protagonist. It also describes her beliefs and her efforts to understand the real meaning of the *Bible*. Besides, it portrays her childlike fears about her insignificant 'sins,' her disenchantment, and the final liberation that she seeks. The repeated reading of the *Bible* and the recitation of the hymns helped her form a vision and mission. She gives a trajectory of her spiritual growth. Her inner courage, strengthened by her spirituality, makes her bold.

The most painful moments of Bama's life are during the days of her stay in the convent. On seeing how the nuns treat the poor and the oppressed, she decides to become a nun herself to serve the poor, resigning the job that she was in. All the people whom she knows well warn her against her decision, with no effect. She is full of dreams of becoming a saviour of the poor through the religious order. But all her hopes and fancies are entirely shattered.

Through the protagonist, the autobiography unravels how the Church exploits Dalits. She comprehends enormous deep-rooted contradictions that lie between what is exhibited as Church to the people outside it and what the real Church inside is. The Dalits are not innocent of what the Church is doing to them, and they are not blind to it either. They feel that they cannot do anything against it as they are economically underprivileged. They are aware of what may be happening inside the Church and the convent. When the protagonist discusses with her family about her decision to enter into the convent as a nun, they warn her about the actuality. But she is stubborn in her decision and realises the truth of their words only when she experiences it. She is aghast by the caste and economic prejudices that she witnesses and experiences there. The nuns in the convent have preconceived notions set about the Dalits and despise them for no fault of theirs. In the convent and the Church, Biblical doctrines are preached, but not practised. The figure of Christ is used as a threat to the innocent commoners to keep them under their control. The protagonist tries to re-read the Bible for its real meaning, not for the meaning given by the Church and the convent. She realises that neither the Church nor the convent provides the actual and factual context of the Bible.

At last, she is forced to exit the convent fighting against her superiors and questioning the establishment. She comes into the outside world empty-handed, no job to fetch her any earning, nothing to support her family or even to herself. She feels estranged from herself and the world outside. The convent has converted her completely. It has drained her of all her courage, confidence, and veracity. To face the reality of the world, she has to recreate and regain her assertive self, shedding off the present shattered self. She breaks the long-lasting silence about the shameful secrets of the Church.

K. Narasimha Rao, in his article "Teleology of the Differential Imperative: Bama Faustina's Select Works," says, "Dr B. R. Ambedkar upheld a quest for Dalit self-respect as against Gandhian emphasis on Dalit quest for self-purification as a precondition for the eradication of untouchability" (62). Dalits quest for self-respect, but at the same time, for them, this self-respect is a by-product of the respect that the 'upper caste' bestows upon them.

The protagonist understands that it is their economic position that keeps them down to dust. When she sees the 'upper caste' people belittling the Dalits, she muses over what they do to the Dalits:

> How was it that these fellows thought so much of themselves? Because they had scraped four coins together, did that mean they must lose all human feelings? What did it mean when they called us 'Paraya'? Had the name become that obscene? But we too are human beings. Our people should never run petty errands for these fellows. We should work in their fields take home our wages, and leave it at that. (15-16)

The Dalits remain poor because they are not given due wages for their labour. They are always in a state of poverty, scarcity, and shortage. The protagonist reflects, "How did the upper castes become so elevated? How is it that we have been denigrated? They possess money; we do not. If we were wealthy too, wouldn't we learn more, and make more progress than they do?" (27). So, they need to find some way out of their present despicable condition and become economically elevated.

In the convent, there is not just caste discrimination; there is linguistic discrimination too. Tamils are mortified. The protagonist says, "... thus far they made us hang our heads in humiliation because of our caste; in this order being a Tamil seems to be equivalent to being a Paraya" (24). In the convent too, her promotion is stopped by a nun just because she does not like Tamil nuns. Her denigrated state infuriates the protagonist.

V

Though in the "Introduction" to *Karukku* Lakshmi Holmstorm writes, "*Karukku* is concerned with the single issue of caste oppression within the Catholic Church and its institutions, and presents Bama's life as a process of lonely self-discovery" (xvii), Bama touches upon gender issue also here.

In Dalit community, like other communities in India, women are the ones to do the household chores, even after they return home from the hard labour of the day. When the older women go out on work, it is always the girl children who have to look after the household chores. In the workplace, there are no equal wages for equal labour. For the same job done, men are given more wages than women. These are the women who rescue men in times of hardship. In the absence of men, women manage by themselves both the house and the village affairs. They are even smart enough to devise plans to safeguard men and execute their strategies successfully when the men of the whole community have to go into hiding. They are daring enough to fight battles in communal riots. But despite all these, men treat women as their inferiors. Women have to be the outlet for the anger and frustration of their male counterparts. Even in children's play, "... the husband coming home drunk and hitting his wife" (57).

When the protagonist leaves the convent and arrives at Madurai Bus Stand, she is terrified to stand there even for a few minutes. "If it is so difficult even to find a means of living, there is also another great difficulty, the difficulty I find in moving about in the outside world, alone. If a woman so much as stands alone by herself somewhere, all sorts of men gather around her, showing their teeth" (119). Woman is seen and treated as an entity, a source of pleasure, and in opprobrious terms too.

E.V.R. Periyar, in his book *Pen Yen Adimaiyaanal?* (Why Has Woman Become Slave?) lists out ten reasons for gender oppression. He says the concept of chastity, which is now attributed to women, should be held common for both the genders, and it should not be thrust upon people. There should be laws in favour of women. Women should come out of their ignorance. It is no longer their ornament. He questions the concept of love and insists on the union of a male and a female-only with mutual consent. He encourages women to free themselves from marriages that do not give them happiness and fulfillment. He also promotes re-marriage for women. He cites examples from religious books and the lives of Gods. According to Periyar, the word prostitution, which is associated with women alone, is contrived to make women slaves. Women should be given a share in the familial property as this will enable them economic independence. Finally, he says that the concept of masculinity should disappear, and only then will there be true liberation for women.

These concepts of E.V.R. Periyar, though, if followed, may bring women liberation, are not complete by themselves unless the concept of education for women is imbibed in it. It is only through education that women can be independent—both economically and intellectually. Periyar insists on that too.

VI

Now the question arises "How the Dalit woman crossed these barriers of hegemony?" All men are equal before God and law. But some are more equal than the others. Dalit women experience this inequality in many forms throughout their lives. As a representative Dalit woman, Bama talks of the myriad forces that push them down and try to keep them under their feet. There are oppressions from all corners that suffocate her. She has to face oppression as a Dalit, as a woman, as an economically backward person, and as a Tamilian. The way she chooses to come out of all these oppressions is education. It is education that helps her to reach the outer world, helps her to aspire to the development and salvation of her community, helps her to liberate herself and raise her voice for her people. From her school days, her brother has been insisting on the importance of education because he sees it as the only solution for their chronic agony. He has experienced the dignity of education once in the library in his village. He tells her, "Because we are born into the Paraya jati, we are never given any honour or dignity or respect. We are stripped of all that. But if we study and make progress, we can throw away these indignities. So, study with care, learn all you can" (17-18). She takes it to heart as she is aware of the plight of the Dalits in the society. She also realises that it is due to the lack of education that Dalits are not able to break these barriers that are in the way of their progress. The Dalits are also very well aware that they are subjugated by the 'higher class' because they are economically backward. Money brings not only comfort and luxury but also respect. Education is a means to earn money. Being conscious of this fact, Bama resorts to education for an elevation in life and to enable herself to elevate the lives of the children of the Dalit community. She says:

> ... because I had the education because I had the ability, I dared to speak up for myself; if I didn't care a toss about caste. Whatever the situation, I held my head high. And I completed whatever I took up, successfully. ... In this way, because of my education alone I managed to survive among those who spoke the language of caste-difference and discrimination. (22)

She chooses to be a teacher so that she will be able to educate poor children. She enters into a convent and accepts the religious order to serve the poor. When she finds that place to be unfit for her purpose, or rather, when she discovers that it does not allow her to carry out her mission of serving the poor, she leaves it against all the odds. She is not sure what awaits her in the world outside. She is not sure what the future holds for her. She is not sure how her family will receive her. She is not married. She does not possess any job. She has to live alone after her parents. All these challenges are there in front of her. But, still, she stands firm in her decision to leave the convent. The only wealth she possesses is her education. With this in hand, she has become what she is today, a renowned writer and a representative feminist of her community. Her voice, which was not paid heed to, is now listened to everywhere. She, who was insulted and looked down on because she was a Tamil, is now a treasured Tamil writer all over the literary world. She, who was despised because she was a Dalit, is loved by the lovers of literature. She, who was subjugated and dominated by the other gender because she was a woman, is now celebrated as a Dalit feminist. She can achieve this because of her steadfast perseverance, undaunted courage, never-diminishing determination, enlightening education, unwavering dedication, thirst for liberation, and her love for humanity. She has a positive approach and outlook, which is evident in the opening positive lines of *Karukku*, "Our village is very beautiful. Even though you don't see much by way of progress or anything like that here, I love this place for its beauty. Although it's only a small village, many different communities live here" (1). This positive energy drives her throughout her life.

VII

Karukku is a critique of the socio-cultural subjugation and the gender 'othering' of the Dalit women. It is an expression of the collective consciousness of the Dalit community and women. As Bama has said in *Karukku*, it means palm leaf, which has sharp separated edges and is like a double-edged sword. It *hurts* who holds it. It may also be interpreted as referring to 'karu,' which means embryo, a seed—waiting for the befitting and perfect time to sprout, to emerge anew. Dalit women, too, are like an embryo, a seed waiting to bloom, waiting to grow. They are in their breeding period, sleeping under cover of autumn, waiting for their spring, in a while grooming themselves befitting their future, fighting against all forms of subjugation. They stand testimony to Hemmingway's words, "A man can be destroyed but not defeated" (91).

As K. Sareen Raj has written in his article "Exploring Dalit Christian Autobiography: A Perspective on Bama's *Karukku*," "*Annihilation of Caste* written by Ambedkar emphasises on the need to destroy the religious notions on which caste is founded. Dalits have been deprived of religious, economic, political, and social equality from the beginning. They became untouchables in their own land, succumbing to the onslaught of the repressive system" (75). There are laws in the IPC formed by Dr B.R. Ambedkar for the uplift of the Dalits. There have been so many amendments after that for the betterment of Dalits. There is a separate quota allotted for the marginalised for entry into educational institutions and jobs. But, despite all these, there is still segregation, subjugation, and social and economic oppressions on Dalits and gender oppression on Dalit women as on all women; the Dalit women being oppressed thrice, or even four times—as Dalits, as women, as the poor, and as the illiterate.

Dalits' battle against oppression will continue until the caste system and gender discrimination vanished from the surface of the globe. There cannot be a better concluding touch than the words of Lakshmi Holmstrom:

> There is, in this writing, a very powerful sense of the self and the community as Dalit, which rejects outright the notion of varna and which, on the other hand, refuses to 'Sanskritize,' to evaluate Dalit lifestyle according to mainstream Hindu values. There is also at the same time a powerful engagement with history, of change, of changing notions of identity and belonging. Bama captures a moment that contains a paradox: she seeks an identity, but also seeks a change which means an end to that identity. (xix)

Works Cited

Bama. *Karukku*. Trans. by Lakshmi Holmstrom. Oxford UP, 2013.

Dhawan, R.K. & Sumita Puri. "Introduction." *Bama: A Dalit Feminist*. Eds. R.K. Dhawan & Sumita Puri. Prestige Books International, 2016.

Hemmingway, Ernest. *The Old Man and the Sea*. Amazon Kindle Edition, Grapevine Publishers, N.D.

https://timesofindia.indiatimes.com/blogs/tracking-indian-communities/anthology-chronicles-deceits-and-pleasures-of-dalit-existence/

Muthukumar, R. *Ambedkar*. Kizhekku Pathippagam, 2013. https://t.me/tamilbooksworld.

Periyar, Thanthai. *Pen Yen Adimaiyaanal?* Periyar Suyamariyaadhai Prachaara Niruvanam, 2004.

Periyaar. *Azhiyattum Aanmai*. Periyar Dhravidar Kazhagam, 2010.

Raj, K. Sareen. "Exploring Dalit Christian Autobiography: A Perspective on Bama's *Karukku*." *Bama: A Dalit Feminist*. Ed. R. K. Dhawan & Sumita Puri. Prestige Books International, 2016.

Rao, K. Narasimha. "Teleology of the Differential Imperative: Bama Faustina's Select Works."*Bama: A Dalit Feminist*. Eds. R. K. Dhawan and Sumita Puri. Prestige Books International, 2016.

8

Journey of Reclaiming Identity in Kaushalya Baisantri's Autobiography *Dohra Abhishaap*

Dr Meetu Bhatia Kapur

India is a land of various hues and colours found in different caste, class and culture. These hues and colours can be seen portrayed in the strokes of festivals, rituals and literature. Every caste paints its distinctiveness through its literature. This literature acts like a window to understand the society and its habitants which somewhere has lost its glory. Literature becomes its pathfinder. The term 'Dalit' refers to backward, untouchable or underprivileged mean persons who are cut or kept disconnected from the society. Since the people from this group were largely involved in doing menial works or jobs, they eventually came to be considered outcasted, poor, weak and untouchable. Being physically and socially eliminated from the society, their living conditions were quite deplorable for them. There was no way for them to raise their voice and fight for their human rights. Even after independence, there is not much change in their social conditions and living standards. Though many social reform movements did take place, but nothing substantial could work against untouchability. The discrimination and prejudice against Dalits continued. The struggles, subjugations and atrocities from high class communities against Dalits were never ending. It is largely felt that it was only literature which could rescue from this condition.

Dalit section started taking help of literature to express their plight and confront their subjugations. Many Dalit writers like Bama Faustina Soosairaj, Baby Kamble, Urmila Pawar, P. Sivakami, Daya Pawar and Baburao Bagul raised their voices with their own stories of pain and suffering, narrating the anguish of Dalit life in original. The situation of the women in Dalit communities was even more painful. They not only had to fight against caste discrimination, but also against gender discrimination – both inside and outside. There seemed to be no saviour for Dalit women and their woes. It was at this crucial junction that the emancipatory project of a Dalit feminist standpoint came to be approached by upper-caste feminists scholars like Uma Chakravarty, Sharmila Rege and V. Geetha. In fact, they proved to be exemplary that it is not just about Dalit women's autonomy to question the caste structure. Any woman who can feel the pain and silent suffering of a woman even if she's a non-Dalit feminist, can hold the responsibility to question casteism as much as Dalit women do, *albeit* from their specific standpoints and lived experiences. It essentially doesn't imply that a non-Dalit feminist speaks on 'behalf' of Dalit women and tries to appropriate their struggles. The statement simply refers to the fact that caste as a structure exploits women at different levels. Therefore not just from Dalit feminist point of view, but from different standpoints of different degrees and measures, they are also the victims of caste hierarchy and not above this oppressive structure.

Savitri Rao Phule, who, along with her husband Jyotirao Phule and friend Fatima Sheikh, was India's foremost Dalit feminist icon in India. She is credited to have fought tirelessly against the feudal caste system and discrimination. The struggles of Dalit women were of greater magnitude largely owing their caste position. They were not only subjugated by the patriarchal set up of their own caste and society, but also largely by the high-class Brahmans. Savitribai Phule and her husband, in such conditions attacked the Indian society. They not only citied the condition of Dalit women, but also of Hindu widows who were equally suppressed and exploited. The condition of Dalits was more pitiable largely because of the hopelessness for them existing from all quarters and also being marginalised and disposed.

Standpoint Theory is largely responsible for conceptualising the Dalit feminist point of view. The origin comes from a feminist school of thought born from Marxism. The testimony of the fact is that the production of knowledge origins from social epistemological positions can be traced in the Black feminist standpoint. This was largely responsible to encourage several narratives by Dalit women. This led to produce feminist knowledge from their own standpoints. Dalit feminist standpoint, therefore, refers to a spectrum of knowledge consisting of individual testimonies of marginalised women's experiences within the larger social structures. Her suffering, subordination, and awareness of her rights remained restricted to the caste question. It was observed that women's writing did express awareness beyond the caste question. The concern of caste and gender was the main focus area of the Dalit female mobilisation.

The era is broadly widely divided into three divisions:

1. Conversion of 1956
2. Women's Movement of 1975
3. Globalisation of 1990

It was only after 1975, that the idea of women's liberation gained momentum. Dalit women came to realise that she was not a commodity to be used, humiliated and eventually discarded. The focus was not on the mythological or Buddhist studies but on the real life stories of the oppressed fairer sex in the society. Writers like Rajni Tilak, Urmila Pawar, Bama,

Kamble and many more felt the pain and anguish of the women in the society at large. They realised the significance of not so significant considered creation of God. It was through their works that the society by large came to value the intellect, space and dignity of women especially Dalit women. What was largely advocated for Dalit men of the society, was demanded for Dalit women also. Urmila Pawar's works like *The Weave of My Life: A Dalit Woman's Memoir* (2008), *Motherwit*, etc. were picked from the air the Dalit women were breathing. Issues largely covered caste, rituals, and traditions from a feminist perspective. The ideological premises therefore got constructed on these pillars of issues.

Within the backdrop of the ideological differences between upper-caste feminists and Dalit feminists, based on their different approach in addressing and situating 'caste' within the women's movement, the call for a 'Dalit feminist standpoint' by Dalit feminists emerged.

To trace the construction of identities, it requires one to engage with historiography. In India, the non-Brahmin women's histories have often been neglected, which otherwise was populated by masculine and upper-caste narratives of nationalism, imperialism and communalism. That is when the feminist historiography stepped in. Rajni Tilak has also expressed how the mainstream women's movement did not adequately incorporate and invoke the ideals of Savitribai Phule, Ambedkar and Jyotiba Phule.

Therefore, re-visioning historiography from a Dalit feminist standpoint brings to light important turns in the women's movement in India—firstly, how Dalit women as subjects were focused on only after 1990s by what was the initial women's movement in India. Secondly, the focus on the engagement with Dalit women's experiences and life testimonies, and finally, Dalit women's agitation to fight their marginalisation in literary and political circles due to their doubly-oppressed position, owing to Dalit patriarchy as discussed by Urmila Pawar, Bama, Gopal Guru and Anand Teltumbde, to establish speaking on their own, and for establishing a standpoint varied from each other as well as from the upper-caste's.

Uma Chakravarti in her article *In Her Own Write: From Dalit Feminist Standpoint* (2012), also captures the shift in Dalit women's agency from speaking through interlocutors to publishing and speaking on their own in front of national and international audiences.

The focus of this paper is to analyse Kaushalya Baisantri's autobiography *Dohra Abhishaap* (1999). This work hints at the double curse a woman goes through- one on the account of being a woman and the other on being a Dalit. Kaushalya became the mouthpiece for such oppressed women at the threshold of patriarchal community. Her autobiography is a glimpse into her life, where every moment, minute and days were a struggle to uphold one's dignity and self-respect, in a society which was more attuned to dishonour the women as their right and privilege. Her boldness and stand against this discrimination was not taken too well either by the patriarchs of non-Dalit community and also by her community too. There are number of highlighting features of her work. Firstly, her work is a firsthand testimonial of the mental, physical and emotional atrocities mated to her by her husband and other male patriarchs. Subsequently, it also brings forth the insults and abuses her mother and her grandmother had faced at the hands of their respective husbands. Aaji, as she called her grandmother, had been considered a bad omen for her husband's family, after his demise. Forcibly pushed into a second marriage, since polygamy was much practiced, she was a "paat"—a woman who had lost her first husband, brought to the house of the second husband at night and who was made to wear a necklace, with an inscribed figure of a woman and to be boycotted from any social or religious participation. She had faced hardships not only at the hands of her second husband, but also his first wife and the family respectively. Aaji was supposedly quite beautiful. This was a reason big enough for her grandfather, called Aajoba to:

> Rebuke her, and display his anger towards her. He used to drink and abuse her, to hide his inferiority. Aaji, tolerated it with all patience as she never had the courage to raise her voice against this. (11-12)

Eventually, she left for Nagpur after facing much; lost her son at the age of eighteen and bowed to the forceful marriage of her daughter, Bhagirathi, Kaushalya's mother. Though underprivileged and poverty- ridden, yet she had better husband than her father to her mother. But unfortunately, even Bhagirathi's life could not be devoid of patriarchal influence. Being illiterate and widow with five children, she wanted to give education to her offsprings; but this was somewhat not well digested by high caste people and the society at large. Kaushalya Baisantri, over her journey of writing this autobiography, gives an insight into her family conditions to let the readers understand the intensity of injustice and oppression faced inside outside—her grandfather, her husband and her sons complemented by the male dominant society. She knew very well that opening of her heart in the form of her autobiography, would definitely not be accepted by them, but she knew that this was the only resort to make the outside world aware about the woes of women and that too Dalit women at large. With five siblings and that too girls, she grew amidst the curse of being a girl child, breathed in poverty, where clay and cow dung was binder for their broken walls and roofs, eating broken parts of rice, washing hair with clay, eating beefs and buying eatables from a nearby graveyard made for Anglo-Indians. A lot of first hand insight into plight of the women was narrated to her by her mother, when she was forced to get married in her infancy, denied education and became a widow in adolescence. Despite all odds and under much hardships, she educated her children for a better tomorrow least realising that the third generation i.e. Kaushalya and her female siblings, would too face the similar consequences. Her elder sister was married off when in school despite many pleads; bore a child every second year—eleven children—all suffering from illness due to malnutrition and lack of proper medical care. She herself was married to an educated IAS officer Devendra in 1947 who was literate but uneducated—the mind frame still followed the old dictum of male supremacy over females. Though he worked for the Dalits, but was far from being sensitive towards females of the house.

> The right to education was denied by him for his sisters; females had no right to voice their opinion and give suggestions. The trend continued for Kaushalya too when she joined him in his house. (100)

Kaushalya, at a very young age had come to understand quite well that the male domination constructed Aajoba to display his masculinity, since the patriarchal society had given him this permit. She could see the trail in her husband too. What was more perplexing was the fact that Devendra, her husband was quite educated and qualified, yet was an alter ego of the males she had grown up seeing around her. Devendra was only reminded of Kaushalaya to satiate his physical urges and the completion of household chores through an unpaid servant- his wife. He could never strike a chord with his children too; deprived his family of the basic necessities. A decorated freedom fighter with no sentiments for the females is what the actual gory picture of Devendra was. The last nail in the coffin came when Kaushalya Baisantri is admitted in the hospital during childbirth and the amount of medical expenses mounts to be more than two hundred. Against this amount, is paid only forty rupees. This was the time, when she decided to file for a divorce which was definitely not only a big step but also a trumpet of breaking free from the shackles of the taboo of being weak, suppressed and oppressed. This was a turning point where like her grandmother, she too decided to fight her own battle and face struggles. Her lineage of living with self-respect and dignity inspired Kaushalya to raise her voice against unacceptable and invalid norms of the patriarchal society.

Kaushalya Baisantri makes effective use of power of the pen to wage a war against unfair and unaccepted male dominance. Through her own narratives of brutalities and sufferings, she had tried to raise awareness about it in her fellow females of that community. The baton had to be successfully passed on as to keep the light of fight for equality on. All the autobiographies and other form of writings, therefore become a tool for Dalit females to break free from the chains of the slavery of caste and sex discrimination.

Each Dalit female writer, with deep profoundness and complicity, brings forth the complex issues of identity, caste discrimination and poverty. There lies the richness of the craftsmanship with testimony of true experiences. The harsh realities of belonging to the lower caste is known and accepted by all the female writers but what emerges is the fact is the battle they have tried to raise against the miserable sufferings and exploitation especially of the females and consequently help them to find a place of dignity and self esteem in the society. The societal format of writing, in Dalit Literature has no doubt drawn significant global attention and is rightly called Dalit Architectural Style.

Work Cited

Chakarvati, Uma. "In Her Own Write: Writing from A Dalit's Standpoint." *India International Centre Quarterly*, Vol. 39, No. 3/4, 2012, pp. 134-145. *JSTOR*, www.jstor.org/stable/24394281. Accessed 25 Aug. 2020.

Dwivedi, Vachaspati. "Kaushalya Baisantri's *Dohra Abhishaap:* A Treatise on Dalit Women's Marginalisation." *Research Scholar*. Vol. 5, No. 3, August 2017, pp. 19-26.

Baisantri, Kaushalya. *Dohra Abhishaap*. New Delhi: Permashwari Prakashan, 2012.

Lal, Panchu. "Confronting Patriarchy: A Study of Kaushalya Baisantri's Autobiography *Dohara Abhishaap*." *Re-Marking: An Analysis*. Vol. 3, No. 5, August 2018, pp. 221-23.

Nagaraj, D.R. *The Flaming Feet and Other Essays*. New Delhi: Permanent Black, 2010.

Sreelatha, M. "Dalit Women Autobiographies: Untold Stories of Anguish." *Research Front*. Vol. 4, No. 4, Oct-Dec, 2016.

Thorat, Sukhdeo. *Dalits in India: Search for a Common Destiny*. New Delhi: Sage Publications, 2009.

Lalmungthani, Melody, Ed. *From Oppression to Liberation through Education Critical Essays on Dalit Literature*. New Delhi: Atlantic Publishers and Distributors, 2013.

9

Women's Struggle from Marginality to Centrality: A Study of P. Sivakami's *The Grip of Change*

Dr C. Ramya

P. Sivakami is a celebrated Dalit writer from Tamil Nadu. She was born in 1957 in a Dalit community. She has done her post-graduation degree in History. After that she thought to take an administrative post. She took up IAS exam and finally became an IAS officer. Being a writer from the core, this job could not give her entire satisfaction to her and she took voluntary retirement from her job and took writing as a full time profession since 2008. Her works deal with the marginalised status of women and the tyranny of men.

An autobiographical novel is a form of novel in which autofiction technique is used autobiographical and fictive elements are merged. The names and places may be changed and the events have resemblance with author's personal life. In the autobiographical novel *The Grip of Change*, Sivakami has used another name Gowri whose life matches with Sivakami. Woman has been depicted as a second-grade gender in her novels and they are loaded with bundles of responsibilities. Vaishali Shivkumar suggests a very famous statement in this context:

> 'Woman is a Dalit from Beginning to End' seems really a naked truth at this stage just because of this struggle of the

> Dalit women against the society, against their own outset and against the traditions their men follow. The patriarchy crushes down the originality, warmth, delicacy, tenderness and even beauty in them. (3)

Sivakami's autobiographical novel *The Grip of Change* also deals with the issue of caste discrimination, gender issues, struggles of Dalits and political tactics. This novel narrates the trial and tribulation of a Dalit woman named Thangam. A Dalit leader Kathamuthu tries to save her from the exploitation but there were some personal motives behind it. V. Sangeetha and V. Peruvalluthi write about this novel:

> *The Grip of Change* highlights the longing of Dalit to resolve them in this society with their own appraisals among other communities. P. Sivakami, an important Tamil writer, is critical of the Dalit community. (144)

At the outset, Dalits have been shown as victims of caste discrimination. They are not given equal status, respect and position in the society. Thangam comes at Kathamuthu's house for his help due to the encroachment of the Udayars. She tells him that she was physically exploited by Paramjothi Udayar, and when his wife comes to know about it, she, with her brothers, beats Thangam brutally and finds the entire fault in her.

Kathamuthu takes this issue very seriously and he takes immediate action against the culprits. He gives her shelter and registers a case against the oppressors. Thangam was misbehaved because she belonged to a low caste and there was no any man to protect her. She started working in Paramjothi's farm for her livelihood after the demise of her husband. Udayars belong to the upper castes of the village and were dominant also having good property. Paramjothi would use Thangam for his sexual desires. Prof. D. Amalraj comments about Thangam:

> Thangam should have stayed in the house of her husband accepting the conditions of her brothers-in-law. Had she

> remained where she should be, she would not have gone through sexual torture outside her home and met with public disgrace. (44)

When Paramjothi's wife comes to know about this relation, she becomes so enraged that she, along with her brothers, beats her mercilessly. They forget all human feelings and drag Thangam through the street to show others what she has done. This description reminds the readers Rohinton Ministry's *A Fine Balance* in which Thakur Dharmsi's goons kill the Narayan and his family members for having the temerity to ask for a ballot paper. They project their dead bodies on the village square so that they may tyrannise villagers. Such incidents explain the atrocities meted out to low caste people in our country. As soon as Paramjothi comes to know that Kathamuthu has taken up of Thangam's case, he feels much regretful of his illegitimate relationships with Thangam, a Parachi:

> He did not fear the police, the courts, the expenditure that he might incur, and the nuisance that would follow. Only the caste concerns made him anxious—the exposure to an affair with a Parachi was humiliating. He would have braved it out even if it had been a murder case of criminal assault. But what a disgrace if he had to own up to a relationship with a Parachi! (32)

Caste discrimination paves the way for the exploitation and oppression. Dalits face all kinds of humiliation by the upper caste people still they must remain silent. Caste antagonism deprives them of their fundamental rights. Revathi Krishnaswami remarks about the casteism:

> Caste disappeared from the realm of discourse even as it remained materialised in social practice. Armed not with ritual superiority but with English education, the upper castes retained control of most economic, political, and cultural resources in the modernising secular nation-state. (76)

Some people relate their caste with their destiny and they do not want to do anything against the caste discrimination they face in their life. All the people on this earth have equal right to live their life. Many social reformers and Dalit activists also have written and struggled for the equality of Dalits. Dr Bhimrao Ambedkar remarks in this context:

> The Hindu social order does not recognize equal need, equal work or equal ability as the basis of reward for labour. Its motto is that in regard to the distribution of the good things of life those who are reckoned as the highest must get the most and the best and those who are classed as the lowest must accept the least and the worst. (85)

Another big issue is that every upper caste in hierarchy considers the lower caste people inferior and that's the reason that such people try to suppress the low caste people. According to Sivakami, the people of the different castes keep quarrelling over the trifle.

Kathamuthu forced the upper caste people to pay for the atrocities meted out by the Dalits. They had to compensate for the rehabilitation and exploitation of the Dalits. He was an influential figure that's why Paramjothi request him, "Kathamuthu, can't we settle the matter in the panchayat? Why should we take a matter concerning a woman to the court?" (74). Paramjothi had to pay ten thousand rupees to Thangam and she gets a bit relief. Kathamuthu's thinks that "Those who bear their suffering in patience will ultimately rule the world" (73) invites disagreement in the village among the educated youth.

The strange thing is that though Thangam is saved from Paramjothi's exploitation yet she has to succumb to Kathamuthu. Thus, the hypocrisy of people has been beautifully narrated by P. Sivakami. There are many Thangams who are exploited by the upper caste people and the people of their own caste also leave no stone unturned to exploit them. Thangam's life is made a hell just because she is a woman—a sexual object for everybody. After the death of her husband, his brothers evicted Thangam from his husband's land and they wanted to molest her. She considered Kathamuthu as her guardian but he also used her. It was like "stepping on shit while walking on a riverbank" (87).

P. Sivakami has written about the life of Dalit women in Indian villages how they have to face multiple exploitations in the society. Other women of the village have to suffer all the humiliation and exploitation silently because they know it well that if their family is not with them who can help them from the society. They preferred to bear everything silently. Here Thangam is a good example who is rescued from one oppressor but her saviour also exploits her later.

Kathamuthi is a Dalit patriarch who gives opportunities to his daughter Gowri to study and thus, Gowri starts understanding the problems of Dalit women. It was her education that she protests against her early marriage because she had seen many things in her own home. She says, "The sufferings that my mother underwent in her marriage! I don't want to be tortured like her by some man" (124).

Thus, education provides her a platform and support to defy her father's decision and she starts working hard for her examination. This incidence resembles with Bama's autobiography *Karukku* in which Bama also prefers to get high education so that she may come out of the cruel clutches of the caste. Likewise, Gowri decides to get higher education in a college. When Gowri crosses the threshold of chauvinistic attitude, disobeying her father's intimidation, she is filled with energy that she has conked out the tyrannical chains. She breaks all the barriers coming on her way and becomes the part of the mainstream:

> During floods, waters from overflowing wells mingle with the waters of huge water bodies, transgressing their

> boundaries. Gowri felt that she had crossed over human-made boundaries—her father, her caste and her village—and merged with the ocean of people. (95)

Gowri's education gives her strength to fight not only for herself but also for other women like Thangam. She condemns her father Kathamuthu's inhuman attitude towards Thangam. She knew it well that her father is taking undue advantage of Gowri that's why when her father rapes Thangam, Gowri vehemently shouts, "Dogs! Dogs in this house! Shameless as dogs!" (93). Gowri has been depicted as a mouthpiece for Dalit women. She stimulates her mother Kangawali and her step-mother Nagamani also for their equal status in the society. In this book, Gowri's life resembles with P. Sivakami's own life that's why it is an autobiographical novel. K. Sachidanandan observes, "Dalit literature empowers the marginalised by retrieving the voices, spaces and identities silenced or suppressed by casteist powers" (14).

Through this novel, P. Sivakami has brought out two women characters Thangam and Gowri from different perspectives. Thangam's life remains full of struggles and exploitations and she has to face many blows of fate one after one. On the other hand, Gowri has been presented as a strong girl who dares to break the patriarchal rules and wants to give equal status to all women.

Thus, this autobiographical novel is an icebreaker for Dalit women. Though they have to undergo the sexual assaults, humiliations, psychological torments and multiple exploitations, yet education may be a ray of hope for the Dalit girls. Thus, it has been given a message to all Dalit women that education can change the lives of Dalit women. Girls like Gowri should come forward to change the social set up otherwise drastic change in the society will be difficult to see in future. Ginni Rani writes about this novel:

> Through the character of Gowri, the ideal of education in recovery of Dalit's condition is also established. This novel postulates a crude stereotype of the patriarchy along with a hopeful vision presented by Gowri. The glimpses of the growing consciousness can be seen in the novel. (Rani 686)

Works Cited

Amalraj, D. "Sex Knows No Caste: A Study of P. Sivakami's *The Grip of Change.*" *Dalit Women's Autobiographies: A Critical Appraisal.* Bijender Singh, editor. Kalpaz Publications, 2016. pp. 39-46.

Ambedkar, B.R. "Caste in India". *Caste* and *Democratic Politics in India.* Ed. Ghanshyam *Shah.* Permanent Black, 2002. pp. 83-107.

Krishnaswamy, Revathi. "Globalisation and its Postcolonial (dis)contents: Reading Dalit Writing". *Journal of Postcolonial Writing*. Vol. 41, No. 1, May 2005, pp. 69-82.

Rani, Ginni. "Articulating the Voiceless: A Study of P. Sivakami's *The Grip of Change*". *Research Scholar: An International Referered e-Journal of Literary Explorations.* Vol. 2, No. 2, May, 2014. pp. 683-687.

Sachidanandan, K. *Indian Literature: Positions and Propositions.* Pencraft International, 1999.

Sangeetha, V. and V. Peruvalluthi. "Women Marginality in P. Sivakami's *The Grip of Change.*" *Shanlax International Journal of English.* Vol. 6, No. 2, March 2018. pp. 144-47.

Sivakami, P. *The Grip of Change and Author's Notes.* Trans. P. Sivakami. Orient BlackSwan, 2006.

Shivkumar, Vaishali. "A Dalit Woman under a Strong Clutch of Patriarchy: A Comprehensive Study of *The Grip of Change.*" *Language in India.* Vol. 13, No. 4 (2013). Web. 3 Jan. 2014.

10

The Hierarchical Deliverance of Sanskrit and its Casteist Nuances: A Study of Marginalisation in Kumud Pawde's Autobiography *Antasphot*

Dr Meenu Dudeja

Every creation of God in the form of a human being has been given equal rights if God has given five senses, one mouth, two hands, and two legs. Then why some people are discriminated? Why they are treated so bitterly? Why society doesn't accept their existence? Are they not a human being created by God? Why people are so discriminated on the basis of their caste and gender? Why they are considered a Shudra? After all what is their fault? Is someone's caste the definition of his whole life? Someone's existence can be the existence of his life? Does his identity depend on caste and gender only? Is there something more than that? Many reformers are doing very good work against gender and caste discrimination. Only a Dalit writer can understand the depth of those humiliations and pains, which others fail to understand so deeply. The narrow mindedness and mental sickness of our so-called modern society remains the main concern of this paper.

Does this women's liberation movement not the movement for the liberation of handful women? It is not the movement for the emancipation of the entire womanhood—Dalit, tribal, untouchable and Muslim women. They are being exploited by caste, gender and poverty. Is it not our duty to think that their exploitation should be stopped? Maximum rape cases have been occurred with Dalit girls. Why Dalit have to bear the pang of customary poverty and persecution always on the basis of their caste. Kumud Pawde, a Dalit woman writer from Maharashtra, tried to show the mirror to the society why Dalit also have the right to be educated. Why they have to face a lot of pain only to earn bread and butter for them? Why are there terrible situations to prove themselves? We have to raise all questions. Why are Dalit girls considered as objects of enjoyment? If there is only one creator then why there is too much difference in His creations. Why is there so much discrimination?

> ...although I try to forget my caste, it is impossible to forget. And then I remember an expression I heard somewhere: 'What comes by birth, but can't be cast off by dying-that is caste. (Pawde 25)

Kumud Pawde, social activist and feminist writer was born in Nagpur, India in 1938 as a member of Dalit community. She belonged to Mahar community which is one of the untouchable communities of India. Her autobiographical work *Antasphot* (1981) is in Marathi language. She has narrated the experiences of her early childhood and youth in caste-based Indian society in the story in "The Story of My Sanskrit" in the anthology *A Corpse in the Well* which is translated by Dalit writer and activist Arjun Dangle. The story has immense potential to raise serious questions about the hegemony of the story. How it has been too much insulted to read and teach Sanskrit—the ancient language of the Hindus. There is a powerful temptation of indelibility of the caste system in the Indian social psyche, but also for Inequality by two most important social categories-caste and gender. Kumud Pawde, her first name is Kumud Somkunwar, who was born in lower caste, narrates how she used to be humiliated for studying and teaching Sanskrit:

According to the principles of Brahmanism should be learnt only by the members of high caste. While the story brilliantly depicts the insurmountable hardship that Kumud Pawde had to face for receiving a job despite possessing a postgraduate degree in Sanskrit, the real twist in the story, comes at the end as Kumud declares how 'miraculously she got the job of an Assistant Lecturer in a government college after her inter-caste marriage. (Pawde 34)

Dalit literature, forced me to think over the intricate relation. How much the two factors like caste and gender have in shaping the identity of a woman. It also speaks about many of the traditional inequalities of Hindu social structure, resulting in making the lives of women and Dalits very miserable. Kumud Pawde narrated the experiences of her early childhood and youth in caste-based Indian society.

The issue is that she belongs to which social group, does not exist in the Indian common public. She have learned against her caste background seems strangely bizarre. The most amazing thing is that a low-caste woman, whether she has the right to learn Sanskrit? Whether she has the right to teach it? It is a terrible discrepancy. A man whose life has these anomalies accumulates become the centre of attraction. Is the attraction of mixed culture and acceptance?

The question is that the one language (Sanskrit) which was not even touched by his caste for so many centuries was now under her control, it was natural to have arguments but if the praise was limited to this personal level, she would have tolerated it but it was all determined. As usual, people started beating the drum of my caste and spread of my knowledge of Sanskrit.

Not only caste system but also two other important problems of society are also to be described. Her maiden name is Kumud Somkwar, born into untouchable Mahar caste. This is the story about how she had to face a lot of humiliations because of her gender and her thoughts about language.

According to the society, Sanskrit language is only the personal right of Brahmin, not to anyone. Sanskrit language is only their fundamental right. A person who belongs to other caste can't have the right to speak or teach this language. If he would teach then have to face lots of problems. Either he is Dalit or Muslim except Brahmin no one can do this. Kumud Pawde has expresses her all story in his autobiography. Situations have not been changed yet. This is a story about her untouchable's hardship obtaining a job after possessing post-graduate degree in Sanskrit. Society is least bother about his qualification they have only one concern—her caste.

Everywhere, every time, her identity is considered with her caste and gender. She has no other identity, no existence. Except it, she is a Dalit and a female. Why our modern society is not trying to understand the reality. Why they are called Harijan? But its real meaning is *Hari ke Log* (People of God).

In his autobiography, she said, on the day of Vijay Dashami in 1971, the Government of Maharashtra organised a meeting in Nagpur to honour the scholars of the Vedas, according to the wishes of the Honourable former Education Minister Mr Madhukar Roy Chaudhary, she had to introduce these respected scholars in Sanskrit language. From the Himalayas to the Kanyakumari these days, the perception of common Indian people had become in their mind that her ancestors should blame themselves if they even listen to Sanskrit voice. And it was strange, today is the same language, which I have to speak. Describing my inner opinions, saying that she could not control her heartbeat, his mind stalled due to anxiety and she was in a state of inferiority.

The clash of her emotions and the clash of public appreciation enveloped her from all around. Women of our caste and studying Sanskrit were forbidden for research. This is how a woman today will introduce these scholars in Sanskrit despite being one of the lowest caste. This was a very big question, it was the beginning of a progressive way of thinking in India itself.

A tornado of mixed emotions always creeps into his mind. Seeing this hatred, she repeatedly slip into the past, while this hatred is familiar to her and she is used to this. The house that took place was surrounded by the homes of casteist Hindus in every way, a seven-eight year old girl like me could not understand what is happening, why this discrimination, on what basis, why this bitterness is there? She writes in her autobiography, about *vatsavitrivrat* and expresses her displeasure towards the false religious beliefs. She writes:

> Are all the scriptures have been written to keep the woman under control? Though such oppressive religious customs are gold-coated, they cannot be admired. Though I was happy in my husband's company, there were many other women who were enduring the pangs of hell in the company of their husbands. Though those women were wishing for the same hell again and again, didn't I have my own duty? Why should I follow such evil customs after being aware of their futility? And shouldn't I explain the cruelty and meaninglessness of those customs to the ignorant women? (Pawde 16)

If one compares the houses, our house is more clean and beautiful than the rest of the houses, from the cleanliness to the dyeing, to the splendour of utensils, the rangoli was everything. This hatred made me to think at a young age, that this feeling inspired me to introspect, the idea of playing and running here and there at this age put me in great dilemma:

> I take a bath with Pears soap daily. My mother applies Kaminia hair oil to my hair and plaits them neatly. My clothes, too, are washed clean... At home, there are always various oils, soaps and perfumes. Besides the girls of our area, other girls of my class also liked to sit with me... My home is cleaner than theirs. (Pawde 25)

One incident shattered my self-esteem. She had a thread ceremony for her classmate's brother, in which she was not invited, but a very curious voice she went there and the result of that, she was interrupted with their response. She started the Sanskrit with the help of her father, but she became a laughing stock in front of the educated people. Is Sanskrit such an easy language? It is very difficult. Is it discouraging to hear that our forefathers have ever learned it? Only her father used to encourage him and his encouragement made him confident and awakened his confidence Sanskrit was a difficult subject. Kumud Pawde writes:

> Like the previous occasion, our educated neighbours made fun of me. Some of them were professors and lawyers. How is it possible? Though you scored good marks in Matriculation, is it so easy to complete M.A. with Sanskrit? One should not boast of one's abilities. Should realize one's capabilities. People were talking. And the amusing aspect of it all was that most of them belonged to our own caste. But their words couldn't deter me away from my determination. I did not respond to them. (Pawde 28)

Kumud Pawde said that she went through all kinds of struggles but she hated crying so much, she never used to cry. Her talent soon became clear and by the time she started college and doing an outstanding performance in Sanskrit. At that time Motiram Pawde, an idealistic young teacher, should run the night classes for the underprivileged children at Haslop College, Nagpur. As educated youngsters were looking for teachers to teach poor children, someone suggested the name of Kumud Sonkuwar. Both of them did work together. They got married but his family was not ready to accept her. But she didn't lose hope and with her strong determination she became successful to settle her family. His autobiography in Marathi titled & Support, published in 11th Marathi 2, lectured his childhood and youth experiences in a caste-based Indian society.

Kumud explains her relationship with his father-in-law after her marriage. He got very annoyed and so obstinate and conservative. He refused to forgive his son for getting married to a Dalit woman even after the birth of his grandson. Kumud writes:

> I was terribly angry. The old man did not cuddle my son, didn't fondle him, didn't put his hand on his head... Though this man was our blood kin, he didn't touch his grandson, as he was born to a Mahar woman. (Pawde 79)

This behaviour is certainly despicable towards daughter-in-law and grandson. She got the full support of his parents to pursue his career, yet he got married. Much oppression and discrimination had to be faced. Her in-laws did not accept her from the beginning so she faced redress within the family and also continued her faith against all forms of oppression. She had a strong voice of women in the Dalit movement Comes recorded in October 2017 at his residence in Nagpur.

After entering high school, she chose Sanskrit an optional subject. She tried relentlessly to stop learning Sanskrit. You are not capable. No one will teach you at home. Her teacher Hatekar had suggested her:

> "...you can become a doctor, can't you?"
>
> "Won't you be able to help the afflicted? That's what's needed among your people." (Pawde 25)

You cannot do this. I used to look at it from my past, but it had no effect on me, the effect of words like *ghrina* and bitter could not even touch my existence. With great keenness and interest, she started studying Sanskrit. She also gave herself a good score. She was highly impressed with Gokhale Guruji by the kind and humanistic behaviour of his family members. But she was always possessed with the fear of her caste being exposed to his family members. As she writes:

> ...the older boy came out bearing plates full of cooked poha. I became nervous, fear crept over my mind. Suppose this lady were to find out my caste? Along with sips of water, I swallowed the lump in my throat as well as mouthful of poha. I couldn't concentrate on what anyone was saying. My only worry was when and how I could escape from there. Suppose someone from the Buldy area were to come here? (Pawde 34)

She completed his BA with good marks. She respected the fairness of her teachers. Now she have started M.A., her department president was a scholar of all India fame, he never liked to learn his Sanskrit and he used to say clearly. His taunts used to paint her room with full of darkness. She had completed her education despite all the difficulties.

But even after doing M.A., she was unemployed. She had no means of job. Standing in the dock of many questions, she answered many questions in every interview and in her desperation; she took some arrows in my body. Took a bold step to get out of the trap. She presented her entire case in writing to the Honourable Shri Jagjivan Ram, the eminent minister of the Union Cabinet. Her words had the power of a sharp sword as it was bleeding from the heart of a man. Words were weeping that were crushed to death under the circumstances such as Jatayu's scream alone in his final struggles.

The minister presented her letter to Pandit Nehru. He was worried that why I had not got the job yet, he proposed to meet me and she was given a prize-money of two hundred and fifty rupees but all this was only for my assurance.

But she was left with assurances. She did not want promises. Promises keep false hopes alive. Research is the fruit of mental peace. She also did MA in English. In the meantime, she got married to an interracial marriage of Indian society. Nature has a different surprise that after 2 months of my marriage, she got a lecturer job in a government college and she is a professor but this question always runs in his heart that the credit of Kumud Somkuwar's job is given to someone. Is not the name of Kumud Pawde? My job depends on my surname? Not on my capabilities:

> After acquiring a non-Dalit surname, he opened up a lot of job officers and was declared a Sanskrit Pandita by the Nagpur College. Eventually Amravati retired from Government College as a Sanskrit department head after decades of being her daughter-in-law. She always said that she would be remembered with her mother-in-law and she was her student. People loved her class.

After facing a lot of pains and sufferings, she never liked to cry. Her son said that I have seen my mother crying only once in my entire life when my Father had lost his eyes, he got all this strength from Dr B.R. Ambedkar's message was to be free, freedom, intellectual freedom and social freedom. Kumud Pawde of Nagpur, Sanskrit scholar and freedom soldier.

There was an ideology of B.R. Ambedkar, at that time, Baba Saheb thinker who wrote the last challenge of a civilised existence, the feeling of changing the caste apocalypse, the fight for social democracy, the vigorous intellectual attack on Brahmanvad, along with the youthful idealism and revolution in Maharashtra. She remember that when due to fear they were not allowed to draw water from the wells, they would get polluted. She would join in queues with women to drink our water. She was a degree holder in Sanskrit but could not get a job yet.

From time to time, various scholars and even women have attacked us very much. Leave the women considered polluted and the new position of the community, the knife which I have very systematically raised is the important caste of modern India. The combined legacy of anti-feminist thinking stood solidly behind our remarks, yet we found the chief professors of Sanskrit making absurd claims, for example, caste is related to birth, that Hindu society is inhuman. When she has left her surname then she got the job.

Works Cited

Pawde, Kumud. "The Story of My 'Sanskrit.'" *A Corpse in the Well: Translations from Modern Marathi Dalit Autobiographies*. Ed. Arjun Dangle. Bombay: Orient Longman Ltd., 1992. Reprint 1994. 24-34. Print

Moon, Meenakshi and Urmila Pawar. "We Made History, Too: Women in the Early Untouchable Liberation Movement." *Gender and Caste*. Ed. Anupama Rao. New Delhi: Kali for Women, 2003. 48-56. Print.

Limbale, Sharankumar. *Towards an Aesthetic of Dalit Literature: Histories, Controversies and Considerations*. Trans. Alok Mukherjee. New Delhi: Orient Longman, 2004. Print.

Pawar, Urmila. *The Weave of My Life: A Dalit Woman's Memoirs*. Trans. Maya Pandit. Kolkata: Stree, 2003. Print.

Guru, Gopal. "Dalit Women Talk Differently." *Gender and Caste*. Ed. Anupama Rao. New Delhi: Kali for Women, 2003. 80-85. Print.

'Caste' https://www.britannica.com/place/India/Caste August 19, 2019.

11

A Sensitive Soul Writing out Its Fragmented Existence: A Study of Kaveri's Autobiography *Tukda-Tukda Jeevan*

Dr Avinash Kumar

All the theories that vouch for an impersonal method of artistic expression are presented with an intriguing game of binaries by the literary genre technically labelled as 'autobiography'. The literary critics are forced to revisit the centuries old question whether an artist is entitled to narrate his own story from a subjective point of view. The subjective-objective narrative technique binary gets complicated in an autobiography when one seeks answers to the question of 'truthfulness' or the social realism in a text. If an author is supposed to give value to the social reality in his/her artistic expressions, the experiencing self of the writer cries for space in creative art. When a writer is writing his/her own story, the experiencing self cannot be denied space in the literary expression. This is the highlight of autobiography writing across continents, especially in the tech-savvy and information hungry generation of the millennials.

A quintessence of discursive objectivity is presented in the autobiography of Kaveri, the widely acclaimed Dalit writer hailing from the erstwhile undivided Bihar. The autobiography

Tukda-Tukda Jeevan (2017) is a powerful rendition of the struggles of a Dalit writer who aspired to create a space for herself by attaining financial independence ever since her first encounter with the social stigma of being an untouchable early in her childhood. The narrative hinges on the fact that the life of a Dalit girl with dreams of independence in her eyes has multiple ruptures. Each experience of marginalisation leaves a rupture in her feminine self that defines her identity. Therefore, the title of the novel also reiterates those scars of fragmentation that played a crucial role in shaping the authorial world view. The double jeopardy of being a Dalit and being a girl is beautifully brought out in the story of Kaveri, which immediately places her work into the rubric of postmodern post-feminist discourse.

In the last three decades, gender studies have focused primarily on how societies have determined and managed sex categories, the cultural meanings attached to the roles assigned to those categories and how individuals have understood/reacted to the identities thrust upon them across time and space. Rather than building a grand narrative of feminist discourse, the focus has been to draw up small/local narratives of gendered roles as socio-cultural constructs that challenge and subvert the overarching established narratives. In other words, gender studies have been naturally intertwined with culture studies, which is crucial to the postmodernist approach to literature. The essential aspect of postmodernism is to incorporate within a broad rubric of cultural studies all schools of thought that subvert the powerful coercive ideological apparatus.

Postmodern theory evolved as an atheistic and anti-realistic system of belief in opposition to the existing concept of Modernism. Postmodernism expands the area covered by modernism by its insistence upon the relevance of fragmentalism and a compulsory skepticism. According to Peter Barry, postmodernism emphasises that 'reality' is beyond the spheres of human understanding and those who claim to have access to the reality are actually displaying their politics of power. He further explains, "The prominence of fragmentation has been featured by the modernist to register a deep nostalgia for earlier age when faith was full and authority intact" (83). Peter Barry goes on to argue that fragmentation for the postmodernists "is an exhilarating, liberating phenomenon, symptomatic of belief. In a word, the modernist laments fragmentation while the postmodernist celebrates it" (84).

The postmodern approach also points out that construction of the binary terms of 'sex' and 'gender' is not the ultimate truth or reality but a politics of power. As the meaning of a sentence or a word should be determined by the reader and not by the author, the reality of cultural and social binaries should also be determined by the individuals through the construction of new identities. With the politics of 'identity', the postmodernists emphasise on empowering the minorities, women, and homosexuals.

In the 21st century, in spite of gender equality gaining primacy across the globe, body has become more important. There are men who still treat women as their property because of physical weakness of women. The domestic violence, rape cases inside home, outside home or in different offices with working women indicate the mindset of men who only see women through their body. Therefore, the question is raised against the existence of the categories like sex and gender, which create huge gap between men and women. The postmodern take on gender does not aim to achieve gender equality. It rather interrogates the existence and the truth of gender on the physical plane.

The gender studies emerged around 1980s and the first area of discussion was how to make a clear division between gender and sex. Michel Foucault in his work *The History of Sexuality* (1979) has empathically challenged the understanding of 'sex' as a biological fact, arguing that sex cannot be simply understood as a biological category; rather it should also be studied as a social practice. Foucault has analysed sexuality with different perspectives and establishes it as a cultural category like gender.

In the backdrop of this theoretical perspective, the opening lines of Kaveri's autobiography are remarkable (translation mine):

> How to begin and where to end the narration of pain inflicted by a barb piercing my soul? The public demands me to write my autobiography. What will happen if a heart that has suffered for long is poked again? A big explosion. I have discovered while reflecting upon my childhood that I was not able to bear injustice at all. The barb of untouchability stung me during childhood, which forced me to drop out from the school. My childhood could not bear that the teacher would drink water touched by upper caste kids and slap me for touching the bucket. (07)

This initial shock leading to the first fragmentation in the life of the author opens up the sluice gates of her further struggles. Born in a Paswan family that was hardly capable of feeding the belly of five children, Kaveri's rebellious response was met with sensible treatment from her grandmother and father. She was taken away to another place located in Sizwa Kolvari. Her education resumed and the conservative social tentacles continued to grow around her concurrently. Unlike her elder sister, she fought with her grandparents to continue her education in a co-educational school and the taboo of keeping distance from the boys was shattered by her. The will power to stand up to the conservative norms hidden in the garb of ethics and morals in an educationally challenged social milieu opened up the channel of knowledge for a young sensitive mind.

At the age of fifteen, Kaveri was married off to a person from a different *gotra* and the next fragmentation of her young adolescent self happened. The autobiography has thrown up some astute questions within the Dalit discourse in rural India.

Whereas the marginalisation of Dalits is generally assigned to a Brahminical or upper-caste dominated social structure across centuries, the narrative of Kaveri revolves around her own community. The biggest challenge before Kaveri is presented by the female members of her own paternal family as well as her in-law's family. The wife of Kaveri's elder brother was extremely rude towards her. Similar treatment was meted out by her mother in-law after marriage. This continues in the next generation as well. Her daughter-in-law hates her in equal measure. The women of her own family are the biggest perpetrators of marginalisation upon Kaveri. This is in stark contrast to the general belief that Dalit women face discrimination only from the upper caste men and women. When she goes to stay in a girl's hostel for her studies, the next caste-based marginalisation is witnessed. However, this is a limited discrimination as the behaviour of girls other than three-four culprits is quite good towards her. She exclaims that a few rotten fishes pollute the whole pond, but those fishes do not represent all the fishes living out there.

The patriarchal system considered the woman's body as an object of pleasure. This jeopardy was painful for a girl who wanted to carve a niche for herself in the society. Here also the biggest threat comes from within the family. She is repeatedly raped by her own husband who has little respect for her except for fulfilling his carnal desires. The younger brother of her husband and a close friend of her husband also attempt to outrage her modesty on numerous occasions, but her husband does not find anything wrong in their sexual advances. The ethical symbol of chastity represented by virginity of wife at the time of marriage is the prime concern of her husband. After her marriage, the woman is just an object of pleasure which can be used by him and his relatives without any social taboo. The woman is supposed to keep silent and bear the exploitation as a part of her existence.

Kaveri revolts against this atrocity and chooses the path of education and financial independence as her liberating agency. She exposes the imbecile masculinity of the Dalit males who seem to be no different from the upper caste Hindus when it comes to oppress the so-called weaker section of their own household. Kaveri grew in stature as a writer after joining the DVC +2 school in Maithon and the autobiography ends on a positive note as she sees a silverlining in the form of her grandchildren. She lives away from her husband and tries to support her son who faltered in his career.

One character who holds the narrative through her absence is the daughter of Kaveri, who died prematurely due to the family condition. Her memory reverberates throughout the text in the same way as Seth feels for her dead daughter in Toni Morrison's *Beloved*. There is a powerful similarity between the two mothers as they struggle to emerge out of the trauma of that loss. The autobiography is also dedicated to her daughter Jyotsana, who died young in deep agony. The modesty of the daughter was outraged at the age of five by a neighbour, with whom Kaveri fought frantically without any support from her husband. As a matter of fact, whenever the protagonist is violated, the husband remains an effeminate mute spectator.

Therefore, in conclusion, the autobiography of Kaveri, *Tukda-Tukda Jeevan* is a brilliant narration of double jeopardy faced by the women from the most vulnerable social section of India. Within the overarching construct of social marginalisation lie several fragmented narratives that escape the critical discourse. These 'local' and 'personal' narratives can be seen as concrete bricks that are joined together to form a grand narrative in the postmodern discourse. The thin strands of family relations are ruptured in these narratives and a composite picture can be drawn only by looking at those ruptures from a clean lens. Kaveri's autobiography gives an insight into the process of her creative oeuvre and allows the reader the liberty to challenge the constraints of legitimising ideological apparatus functioning with the power structures of Indian society.

Works Cited

Barry, Peter. *Beginning Theory*. Manchester University Press, 2002.

Foucault, Michel. *The History of Sexuality*. Vintage, 1979.

Kaveri. *Tukda-Tukda Jeevan*. Isha Gyandeep, 2017.

12

The World of Dalit Women in Viramma's Autobiography *Viramma: The Life of an Untouchable*

Dr Suruchi Sharma

Untouchability was one of the biggest problems in India and this practice has only been mitigated not eradicated even after the enforcement of legal laws by the government. Laws can be made by the government but it is very difficult to change the mentality of the people. Though many dalit women writers from India have written their autobiographies in regional languages, yet only few autobiographies are available in English. Most of these autobiographies have been translated from other languages but there are few dalit women's autobiographies which have been told by the autobiographers to someone else, and those people have recorded the life of illiterate dalit women. *Viramma: The Life of an Untouchable* by Viramma also belongs to this category.

An autobiography is an authentic record of one's life and it has all realistic depiction because all the incidents of the author's life are revealed through him/her directly. That's the reason, autobiography remains more appealing to people. Shweta Singh writes in this context:

> An autobiography with its claim of genuine remembrance and retelling can also have a counter-claim of genuine

> forgetting and omission as is evident from the treatment of women in male autobiographies....Dalit women not only questioned their victimisation but also spoke for the upper and the middle class women who met the same fate at home. (46)

The life narrative of Viramma has been written in different chapters. The first chapter of this autobiography "A Childhood in Velpakkam" narrates the life of her grandparents. Viramma describes that her family belonged to an untouchable community called serfs. Her grandfather Samikkannu was a sorcerer and one day he brought another pregnant woman in his home. Nobody dared to protest against his decision. He went to Madras to work in coconut plantations. Her grandmother remained alone in the village and it was very difficult for her to stay alone:

> The separation was heartbreaking for the grandmother though. She was always crying and lamenting and wishing that the boys would come back, or at least her son Nadeshan. Night and day, she tried to think of ways to bring him home and she decided to talk about it to her sister who lived in Ranganam. (2)

Viramma's mother's name was Pattu. She had seven children as in that time these people did not know much about the family planning methods. At the time of Viramma's delivery, her father was sitting with his head in his hands and at the birth of a girl child, he said, "Hey, here's another little bitch been born!" (3). But it was an auspicious day and that's why she was named as Viramma.

Viramma tells her story how she became a woman. It was a strange and shocking experience for her when she saw blood under her thighs. She was unable to understand why it has happened with her because she had not received any cut or injury. When the elder women of the family came to know about it, they were not a bit surprised. Viramma was kept in a separate place and a special tonic was given to her so that her uterus may become strong and she may be able to give birth to strong and healthy children in future. She is told that she has become a woman and she can live with a husband now. The family members become busy in the ceremony and they had to borrow amount for it. After this incidence, Viramma was married soon:

> I was still a little child, innocent, happy and flat chested when it was decided that I should get married. Big sister Ellamma, one of my much older cousins, had been given to a family from Karani. When she heard that my future parents-in-law were looking for a daughter-in-law she let them know that an ideal little girl in Velpakkam the village where she was born. (15)

Her sister Ellemma brings marriage proposal for her from the village where she was married. Viramma's mother feels happy that Viramma will be married in a good family and her sister will help her out in case of any need. Viramma tells about it, "I knew they were talking about me, but I only heard snatches of sentences, 'She will be happy. ... She will work well...Ellemma will be there to look out for her...Karani's not far, we'll be able to go and see her a lot' ..." (15-16). Viramma told her mother that she did not want to get married at this age. She sobbed days and night but nobody listened to her. Viramma tells everything about it, "I sobbed day and night. I begged my mother not to give me away in marriage. I would be good. I would stop all the games, I'd work hard, I'd bring home lots of money" (16).

In the chapter "Destinies of Children" Viramma speaks about the problems of women and dalit children. She tells that dalit women would breastfeed for at least three years so that they may not have another child soon. These women had to keep their child everywhere and they were forced to do every work. They wanted delay in the birth of the next baby just because they must leave their child alone while working and this child remained at high risk.

Viramma tells the horrible experience of her first night. She was merely an immature girl at that time and did not know properly what actually happens after marriage. That's why when her husband came close and touched her in the dark, she cried loudly and her mother-in-law immediately came to calm her down. When her husband touched her again and started making love with her, it remained an awful experience with her. She tells her husband in a resented voice, "I want to go back to Velpakkam, I want to go back to my mum, I'll tell her everything that's happened to me here" (41). Her husband knew everything and he just tells her to calm down. She faced almost the same problem the next night also but her husband told her that he would keep her happy but initially she will face some problems but she will enjoy later. She was feeling like a caged bird in her husband's house. Dr Sigma G.R. writes about Viramma, "She was thinking like her kidnapping news with the consent of her family members" (Sigma 76). Baby Kamble also writes in her autobiography:

> In those days, it was the custom to keep women at home, behind the threshold. The honour enjoyed by a family was in proportion to the restrictions imposed on the women of the house. When no one could see even a nail of the woman thus confined within the four walls of the house, then this 'honour' became the talk of the town—a byword among the relatives and friends in the surrounding villages. (Kamble 5)

Viramma narrates in this autobiography that the life of Paraya women was full of all the challenges because they had to do all the domestic chores and they had to go for the work also. Their economic condition and social status were low that's why they would become the easy prey of the upper caste people. Their own respective husbands would not give them any respect while the upper caste people would get attracted to them so easily. She narrates:

> Those gentlemen of the ur talk a lot about the uncleanness of Untouchables, but our holes always turn them on. We're the ones they get up to all their dirty tricks with; it makes you think our juices taste better than their wives! (52)

Dalit women did not have sufficient money. That's why they had to go to the cheaper hospitals for the treatment. Doctors and other staff also tried to exploit them. Viramma narrates that poverty is like a curse for these women. She narrates how doctors would touch them in hospitals, "The doctors pretend to listen to our hearts so they can feel our breasts.... That's happened to more than one of us. We're harassed nonstop down there" (52). These women had to bear everything silently.

Sometimes other caste women would come in the demand of their milk especially when their children would get ill. Viramma tells that her milk was nutritious because they eat various types of milk and other food also while the upper caste women would eat only green vegetables.

Viramma narrates about the crime committed by Dalits. In the chapter "The Caste of Thieves," she narrates about the caste of thieves. She writes that Kempari men and women are thieves, "It's their families' trade" (151). The women of this caste also go for stealing from one town to another. Their target remained the metro-cities and they never harmed the village people. The men would rob the banks and the women would steal from temples, festivals and fairs. It was a strange thing that these women would wear very good dresses and would speak several local languages so that other people might not have doubt on them. Viramma further writes, "Besides, they really are rich. The real rich couldn't match them!" (151).

These women would perform this task in the groups and they would use some spray and cut the jewels with the gold-cutting stone. They were so expert that nobody could notice them, "They know all the techniques, eh, it's their trade!" (152). Sometimes the children would help them and they would take the jewels to a man who would stand at little way off. These women were not afraid of anything and sometimes the police would come and arrest them. Viramma writes about it:

> Sometimes we were sad for them and we'd cry: poor women, take away by the police like that, the shame of it! We'd say to them, 'You're as beautiful as sugar candy, why do you steal? Why do you have such a trade?' But it didn't embarrass them at all. (152)

Viramma writes about the caste discrimination also in this autobiography. She writes that Raddiars belonged to the upper caste and the other castes such as Mudaliars, Naikars, Gounders, etc. were below them. The Reddiars would never go to work, instead they would put many others for the work. Even the women also stayed at home as Viramma writes, "Their women don't work and they never go out" (156). Baburao Bagul writes about the misfortune of the dalits in his poem "You Have Made the Mistake":

> ...That's why I say—
> You have made the mistake of being born in this country
> Must now rectify it: either leave this country,
> Or make war.... (*Poisoned Bread* 81)

Viramma writes that they would fear the most from the Reddiars and they would never speak in front of them but when they would work for the Naickers, they would make fun of them. Viramma writes how they would cut jokes with the Naiekar people. She writes about one occasion:

> 'Yennayya! You never stop giving your wife children! She's pregnant every year like a bitch and you'll lose your strength, you won't have anything left, even if you eat melted butter and curds. Come over here a bit, ayya, come and see if you

> strength is a match for us beef eaters when it comes to real work like this!" (157)

In this autobiography, Viramma tells about the dalit consciousness through radio broadcasting and through the announcement on loudspeaker. Some people motivated them to stay united and fight for their rights. She writes how the announcement would go like:

> Come people of the colony! Come and educate yourselves! Come to evening lessons, adults and children, for people who can't read and for people who can't write! You'll see that when you're educated, you won't be treated like you are now! You won't be a lower caste anymore!" (181)

Some young educated people would inspire dalit people to join their movement. These people would persuade the elders not to send their children to work at low wages. They would convince dalit women not to work on the low wages. They wanted hike in their wages so that dalit people may live their life with respect and dignity, "Demand an increase in your wages! Five rupees for the women, ten rupees for the men!" (181).

The party workers would leave no stone unturned to bring a change in dalit people's life. They would tell people that it has been a long time since they are being harassed, suppressed and exploited, but now they must be aware about their rights. This *kaliyugam* should go to an end and an ideal world should be created where all the people have equal rights and there is no discrimination on the basis of caste, class and religion.

Thus, it is clear from this autobiography that the life of dalit women remains full of problems because they are given multiple responsibilities and they don't have enough money to run their respective families. That's why they had to do many manual works like men so that they may be able to bring bread for their family members. Showkat Ahmad Naik writes:

> Dalit autobiography, a recent offshoot, introduces a new world of experience in Indian literature. It widens the range of expressions and makes use of the Dalits who have been excluded from the mainstream Indian society and discriminated, exploited, humiliated and marginalised on the basis of low caste status. (Naik 278)

Works Cited

Dangle, Arjun, ed. *Poisoned Bread: Translations from Marathi Dalit Literature*. Hyderabad: Orient BlackSwan, 2009.

G.R., Sigma. "Role of Marriage in Shaping a Dalit Woman's Identity: A Study of Dalit Memoir *Viramma: Life of an Untouchable*. Ed. Bijender Singh. *Dalit Women's Autobiographies: A Critical Appraisal*. New Delhi: Kalpaz Publications, 2016. pp. 69-78.

Kamble, Baby. *The Prisons We Broke*. Trans. by Maya Pandit from Marathi *Jina Amucha*. New Delhi: Orient BlackSwan, 2009.

Naik, Showkat Ahmad. "Contradicting Monologue: Dalit Autobiographies as a Counter Discourse." *Research Journal of English Language and Literature (RJELAL): A Peer Reviewed (Refereed) International Journal*. 3.3. (July-Sep 2015): 278-282.

Singh, Shweta. "Representation of Dalit Women in Dalit Men's and Women's Autobiographies." *The Delhi University Journal of The Humanities & The Social Sciences*. Volume 1: 2014. pp. 39-47.

Viramma; Racine, Josiane and Racine, Jean-Luc. *Viramma: Life of an Untouchable*. London and New York: Verso, 1997.

13

Triple Marginalisation of Women in Mukta Sarvagod's *Mitleli Kavaade: Closed Doors*

Dr Kusum Kanger

> Dalit literature is one which acquaints people with the caste system and untouchability in India, its appalling nature and its system of exploitation. In other words, Dalit is not a caste but a realisation and is related to the experiences, joys and sorrows, and struggles of those in the lowest stratum of society. – (Dangle 265)

Time never stops for anybody and the most important feature of the time is that it constantly keeps changing and assuages our pains accordingly. Human beings are slave of time and time can make a king a pauper. It is generally considered that time and circumstance keeps changing. Human beings just need to have a little bit patience in this context. Dalit women writers have revolted against the patriarchal set up and had to indulge in acrimonious arguments to create their own place otherwise there was no chance that the male-dominated society of India may happily provide them equal opportunities.

The doors of opportunities and rights were closed for Dalit Women even up to few decade back. Present autobiography *Mitleli Kavaade* (*Closed Doors*) by Mukta Sarvagod is a personal narrative in which she describes the bitter experiences of her life and community. The vicissitudes and pangs of her life come to the fore.

Dalit women started writing much later than men as they were deprived of their right of education. Any autobiography by dalit writer reveals the facts and events of a writer's life. Most of the dalit writers have written autobiographies so that people may understand their pains and may not do caste-based discrimination with them. In the autobiography *Closed Doors*, dalit women find their doors shut at every place whether it may be a school, college, office, hospital or a temple.

Mukta Sarvagod's autobiography satirises the social evils such as exploitation of dalit women, suppression of women, gender discrimination and untouchability. Dalit women's life has been the main focus of this autobiography. Mahar women's problems are neglected by other Mahars men and the upper caste people also do not pay any attention to them. These women have to face humiliation in their life due to their low caste. Dr Beena Agarwal writes, "Caste is a man-made institution confined to transitory ends. It can neither strengthen nor spoil the dignity of marriage" (Agarwal 87).

In her autobiography, Mukta Sarvagod depicts many problems she faced in her life. Her father worked in the Indian railways. She was admitted in a primary school in Puntambe when she was five-year-old. In that school, the teachers and students belonging to the upper caste always humiliated the low caste students.

Mukta describes that her teacher would teach all students equally on the blackboard but when she would check the spellings of words on students' wooden slates, he would call every student one by one but she was not called close to his table just because she belonged to an untouchable community of Maharashtra. She had to throw her slate onto the table from a safe distance so that any part of her body may not touch her teacher.

Untouchability is a social evil which is still rampant in the rural and urban areas of India. Many people get good education but they remain so conservative in their thoughts that they are unable to understand that God has made all human beings without any discrimination. This discrimination is only the product of human mind which is unjust and condemnable.

There are many literary texts in English literature also which are based on untouchability. If we look at the works published in Indian Writing in English, we find that Rohinton Mistry's *A Fine Balance*, Arundhati Roy's *The God of Small Things*, Mulk Raj Anand's *Untouchable*, U.R. Ananthamurthy's *Samskara*, Aravind Adiga's *The White Tiger*, Tagore's *Chandalika*, etc. works deal with the same problem of untouchability. In *The White Tiger*, Balram Halwai also tells the difference between the upper caste and the lower caste people, "A rich man's body is like a premium cotton pillow, white and soft and blank. *Ours* are different....The story of a poor man's life is written on his body, in a sharp pen" (Adiga 26-27).

So far as dalit autobiographies are concerned, most of the dalit men and women writers faced this problem in the twentieth century because the people at that time were less educated and they never thought that education can help change their lives.

Though Mukta Sarvagod was very intelligent in her studies yet she had to face the inhuman treatment from her teacher. Her teacher would throw the slate on the floor after marking and she would collect it from here. Thus, a dalit girl was learning less the lessons of education and more the lessons of untouchability through her teacher. She would feel humiliated in front of other students.

Mukta as a child faced many caste atrocities. She could not touch the vessel filled with water in the school. Other students would sprinkle water on her wooden slate and then she would clean it. She describes in her autobiography how many Mahar and Mang community children were deprived of their education due to lack of resources, awareness and discrimination. It was considered a daring act to send their children in school.

It was a generally held notion in ancient time that the education is meant only for the upper caste children and the low caste children need not get education because their work does not require any education. The teachers belonged to the upper caste in those schools and they did not like the students belonging to the low caste.

The equality in the school and college education came when the faculty recruitment was also initiated on the basis of category of teachers. As soon as the teachers of low caste joined the educational institutions, they became the protectors of the rights of the low caste children and the upper caste teachers stopped humiliating the low caste children because now the teachers also had fear in their minds that they may lose their jobs also.

When Mukta Sarvagod's father was transferred to Agra, they had to vacate the railway quarters and they had to live outside. She narrates some social evils prevalent in dalit community. Dalit men would sit idle at home and the women had to work to run the family. These women would take care of their children, did all the household works and would go for work. Still the men would show regard for these women. Such men would quarrel with the women and ask money from them to drink wine.

Mukta Sarvagod describes that the other women were also not happy to see dalit girls going to school. The illiterate women of their communities would criticise and abuse her when she passed from the lanes. They considered that a girl should not study in school as she must get married in the early age and should give birth to children. Thus, she was harassed by the people of her own caste and the upper caste.

She was not only the only person who was suffering from this kind of problems. Urmila Pawar also writes in her autobiography that the women of her caste would go to bring firewood on their heads and they would tell the stories of marginalisation of other women. Baby Kamble also writes the same issue in her autobiography *The Prison We Broke*, "My father has locked up my aai in his house, like a bird in a cage (Kamble 5). Phoolan Devi was brutally raped and tortured by the upper caste people. Bama notices how an old dalit man was not allowed to touch the eatables belonging to the upper caste people. She had to face the discrimination in the convent school.

Dalit women's life was very tough as they were depended on the leftovers. They had to clean the gutters and lanes; they would collect dung with a shovel and make cakes; they chopped the trees for cooking food and they had to do other works also assigned to them by their mistresses. Sharmila Rege also writes about it, "By this time, it is already afternoon. They collect all the leftover....this is the life, if one can call it by that name, of all Mahar women! (qtd. in Rege 148).

Mukta Sarvagod decides to bring a change in the status of women. She joined a Mahila Mandal so that she may do something for the upliftment of women. She gives a new direction in her life. This life gives her much inspiration and enthusiasm to work for the untouchable women. These women made containers together so that they may become self-dependent:

> Encouraged by their husbands, the women worked hard and made the containers, stringing them on the walls from the ceiling to the floor. Their tiny homes were crowded with these containers. When 80,000 such containers were ready, a wholesale merchant from the main vegetable market was invited to see the goods, and discuss prices. (Rege 151)

When the merchant came to see the containers, he saw that these containers were made by dalit women because he saw their arms were tattooed with pictures of trees and flowers. There was a portrait of Dr B.R. Ambedkar also on the wall. He immediately left the place saying that he will tell later. Mukta came to understand the intention of the merchant and she contacted the Mayor and the editor of a newspaper to put pressure on the merchant. It was argued that they know it well that these containers are to be used for the temple offerings and nobody will accept the offerings if people come to know that these containers are made by a Mahar woman. They tried to sell the containers to someone else but nobody was ready to buy them and ultimately they had to throw away these containers.

Dalit women were untouchable for the upper caste people but the same dalit women were physically exploited by them. The husbands of dalit women also beat them mercilessly and treated with them mercilessly. This autobiography records not only her own life but the life stories of the people of her community.

Dalit women were depended on mercy of the men of their own family as well as the upper caste people. They had to please their own life-partners and they were forced to please the bodily hungers of the upper caste people.

The duty of Mahars was very tough. They were generally assigned those tasks which were generally not done by anyone else. They had to clean the dirt, carry the dead animals, protect the dead bodies, clean the drains, road and sewerage etc. They were given such tasks also in which their life was also at high risk. They were given importance at the time of solar eclipse only because it was considered that the alms given to such people will save them from the misfortunes.

The Mahar women would do all the duties assigned to them. They had to work from early in the morning till late night. They were depended on the men for everything. They did everything otherwise they knew it well that their children would sleep hungry. Thus, the Mahar women had to compromise with their soul and they had too many works which were against their wish. Ruchi Tomar writes in this context, "Not only patriarchy and caste but also class divides Dalit women by bringing the embourgeoisment and Sanskritisation. Dalit feminism must respond to the complexity of salience of class and the differences create by the caste-ridden society" (Tomar 2).

Mukta Sarvagod has realistically brought out the pains and problems of dalit women and her community in her autobiography. She wanted to open new avenues for the dalit women. She tried a lot to improve their condition and to give them equal rights. Thus, this autobiography vividly narrates the patriarchal pressure on dalit women, their fragmented self and marginalised status. Dr Deepika Rani comments about this autobiography that "*Closed Doors* is an autobiography that brings the pain and agony of Dalit women from the deep waters on the surface so that it should be realised by others" (Rani 97).

Works Cited

Adiga, Aravind. *The White Tiger.* New Delhi: Harper Collins Publishers, 2008. Print.

Agarwal, Beena. *The Plays of Rabindranath Tagore.* New Delhi: Satyam Publishers, 2003. Print.

Dangle, Arjun, (Ed.). *Poisoned Bread: Translations from Modern Marathi Dalit Literature.* Hyderabad: Orient Longman, 1992. Print.

Kamble, Baby. *The Prison We Broke.* New Delhi: Orient Blackswan, 2009. Print.

Rani, Deepika. "Marginalisation and Subordination of Dalit Women in Mukta Sarvagod's *Closed Doors.*" Ed. Bijender Singh. *Dalit Women's Autobiographies: A Critical Appraisal.* New Delhi: Kalpaz Publications, 2016. 87-97. Print.

Rege Sharmila: *Writing Caste/Writing Gender, Narrating Dalit Women's Testimonios.* New Delhi: Zuban, 2006. Print.

Sarvagod, Mukta. *Mitleli Kavaade* (Marathi). Amalner: Chetashri Prakashan, 1983. Print.

Tomar, Ruchi. "Dalit Feminism: A Transformation of Rejection into Resistance." *The Criterion: An International Journal in English.* Issue 12, February 2013. 1-8. Web.

14

Dalit Women the Most Dalit among Dalits: Reinterpretation of Marathi Dalit Women's Testiminios

K. Sunitha Devi

Maharashtra is a state to provide a fertile land to give birth many Dalit autobiographies written by both men and women. Numerous Dalit autobiographies have been published in regional languages and in English. Sharankumar Limbale's *Akkarmashi: The Outcaste*, Omprakash Valmiki's *Joothan: A Dalit's Life*, Laxman Gaikwad's *Uchalya: The Branded*, Y.B. Satyanarayana's *My Father Balaiah*, Daya Pawar's *Baluta*, Arvind Malagatti's *The Government Brahmana*, Laxman Bapu Mane's *Upara: An Outsider*, Vasant Moon's *Growing Up Untouchable in India*, Balbir Madhopuri's *Changia Rukh: Against the Night*, Sheoraj Singh Bechain's *My Childhood on My Shoulders* etc autobiographies are very famous from Maharashtra.

Likewise some Dalit women writers have also written their autobiographies in Marathi which are also important from different perspectives. Some autobiographies like Urmila Pawar's *Aayadaan*, Baby Kamble's *Jime Amucha* etc have been translated into English, and still there are some autobiographies both in Hindi and Marathi which unfortunately could not be translated due to any reasons also should be given space.

Among such works Janabai Kachru Girhe's life-narrative *Marankala* (*Deathly Pains*) is a wonderful read which narrates that there is hardly any Dalit woman's autobiography which is not pregnant with the pain of a woman. In these autobiographies, the marginalised status of Dalit women is the main theme. Women have to suffer a lot in their life. When Sharmila Rege talks with Kumud Pawde's life-narrative *Antasphot*, she observes that Pawde tries to call her work a critical narrative rather than an autobiography. Sharmila Rege writes:

> *Antasphot*, unlike many of the Dalit life narratives, does not keep to a linearity of life experiences. More importantly, as the first published narrative by a Dalit woman...it proves wrong the usual male-centric criticism about women's life narratives being merely emotional outbursts. (Rege 228)

Dalit women's autobiographies are the saga of the personal agonies in which the subjugated position of women and their suffocated life has been narrated. It is generally seen that Dalit men writers have never mentioned or less mentioned the pains and problems of women. They have taken the theme how the upper caste people have suppressed Dalit men. They have merely described the incidences related to their kiths and kins but they seem to be negligent towards the women in their own community. In this context, when Dalit women writers emerged on the literary platforms, they brought it in front of the society that they are being harassed by the other women of their community, men of their family and the upper caste people. Thus, Dalit women are triply marginalised. Both the autobiographies have one thing in common that these autobiographies are the stories of sorrows, suppression and exploitation. It has been rightly said that, "Despite their differences, male autobiographies project a central consciousness, trace self-development, reflect mobility... (Jain 285) while Dalit women's autobiographies depict the pain of the writer herself and other women of her community.

Urmila Pawar in her memoir *The Weave of My Life* narrates the pain of the women of her community and the discrimination between the upper and lower castes in her school. The women of her community had to cut wood from the forests and then selling wood in the remote market was not as easy task.

Shantabai Dhanaji Dani describes the problem of hunger in her autobiography *Ratrandin Amha*. They had to cook the cheap food in their family. Bhakri, onion-chilli powder, and salt was in their food. They had to eat bhakri cooked in the morning.

Urmila Pawar writes in her autobiography how the upper caste girls would bring delicious dishes for their lunch while she could never think about such good food in her home due to her poverty. She writes, "However, I never asked myself the stupid question, why we do not prepare such dishes at home? We were aware, without anybody telling us, that we were born in a particular caste and in poverty, and that we had to live accordingly" (93). Pawar writes that at that time people were highly impressed by Ambedkar and the conversion into Budhism was in practice. Dalit people had also started performing rites and rituals according to Buddhist religion. She narrates how once she went at her sister-in-law's place with her nieces. When they asked rice repeatedly, the cook asks about their identity and when it is told to him by someone he calms down:

> 'Whose daughters are these anyway?' He burst out. 'They are eating like monsters' then someone answered 'they are from our Sushi's family! Daughters of Arjun master!' On hearing this, the host came forward. 'Oh! Are they? All right, all right let them eat as much as they want! Serve them well!' The cook returned with more rice but being called monster was not easy to digest and we politely declined. (117)

Urmila Pawar narrates her school experience that once all her classmates decide that each girl will bring some dish from her home tomorrow. The upper caste girls decide that they will bring something eatable but when Urmila asks them what should she bring, they tell her that she must bring money only. It was said to her because she belonged to a low caste and the upper caste girls would not touch her dish. Urmila writes about it:

> They did not allow me to touch anything. However, we all ate together. I really enjoyed the meal. The next day I was horrified to hear that my eating had become the hottest topic for juicy gossip. Girls were whispering in groups about 'how much I had eaten'. (110)

Urmila Pawar writes in her autobiography that she was not good at English and her English teacher would scold her for it. Urmila records her teacher's statement in these words, "This is English, the milk of tigress; it is not easy, like acting in plays." (160). She narrates that the sexual exploitation of Dalit girls is very common. She narrates how her maternal uncle would touched her from an evil intention, "My maternal uncle plays dolls with me and pretends to be my husband drags me into an alcove and presses me hard." (125). Urmila Pawar narrates her first night experience after her marriage. She gives a frank description of her husband's poverty:

> "Never mind! My husband's hands were groping all over my body. The tiny room with its peeling walls, the single iron bed with its creaking iron strips, the smelly, moldy mattress with hard lumps of cotton, the dirty, stained, old bedspread, the flat hard pillow smelling like a naphthalene bag... (183)

Her husband Harishchandra did not like her getting education and taking part in Dalit women's movements, she had to give her salary also to her husband. "When I got my first salary, I could not believe that all that money was mine; that I could spend it the way I liked. Before my marriage, I used to hand over my salary to my mother; now I started handling it over to my husband. If this is not like deliberately offering head for the butcher's knife, what else is it?" (208).

Kumud Pawde's *Antasphot* (*Thoughtful Outburst*) is also about Mahars's problems in Maharashtra. She narrates how in 1946 Mahars were attacked by the Hindus in Nagpur. Mahars also kept them mentally prepared to retaliate. Situation was so tensed that Mahars also decided to do or die. They collected weapons from each family. The people who did ironworks made weapons for them. Even the children and women were prepared to face any kind of adverse situation.

> Every family had knives and sharp instruments for slaughtering fowl and cutting vegetables. The wrestlers and their masters also had swords.... Blades and nails were being attached to sticks. Women were being taught to use the rope hoopla and sticks. Children were given the job of collecting stones and bricks, piles of which were lying at different places in the colony. (Rege 237-38)

> Kumud Pawde describes her experience that she had to face many problems in getting Sanskrit as a subject and even after becoming a Sanskrit professor; she has to face many difficulty because the upper caste students and teachers did not treat her like other upper caste teachers.

Shantabai Dhanaji Dani's life narrative *Ratrandin Amha* (*For Us—These Nights and Days*) is another autobiography that depicts the Ambedkar's thoughts that a Dalit woman remains the most Dalit of all. She had to remain under pressure of Dalit and upper caste patriarchs. Dani narrates how even a well-educated Dalit woman remains at the mercy of her husband:

> A Dalit woman's husband could impose his male ego on his wife. I am well educated but still a woman born in the Mahar caste after all. Because of the very progressive ideological stand of Dr Babasaheb Ambedkar I was able to become president of the SCF of Nasik district. (Rege 113)

Though Bama is from Tamil Nadu yet without the mention of her autobiography Karukku, this work will be insufficient. Bama narrates how she faced gender discrimination in the society and in convent school. She tells in an interview, "True. How can I think of my life as one individual's? I am a Dalit and a woman...therefore it is my community which makes me what I am...my story is my community's story" (Mangai 116). Pramod K. Nayar's writes that Karukku "highlights the complicity between class and caste in post-independence India" (Nayar 84).

Bama notices that Dalits had to face discrimination in the society. They were not allowed to touch the articles belonging to upper caste people. When she was mere a child, she used to go to school on foot. One day she saw an old man holding a packet of pastry with a string. She could not understand it and when she asks her brother Annan about it, he tells that being a Dalit he cannot touch it. Bama raises question about this discrimination:

> Are Dalits not human beings? Do they not have common sense? Do they not have such attributes as a sense of honour and self respect? Are they without any wisdom, beauty, dignity? What do we lack? They treat us in whatever way they choose, as if we are slaves who don't even possess human dignity. (Bama 24)

Dalits were not allowed to enter temple and they could not touch the upper caste people. This discrimination is prevalent in Indian society since ancient time. The poor Dalit people did not have sufficient grain and vegetables to cook. Bama writes about it in her autobiography *Karukku*, "Usually in our street, no one cooked at noon. It was only in the evening that people cooked rice, made a curry; at other times it was always kuuzh, millet porridge" (Bama 7). In present time also, there are many poor, Dalit or backward class people who do not get sufficient food to eat. Bama writes that even the police would discriminate with them. She resists against this corrupt social system and writes, "Here we are struggling just for this watery gruel. So how will the police or the Government be on our side?" (Bama 31). Bama vehemently shows her wrath at the humiliation and exploitation of Dalits. She thinks that Dalits must not rely upon their fate. She writes that Dalits should come forward to fight against wrong system. She writes, "We must not accept the injustice of our enslavement by telling ourselves it is our fate, as if we have no true feelings; we must dare to stand up for change" (Bama 25).

Baby Kamble's narrative *Jina Amucha* was translated by Maya Pandit as *The Prisons We Broke*. This autobiography has the Ambedkarite discourse. Maya Pandit, the translator of the book, writes in the introduction of the book *The Prisons We Broke*:

> Baby Kamble's narration reflects her love for her people without seeming to glorify their terrible condition. Outrage against the inhuman conditions of existence and love for her suffering people originally fused to evolve a self-critical and yet humane and mature tone (xiv).

Baby Kamble criticises the well-educated Dalits who have not imbibed the ideology of Dr B.R. Ambedkar and did not motivate other people also for their upliftment by getting education. She thinks that it is the responsibility of the educated people to work for them as Dr Ambedkar did. She writes that, "Education, prosperity, and comforts should not make me to forget the problems of society" (123). In this autobiography Baby Kamble has discussed the position of Mahars from pre-Ambedkar days to the present time. The transformation in their lives due to Buddhism has been one of the themes in this autobiography. "There will be outcastes (untouchables) as long as there are castes and nothing can emancipate the outcastes except the destruction of the caste system" (85).

Shantabai's *Majya Jalmachi Chittarkatha* is about the conflict between the upper and the lower caste people. She writes how she faces many hurdles in getting her education. She could not save herself from the sting of the untouchables. When her teacher sends her to her classmate Shaku's home, the latter's mother warns her to stay away just because she belongs to a low caste. Her parents also were not happy at her birth just because she was a girl. Her father did not have sufficient money to send her in a neighbouring village to study.

Though there are many Dalit women's autobiographies in regional languages now but among them Baby Kamble's *Jina Amucha* (*The Prisons We Broke*), Urmila Pawar's *Aayadan* (*The Weave of My Life*), Shantabai Kamble's *Majya Jalmachi Chittarakatha* (*Kaleidoscopic Story of My Life*), Kumud Pawde's *Antasphot* (*Thoughtful Outburst*), Janabai Girhe's *Marankala* (*Deathly Pains*) etc are famous. All these autobiographies beautifully depict the miserable plight of Dalit women and their community.

Works Cited

Ambedkar, B. R. *Writings and Speeches*, ed. Vasant Moon, Vol. 5 and 12. Bombay: Education Department, Government of Maharashtra, 1979.

Bama. *Karukku*. Trans. Lakshmi Holmström. Chennai: Macmillan India Ltd., 2000.

Girhe, Janabai Kachru qtd. in Rege, Sharmila. *Writing Caste/ Writing Gender: Narrating Dalit Women's Testimonios.* New Delhi: Zubaan, 2006.

Jain, Jasbir. *Writing Women across Cultures.* Jaipur & New Delhi: Rawat Publications, 2002.

Mangai. "Bama." *Storylines: Conversation with Women Writers.* Eds. Ammu Joseph & et.al. Delhi: Women's World, 2003. 111-120.

Nayar, Pramod K. "Bama's *Karukku*: Dalit Autobiography as Testimonio" *Commonwealth Literature* 41.2 (2006): 18.

Pandit, Maya. "Introduction." in Baby Kamble. *The Prisons We Broke.* Trans. Maya Pandit. Chennai: Orient Longman, 2008.

Pawar, Urmila. *The Weave of My Life: A Dalit Woman's Memoirs.* Trans. Maya Pandit. Kolkata: Stree, 2003.

15

A Memoir of Conflict: Reading Dichotomy in Shilpa Raj's *The Elephant Chaser's Daughter*

Guni Vats

> The two worlds I lived in had become overwhelmingly irreconcilable. I found myself stuck between them, tossed mercilessly from one to the other. When one set of values and traditions confronted the other, a meeting of the minds was out of the question. (Raj 151)

Shilpa Raj's memoir *The Elephant Chaser's Daughter* is a reminisce of conflict; conflict of 'a home' and 'the home', conflict of stereotypes and progress, of East and West and the story of a young girl balancing her life through all the dichotomy. The piece of literature is amongst the first memoir ever documented by a Dalit woman. Raj's memoir is not an autobiography a reader would expect from a Dalit woman, but a bildungsroman. It is the story of the four-year-old Shilpa moving to Shanti Bhavan, to experience a world no one in her community would have ever dreamed of. It is not the helpless cry of the oppressed, but the Ambedkarite celebration of education uplifting children of untouchables to become responsible citizens of the nation. Shilpa unashamedly recounts the horrors of domestic violence, of harassment, of the vicious circle of debt and the community drowning in the horrors of country liquor. Hers is a story of an outsider in her home and a home in the outside world, where she was not meant to belong. It carefully deals with the nuances of sibling jealousy, family expectations, and the tight grips of community superstitions that have fettered the Dalits for decades. In the village of Thattaguppe, the word of landlords was the word of justice and the Shanti-Bhavan-educated Shilpa refused to give up her authority of opinion. The memoir deals with the seriousness of caste and untouchability in the lives of these children who have the privilege to study but have to return to the darkness of age-old traditions. Through the snippets of her past and struggles of her present, Shilpa Anthony Raj weaves a narrative of hope and freedom.

Identity is a societal construction and confirmation of a name that exposes the caste, religious, and financial standing in society. Identity is not the description of an individual but the place that the society has pre-determined for the individual to remain confined in. Shilpa Anthony Raj began the journey to change how she would be viewed along with twenty-three other children, when a blue jeep parked in her village, cutting across the densely woven structures of caste and hierarchy. It was her father, a man who would drink and beat his wife while spending his time with other women of the village, adamant at getting his daughter admitted to the school that promised the only hope for them to become more than they were destined to be. The elephant chaser fought his wife tooth and nail and swore that he would educate his daughter even if it meant he would have to go hungry. The fight of a father to get his daughter educated was condoned and he was called names, but he bore every insult for a future none could envision. Education is not important in the Dalit sectors of India. Despite the reservation laws and political promises of their upliftment; they remain untouchables. Education is costly and worthless for people who would never be allowed to step foot in the places of the sanctity of upper castes. Women bear the worst of it; where their menstruation is celebrated, they are pushed on the paths of marriage and childbearing, with husbands who are elder, drunkard, and violent. Education is a distant dream and Raj's memoir proves how it is essential in the becoming of someone you were not destined to be.

Shilpa's grandmother would always say that destiny is what is written on the forehead. This destiny is challenged by Shanti Bhavan, a school meant to uplift the most oppressed. Shilpa is caught between the dichotomy of the destiny of her past and the opportunity of her future. The Christians of Thattaguppe were Hindu converts, who had escaped the clutches of religion but had found themselves still stuck in the hierarchy of caste and untouchability. Bearing an ancestry of Hinduism, they were haunted by the superstitions and ancestral interference in their lives. Shilpa's conflict is with the demons of the superstitious past and the progressive future that Shanti Bhavan promised. Shanti Bhavan was a heaven of opportunities that preached equality. A haven for the children of Dalits, it was an institution committed to touching their lives holistically. They were taught to be free and responsible at the same time. They were taught human values and were pumped with the self-confidence they would require to face the real world and carve a place for themselves and their family. Shanti Bhavan is an institution that promises to break the chain of oppression, while the caste hierarchy vows to confine Dalits in the swamps of untouchability. Author's home in the village is a testament to gender inequality, obsessive drinking habits of men, and an unfair patriarchal setup where women are meant to cook and clean and bear children. Shilpa is caught between the dichotomy of two, her memoir is her struggle to emerge as her person, an amalgamation of the best of both worlds.

The becoming of an adult is a continuous process of construction that evolves from the society outwards and the psychological identity inwards. The amalgamation of the two is important in constructing 'self'. Julia Kristeva takes forward the argument of psychoanalysts and applies it in linguistics to determine how a thetic phase occurs post chora that determines a subject. A subject-in-process is Kristevan way of explaining how the interaction keeps forming and deconstructing meaning in the forte of language that one speaks and internalises, 'intensifying the semiotic disposition means identifying the shift in the speaking subject, his capacity for renewing the order in which he is inescapably caught up; and that capacity is, for the subject, the capacity for enjoyment.' (Kristeva 29) Shilpa's language of the outside world and inner conscience suffered the thetic-break twice. She has psychologically broken away from her mother's body as the other, realising later that her father had never wanted her to have born and was planning to dispose of her. A second thetic phase occurs when the blue jeep breaks her from the outside world that had constructed her conscience, to begin with. At Shanti Bhavan, not only the world around her changed, but her realisation of herself as an individual went through a sharp re-significance.

> Until I came to Shanti Bhavan, I had never thought about looking pretty. Most of the time I was dirty and wore simple clothes sewed from my grandmother's worn-out saris. Occasionally Amma cut my hair, crookedly, with blunt scissors...no one talked about hairstyles. I had never washed my hair with shampoo, warn shoes, or put on face lotion. But the absence of those luxuries didn't matter then as I didn't know they existed. (Raj 37)

Her first memories at her 'new home' were one of self-hygiene. She used shampoo for the first time and combed her hair well. She squeezed the flavored toothpaste on the toothbrush to taste sophistication. The identity of being dirty associates itself with being Dalit, Shanti Bhavan washed that identity off. They were taught to concentrate on their appearance, to learn posture, to learn cleanliness, and appear put-together. They were woken up at dawn and encouraged to clean after themselves and tend to their gardens. The residential school taught them mutual respect and equality, an important lesson at building the self-esteem, that they had never learned back home. Shanti Bhavan was stark different from their villages, set up in a vast piece of land in known terrain, it was a gated haven of security and progress. The trauma of breaking away from the parents could be understood when the young students would call their wardens and teachers 'Aunty' or sometimes even 'Mummy', and Dr George would be called 'Daddy'. Children at Shanti Bhavan had two sets of parents, Amma and Appa back home and Daddy and Aunties in the school. Siblings were soon replaced by classmates, a diverse group that had come from similar backgrounds who could understand each other and help each other build. The competition was from the outside world, Shanti Bhavan was protected. The existence of Shanti Bhavan and their own homes created a sense of the otherness of self. The life back home became so alien to Shilpa, that she would resent staying in shabby lanes amongst drunkards and molesters, 'observing the lives of those who lived in the shabby huts on either side, a sense of my own insignificance overwhelmed me...' (158). When the family becomes an outsider and the outside world becomes family, a strange sense of alienation takes over, one that shreds the inner self and forces identity in distress.

The *ghar-bahar* conflict takes a new turn in Shilpa's journey, where signification shifts and meanings change. 'Negating or denying the symbolic, without which he would be incapable of doing anything, the subject may imagine the thetic at the place of an object or a partner' (Kristeva 114). Tagore's conflict of the Home and the World, expressed in his 1916 novel, takes a new meaning in Shilpa's memoir. Moving from her village to the residential school at four years of age, shifted meaning in her life. Sharp contrasts are documented in her memoir, from the treatment of girls and boys to the importance placed to human values, they were brought up in a world much ahead of the times of her village. She was torn between her two homes, so much so that she would feel an alien at the home she was born in, and feel guilty in her place of bringing up. The two homes were not different only in the context of the space they were situated, but the virtual times they existed were different. In her writing, Shanti Bhavan moves with rapid energy of enthusiastic progression while the village rots in its stagnant lanes. The school is filled with exciting possibilities, and the village is frozen with shattered dreams. The writing and pace, the semiotic governs Raj's symbolic; the hurried paragraphs are dedicated to her life at school and the slow, unsure, confused passages are given to her village. The two worlds are so different than when the first time parents come to meet their children at Shanti Bhavan, they fail to recognize them.

> Plenty of confusion erupted since some parents could no longer identify their children. We looked so different to them, dramatically transformed by our clean clothes, full cheeks, haircuts, and huge smiles. Some mothers embarrassed themselves by grabbing the wrong child... (Raj 45)

The conflict of the homes ran deeper in the psyche of the author. Once the meanings shifted, the understanding of the world changed. The aesthetic of the man-woman relationship and its acceptance deconstructed. The village taught her that men had the sole ownership of knowledge and only they could make decisions. Whatever the father said was to be treated as the final word, and this hierarchy deepened in caste circles when whatever the landlord said was to be treated as the word of wisdom. Shilpa had witnessed many instances of domestic violence in her home when the drunk father would slap and beat his wife blue. Shanti Bhavan taught her that men and women were to be treated equally and that nobody had the right to decide for her life until she consents. The country liquor was so prevalent that she in her innocence believed that it was only normal for a man to drink, it was later in Shanti Bhavan that she learned that excessive drinking is a disease. While the village gossiped and treated every relationship frivolously, Shilpa had learned to voice her opinion sensitively, she would even act as an intermediary in the fights of her parents, though she would lose at the end, 'Contrary to the widespread village notion that girls should not voice their thoughts, I put my disappointments and frustrations on full display. Playing parent to my parents was the most difficult task I had ever undertaken' (Raj 211). She grew up to understand the oppression that her mother had to face, but also the history of hardship her father had to endure to become whatever he was. She was raised to be a mature young lady, who was not a victim of the violence but a mediator who swore to resolve things respectfully.

> I couldn't help seeing myself as an outsider and that realisation made me terribly sad. How would I ever fit in to a permanent life in the village? How would I find in myself the qualities those women in the fields had found? (Raj 161)

To be a woman of the village and to be a woman in Shanti Bhavan were very different in their inception of the concept of 'a woman'. Thattaguppe trained its women to be good, decent, 'dutiful' wives, 'Most men in the village preferred obedient, dutiful wives.' (113) Menstruation was marked as the threshold of marriageable age for young women in the village, while Shanti Bhavan encouraged them to study and aspire to good-paying jobs so they could break free from the vicious circle of caste oppression. 'Ever since I started my periods, I had been treated differently. Grandfather instructed Grandmother to set aside a glass of milk occasionally, as he strongly believed that girls who had come of age needed to be strong and healthy' (Raj 117). Once the girl reached the marriageable age, she was protected like the cubs are protected. Every moment she stepped out of the house, she had to be accompanied by a guardian. She was treated as a precious property. Kavya, Shilpa's younger sister would crib that she didn't have periods when her elder sister enjoyed the privileges of a menstruating woman. Her education was not worth any attention because she was a girl, she was pre-determined to get beaten by her husband and give in to her domestic duties. 'My education meant nothing to them. They couldn't see its value, especially since I was a girl' (Raj 133).

The memoir that recounts the fantasy-haven of Shanti Bhavan is also burdened by the tales of oppression painted in the dark lanes of the village. The village wisdom that forbids the girls to wander alone or even to talk to boys collectively hushes any instances of molestation carried inside their homes. Women were the most vulnerable when left alone with their families. Shilpa writes about her experiences with her uncle, experiences of harassment, and molestation. '...I felt strong hands press down on my collarbones in a tightening grip. I felt my uncle's cheek gently rubbing against mine. His moustache tickled me as he slowly traced the side of my face with his lips, I then felt his lips moving from my cheek to my mouth. I froze...I didn't know whether I was more anxious or ashamed' (Raj 136). The sexual harassment at home was later conveniently justified by her grandmother because she was intended to marry her uncle nevertheless. Even when she tried to speak about it at school, her grandmother straight away refused any such activities and Shilpa was forced to the trauma of guilt and shame in an act where she was the victim. The alienation at home proved so strong and traumatic, that when once Shanti Bhavan struggled the fear of closing down and Shilpa feared never going back, she almost gave up to the wishes of her family and agreed to marry her uncle. The self, the other, and the otherness of self were the paradigms that pushed the author towards a conflicted trauma. She was a bright student and an enthusiastic writer dreaming about becoming a journalist and within a month, she was tiptoeing her way to her uncle's cot to demand his attention. The desperate need to be accepted by the family drove Shilpa to almost give up her dreams of a better future and surrender to the laws of the land.

Caste and gender were the realities of Shilpa's life. The school could have offered a protected universe, but the practical life threw them back in the clutches of reality. The author writes about the stories of women disgraced, a colleague who had dropped out of school and was now entertaining drunk men of the village, pregnant. She remembers the saga of a classmate's mother who was burnt to protect her honour, and the son covered his hands with gloves hiding burnt wounds from trying to save his mother. Trauma was never an alien feeling for Shilpa or other students of Shanti Bhavan, but they had together learned to overcome it and use education as a tool to write their destinies. 'Boys didn't look down upon girls. It was beautiful to realize that the same boys who witnessed their fathers kick, burn, and emotionally destroy their mothers would never raise a hand to a girl or make her feel less worthy' (Raj 226). The realisation that the children who came from violent backgrounds could change their outlook is a very important lesson of her memoir. It changes how society sees Dalits; it breaks the vicious circle of oppression. Shilpa Anthony Raj was a sensitive passive audience to the stories she heard at school, but her relationship with her younger sister and her parents define how she viewed oppression and discrimination.

We are introduced to the image of Shilpa's Amma through the initial resistance of her willingness to separate her daughter from her. She remains a passive object for the story author had weaved through the life experiences of her father. She was the woman who was wooed, beaten, and cheated. She was the mother who had transpired to distance her daughter from her husband. It was only later, through Shilpa's words that we trace Sarophina's existence. A strong woman, determined to carve a world of her being, left her children in the village and went to Singapore as a house help. Shilpa resists and revolts her mother's absence but soon gets habitual. Her thetic break from her mother occurs thrice in her lifetime, at her infancy, when she is sent to Shanti Bhavan and when the mother decides to go to Singapore. Years pass in her absence and Shilpa grows distant. The mother does return, but her presence is alien. In the story of Shilpa's alienation, her mother's absence plays a drastic role. She learns how to be a woman from her actions and falls in the crevices of dichotomy the moment she learns her mother's dubious intentions. A woman who would fight her husband all day would give in a matter of seconds to only pacify him. Her mother was the mystery she could never solve.

> In the space of a single second, all her bold declarations of wanting to be free of my father's tyranny vaporised and her emotional dependence on him was exposed. She couldn't consider living alone in a village where single women are not safe. I was furious with her for behaving as though it was all her fault... (210)

Kavya's death (or suicide) is how the memoir begins and ends, all rest is Shilpa's effort to understand her sister's death. Kavya and Shilpa are the personifications of the conflict that Shilpa writes about. While Shilpa gets the privilege of studying in Shanti Bhavan, Kavya is left to get educated in the local school. A fiery spirit, she is a free-soul who wanders through the village with an air of belongingness. While Shilpa is always an alien, a visitor, Kavya is the daughter of the village. Shilpa gets to write her destiny and Kavya is left to suffocate in the streets rotten with country liquor. Shilpa's conflict restricts Kavya's freedom. The constant comparison and the tormenting reality that she would be stuck in the oppressive hierarchical untouchable community, Kavya dreamed to fly away from the fetters. The vocal resistance at her mother's claim of love, the resentment at Shilpa's biased treatment created a valley of complex amidst the siblings who were meant to support each other. Shilpa, the eldest daughter was always an outsider to the close bond that her siblings, Francis and Kavya, shared. Though she dreamt of constructing a better future for them, she could never instigate the hope in Kavya. Kavya eloped, a young adolescent girl left her home with boys who could offer her a material pleasure. She called Shilpa after months, pleading her to be accepted back in the village, but all that returned was her corpse. A corpse of a girl who dared to break the rules of the patriarchal, oppressive community was not even accommodated a burial place amongst the villagers. Her death was scorned at as her life was, she was buried in a corner reserved for unnatural deaths. Kavya's death was Shilpa's thetic break from her village.

> The men placed Kavya's coffin by the side of a small, deep pit that a few relatives had already dug for the grave at a far corner of the yard in the secluded section reserved for those who died in unholy ways. It was hard for me to understand how my sister, even in death, could be relegated to lowliness in the same house of God where she used to worship. (Raj 242)

Shilpa's dichotomy was resolved in the death of the only person who made her village home. At Kavya's death, a relative told her to go and never return because nothing was left for her in the village. Shilpa returned to her home, Shanti Bhavan straight from the burial grounds. The conflict of being and becoming is never resolved in a human subject, but what happens when the signification of meaning is in a perpetual contrast? Shilpa's memoir is a celebration of her opportunity at Shanti Bhavan but is also her wail of irreconcilable grief at the loss of her other self, her sister. Being brought up in a haven where boys and girls were treated equally, she would never be able to forget how women are trivialised back home. Her attempt at understanding her sister's death takes her deeper to a voyage of oppression, the conflicted lives that never had a chance to absolve themselves. Being called an 'American Desi', or taunted at her accent and education, she would never take offense because she realises the sacrifice, she and her family had to make her who she is. The dream of breaking the vicious circle of illiteracy and oppression doesn't get resolved by a school or twenty-four children who spend fourteen years of their lives trying to rewrite their destinies. They live in a perpetual state of conflict of self and other, of belonging and alienation, but they are the only hope of their families to dare to dream of something bigger than the fate they are forced to. Shilpa is the elephant chaser's dream of entering *Gunna's* kitchen, an area warded off-limits from the untouchables.

> Who could have ever imagined that the girl in the far corner of the stage once begged on the streets, that the boy in black tie smartly turning his partner was the son of a construction labourer, or that the tall, slender girl dancing off to the side had watched her murdered father's body burn on a pyre? (Raj 230)

Works Cited

Ganguly, Debjani. *Dalit Life Stories. The Cambridge Companion to Modern Indian Culture*. V. Dalmia and Sadana, editors. New Delhi: Cambridge UP, 2012, pp. 124-141.

Guru, Gopal. "Dalit Women Talk Differently: Gender and Caste." *Economic and Political Weekly*, 1995, pp. 2548-2550.

McAfee, Noelle. *Julia Kristeva*. Routledge, 2015.

Morris, Thomas D. *Southern Slavery and the Law, 1619-1860*. U of North Carolina P, 1999.

Raj, Shilpa. *The Elephant Chaser's Daughter*. New Jersey: Worldview, 2017.

Waugh, Patricia, and Rice Philip, editors. *Modern Literary Theory: A Reader*. Oxford UP, 1989.

16

Modernity and Gender Negotiations: C.K. Janu's *Mother Forest* in Kerala Feminist Iconography

Anusha A. J.

The dialogue on gender and modernity in Kerala has been delegated in the public and academic sphere since the last decades of the twentieth century vis-à-vis its engagements and responses to the social geopolitics. The iconography of the 'Feminazis', 'Feminichis' and related jargons has seeped through the collective unconscious of the people in the narrative of Kerala, has come to the fore from a deliberation or the lack thereof of navigating the politics and potentials of a movement as of the nature of Feminism. The state has been a sustained witness to a series of ecriture feminine, in the form of generic outlets as life writings in prose and poetry, novels, short stories and social commentary that modified and re-codified its narrative on women and the politics of their existence. From these, the paper would attempt to read and analyse social activist C.K. Janu's seminal autobiography *Mother Forest* as a foray into the notion of indigenous feminist iconography and its complicated threads of negotiation with the ideas of modernity and gender roles in the public sphere. While doing so, it would also attempt to place the narrative and its writer in the larger discourse of feminism in the state across time.

The study on language as a powerful mediator of changing paradigmatic syndications in the politics of gender had emerged in the long 1970s with scholars by the likes of Kate Millet, Elaine Showalter, Sandra Gilbert, Helen Cixous, Susan Gubar, Toril Moi among others. While these scholars have been instrumental in opening up the platitudes of a literature hidden and manipulated by the restrictive codes of patriarchy, conventions and othering, this has initiated a deliberation on the articulation of a gynocentric (Showalter) narrative amidst the established structures of phallogocentrism (Derrida). Consequently, generations of gaps in the historiography of women and their narratives were unearthed and subjected to scrutiny with a serious critical interest, particularly in Europe. However, Betty Friedan's notion of 'feminine mystique', Alice Walker's 'Womanism' and the critique of Eurocentric White feminism directed the necessity of diverse engagements with different parameters in feminism as a social movement for women across the world, including the identification, articulation and dispersion of pro-women literatures.

As the waves of feminist movements and empowerment narratives helmed a favourable negotiation in suffrage in as early as 1935 and later through the aforementioned deliberations, there arose a consistent influence and cogitation on women's identity and their narrative of the selves in the India of 19th and 20th centuries. Remarkable activists streamlined the political leadership and catered to generating a sort of mobilising power and sisterhood among the women then, including Annie Besant, Margaret Noble etc. While upper caste Hindu leaders like Sarojini Naidu and Vijayalakshmi Pandit attained a sustained visibility in the highly problematic hierarchical historiography, Adivasi and other minority women clusters failed to be etched in the written archives of the country. They were thrice removed from their self by means of colonists, the upper castes and patriarchal structures within their community, but Jhalkaribai, Kuyili, Uda Devi, Sabitri Dev, Putalimaya Devi Poddar have had to fight the repression and bigotries of not only these then, but subsequent generations in ink as well, to place themselves in the currency of not only Dalit epistemology but also in the larger structure of metanarrative.

In Kerala, the initiations of modernity and proliferations of feminist ideals could be traced back to the early decades of the nineteenth century with interjections of rebellions against untouchability and social evils. The Kerala Nadar women's movement in a fight for claim and rights over the sartorial orientations of the physical selves called the Channar Revolt (1813-1859) was foremost in the salient directive towards the possibilities of vocalising the self. But does modernity articulate from the universal awareness of the individual as spaced not in a vacuum but the psychosocial bodypolitics of parametric fragments or transcending the awareness to a mass struggle? How does it fare in Kerala among Adivasi women? The following reasons have been succinctly presented as catalysts in the state:

> The introduction of colonial education, the increase inprinting presses and the proliferation of books and the creation of a dynamic public sphere, the emergence of a new English educated middle class all contributed to the creation of modernity in Kerala. However, an understanding of modernity in Kerala resists fixed genealogies (of the region), connects diverse fragments and also creates ruptures, breaks and discontinuities (Bose and Varughese 12).

The "dynamic public sphere" however failed to address the questions of women's progress and many writers took up these failures in their books as is the case with *Agnisakshi* by Lalithambika Antharjanam and *Premabhajanam* by K. Saraswathi Amma. Though sites from a hierarchical upper class milieu, it dares to point out the fissures that modernity or rather masculine definitions of modernity depraves women. Women of all caste, class and regional affiliations, who realised the power of mobilisations, were left to fret in the domestic and caste space charted out by the reformed men of the century. However, the meagre reforms of gender which succeeded the social reformation were meant for the upper caste women, as J. Devika says. The premier novel in Malayalam *Indulekha* by O. Chandumenon argues for educating the Malayali women but staunchly places her within the caste system by means of her social dialogues and iconography. Drawing from Sangari and Vaid, the literature especially Malayalam women's magazines that came out of the causes of modernity was rather "the recasting of women into companionate marital relationships and attendant familial duties" (20). While the notion of modernity transcribed to somewhat a movement against ills of the tradition in the state, the tradition or cultural definitions was marked by the definitions vis-à-vis the upper Nair-Namboodiri castes. Therefore, there were sans visibility groups of women who barely existed in the system of modernity even in the twentieth century. The lack of inclusivity and equality in the access to education, property, economy and therefore the stabilisations of the nation-state, made modernity a problematic surface to navigate for the Dalit women in the margins.

It was the disillusionment with the land reform movements in the wake of millennium that brought the iron-lady of Muthanga at the forefront of the Dalit feminist iconography. Her Kudil Ketti Samaram (Sit-in Strike) and the subsequent rebellion in the organised leadership of Adivasi Gothra Mahasabha has been instrumental in dispersal of public sphere engagements on Adivasi rights on productive land and bring visibility to their cultural consciousness which was submerged under the qualms of bureaucratic reigns for urban modernity. Both Janu and the text have been subject to scrutiny by scholars regional, national and the international in Malayalam and English. Across time there has arguments been placed on the narrative of the self and the performative self. While Pramod K

Nayar, identifies and Janu's self in the narrative of her community, Rakesh Ramamoorthy points to the existence of the exotic and the modern as a performative engagement amidst the vocabulary of the text. However, the paper argues that she is an autoethnographic self as she reflects and narrates a feminist modernity that lies in community of sisterhood for change and empowerment. In the aforementioned sentence, the semantics of phrases used from self to feminist to modernity to empowerment invokes divergence to the metanarrative of the same in the state.

C.K. Janu was born to the Adiya, an indigenous community from Wayanad, Kerala. Her autobiographical narrative though mediated by author Bhaskaran and translator Shanker is a seminal draft on her community and her resistance since the 1970s from her birth. Born as an Adiya, her narrative of the self carries with it the ethnography of the group and their cultural imaginations and codes. The text presents a transformative lucid in the movement from part one of her childhood tribulations to part two of growth of political consciousness. Struggling from the marginalisation, culturally exhumed to be primitive and ordained to slave at the garbs of the conventionally hierarchical high and the caste conscious modern, Janu's childhood was spent between being a maid and a daily wage labourer earning meagre amount in a burgeoning economy. Deprived of their own lands in the name of building the modern nation and its global infrastructure tagged economic liberalisation, the adivasis in India including Janu have seen a perpetual conflict with the dialogue of the "mainstream India" (Collu, 1999). Her usage of informal oral rhetoric (mediated not muted) and strong identification with 'we' instead of 'I' which collates into her autoethnographic self holds a history that has been necessary to be retrieved for the sake of the feminist movement as well as discussing the ambivalence of modernities in the state.

The rhetoric of modernity and feminism during the course of the text in the state was at a point of awareness and paradigm shift in the sense that an attempt was made to integrate but not assimilate, women of marginalised castes to the dialogue of gender and development. With the presence of people like Sara Joseph and Ajitha, there also featured a politically intense deliberation on the sexuality, gender and grievances of these women. Ajitha's Anweshi and Sara's Manushi were societies helping mobilise the women and syncopating their solidarity with all women under duress. Sara Joseph has also been credited with ushering an era of 'pennezhutu' (womens' writing), a series of critical ecriture feminine in Kerala. As Maya Subrahmaniam points out this was a archive in time when:

> The Indian Association for Women's National Conference in 1984 in Trivandrum also brought women together and facilitated group activities. However, unlike the women's groups in the large North Indian cities, which were primarily, composed of academics at universities and colleges, feminist activists in Kerala included journalists, teachers, lawyers, doctors and others. There were few working-class women who were in unorganised or daily-wage sectors in the movement, since they thought the trade unions took care of them properly. (4)

While Janu was invisible in the pantheon of who were feminists then, her feminism and political activism took shape under the need to fight for land reforms. She under the aegis of the Left which was calling for equity in land distribution and access in the economy, took up a strike for 48 days in front of the Secretariat in Trivandrum demanding that land that was taken away from them in the name of model of development and destroyed with monoculture be redistributed for them to safeguard and sustain. Is Janu a Feminist? The tribal woman and her vocabulary of empowerment depart from the mainstream feminist agenda in the sense of what Jeffrey Rubin addresses as "actions involving consciousness, collective action, and direct challenges to structures of power" (245). While this might seem reductionary, Sangeetha Verma believes that this collective action for the indigenous woman stems from "not abstract ideas of change but collective knowledge derived from the lived experiences of their community" (223). As the mainstream feminism which focused on the nuances of furthering the promises of colonial modernity for the female gender in the state was based on rebelling the flawed traditions, the feminism of the indigenous women is deeply entrenched in her community and its progress. That being said, as modernity inculcated the notion of identity of individual rather than the community, condemned caste consciousness and discriminations, rose up against communalism, the Indian notion of modernity and its "imagination has never been cut off from what existed earlier" (Chakrabarty 21). In Janu's case, the tirade against the mainstream Kerala modernity is meted out with her indigenous modernity which "is secular and inclusive of all, the living, the nonliving, and the earth herself" (Verma 223). Janu's *Mother Forest* in lieu of its title itself has positioned and placed itself in a critical terminology on their community and its claims to the forest land. While most of the mainstream feminists as seen belonged to a literate urban modernity, Janu was illiterate until she took part in a state literacy campaign. The question of access to realm of education did not however deter her from stating and charting out her feminism and modernity based on the notions of sisterhood and resilience that was barely brought into the consciousness of women in the state by societies and social activists, but already existed as a sense of community and collective action in Janu:

> Unity in everything originates from our women. They have something in common that shelters us from meaninglessly adopting the ways of civil society. They have enough resilience in them to stand for what they feel is right even though they may have to suffer a lot for it. It is among our women that our traditions and the way we dress live on even now. Theirs is a resolve that is hardened by the wind

> and the rain of the forest in the face of other difficulties. (Janu and Bhaskaran 53)

Not only is she conscious of the rationality behind the sisterhood but also considers it a mode of resistance which incorporates the dissent against subjection to poverty, social isolation, environmental destruction and caste discrimination. As mentioned, Janu's usage of the term "*nammal*" (We) in reference to herself throughout the narrative rather than 'I' also therefore argues for an assertion of an autonomy for the community, the individual and the forest amidst the mainstream social movements. Scholars of indigenous feminism have time and again deliberated about the significance of oral literature in protest and identity assertions. Janu's oral expressions of her life story also engage a synergy with the identity and the native language against appropriations. While the permission to a translation might be seen from the mediation, however, with the difficulties in the same, it is Janu's narrative that is subverting and pointing out the insufficiencies of the "rotten" dominant language to accommodate their strong heritage and sisterhood (Janu and Bhaskaran 34).

The text posits a strong rational sisterhood and bonding that nurtures and rebels. Her community featured women who resisted the sustained invasion of civil society but never romanticised few of the customs of their past. Though Janu has manifold complaints against the abuse of "tribal innocence" especially of women, she reiterates that they fight the abuse without relegating the victims to isolation, there are no taboos in being "single, widowed or abandoned" (Janu and Bhaskaran 67). While the colonial modernity and urban modernity purported by Kerala model of development has been protesting against these taboos in the mainstream, such things did not exist in Janu's communal consciousness. Her modernity is dynamic in her political and vocal questioning of systemic oppression, while calling for sustainable progress of the cultural heritage and the ecological balance of the land. It also asserts her definitive cultural presence within the state while not being assimilated to the complex homogeneity of the mainstream. Janu's recollection of a bitter incident of children especially girls separated from family to be 'civilised' resonates a deep resentment in their transgressions. Her protest of the same would then witness her locating and transgressing by herself a space of significance and a rational democratic infiltration of the mainstream where neither she nor her community was attributed to "modernity". As 'modern' men and women fought through the discriminative conventional traps of religion, Janu on the other hand has seen no "fair fat gods or goddesses" (40) but rather lived with a strong sense of ancestral and ecological gratitude. Further, her modern trait of rationality is definitive in her argument for an evolution of her community in the new social movements and milieu complemented by equity and respect for each other.

She also thwarts the notion of a modernity set in its phallocentrism and masculine tangentials. For her, the women she has seen and grown up with within her indigenous group have been more responsible and prone to practical life than men who waste away much mostly in chasing after the encroachments of the civil society. Her vehemence with their changing lifestyle of consumption in alcohol and tobacco is seen throughout the text. Janu argues and reiterates favouring women as power central to their community structures that,

> Women always take up more responsibility than men. This is so in other communities too. Women go to work in the fields. Digging, sowing, preparing the fields and any kind of work on land. Also, taking care of the little ones in the hut ...Our community can surely grow only through the togetherness of our women (46-47).

In Kerala of the twentieth century, too, is one of intense loss of productive and cultural resources on the one hand, and reduction to a governmental category to be supervised and managed by the state on the other—within the framework of a certain 'bureaucratic modernity'.

In conclusion, the text and its concerns is and has been historiographically significant in that it brings to the fore a story of a community and a feminist who fought a resistance against the pernicious effects of colonial modernity. She in turn attempts to narrate and situate a rationale of a feminism based on existing sisterhood within her community. She also directs the facts that Adiya women are more rationally modern than men for they have more individuality and perseverance in resistance. Therefore, Janu's narrative been instrumental in initiating a dialogue in state on the Adiya community and the adivasis in general, from a critically nuanced perspective especially on gender and modernity, as the text arises from the very existence of self, at interjunction of personal, political and social, than a third person observer narrative filtered in biases. Seventeen years down the lane, though Janu is still strongly vocal about the tribal grievances, her conflict with both Left and Right wings has downplayed her visibility in the mainstream. But the text speaks of a political transgression and defining moments of indigenous modernity that has shifted the episteme on adivasis and the women in the state and by means of the translations, national and global.

Works Cited

Bose, Satheese Chandra, and Shiju Sam Varughese, editors. *Kerala Modernity: Ideas, Spaces and Practices in Transition*. Orient BlackSwan, 2017.

Chakrabarty, Dipesh. *Habitations of Modernity: Essays in the Wake of Subaltern Studies*. Permanent Black, 2004.

Collu, G. "Adivasis and the Myth of Independence: Mahasweta Devi's 'Douloti the Bountiful." *Ariel*, Vol. 30, No. 1, 1999, pp. 43-57.

Devika, J. "Negotiating Women's Social Space: Public Debates on Gender in Early Modern Kerala, India." *Inter-Asia Cultural Studies*, Vol. 7, No. 1, 2006, pp. 43-61.

Janu, C. K., and Bhaskaran. *Mother Forest: the Unfinished Story of C.K. Janu*. Translated by N. Ravi Shanker, Women Unlimited, Kali for Women, 2004.

K, Beena M. "Women Autobiographies in Malayalam before and after the Feminist Movement A Comparative Study." *Mahatma Gandhi University*, 2014. *Shodhganga*.

Nayar, Pramod K. "Indigenous Cultures and the Ecology of Protest: Moral Economy and 'Knowing Subalternity' in Dalit and Tribal Writing from India." *Journal of Postcolonial Writing*, Vol. 50, No. 3, 2013, pp. 291–303.

Panikkar, Chitra. "Articulating an Identity: The Autobiographical We." *Samyukta*, Vol. 9, No. 1, 2009, pp. 262–271.

Ramamoorthy, Rakesh. "Modernity At Arm's Length: Strategic Exoticism in *Mother Forest: The Unfinished Story of C.K.Janu*." *Literary Endeavour*, Vol. 10, No. 2, Apr. 2019. pp. 226-230.

The Rhetoric of Jacques Derrida I: Plato's Pharmacy. www.jstor.org/stable/20129336.

Roy, Pragya. "6 Forgotten Dalit, Bahujan and Adivasi Women Who Fought For India's Independence." *Feminism in India*, 15 Aug. 2020. https://feminisminindia.com/2020/08/15/dalit-bahujan-adivasi-women-fought-indias-independence/ Accessed 20 August, 2020.

Rubin, Jeffrey W. "Defining Resistance: Contested Interpretations of Everyday Acts." *Studies in Law, Politics and Society*, Vol. 15, 1996, pp. 237-260.

Sangari, Kumkum, and Sudesh Vaid. *Recasting Women: Essays in Colonial History*. Zubaan, 2013.

Showalter, Elaine. *A Literature of Their Own*. Princeton, 1977.

Subrahmanian, Maya. "Autonomous Women's Movement in Kerala: Historiography." *Journal of International Women's Studies*, Vol. 20, No. 2, Jan. 2019.

Turner, Elen. "An Unfinished Story: The Representation of Adivasis in Indian Feminist Literature." *Contemporary South Asia*. Vol. 20 No. 3, 2012, pp. 327-49.

Verma, Sangeetha. "The Chalice and The Elixir of Life: The Female Quest for an Eco Ethic in Autobiographical Narratives." University of Calicut, 2015. Shodhganga.

Whitinui, Paul. "Indigenous Autoethnography." *Journal of Contemporary Ethnography*, Vol. 43, No. 4, 2013, pp. 456-487.

17

The Struggles and Empowerment of a Dalit Woman: A Study of Shilpa Raj's Memoir *The Elephant Chaser's Daughter*

N. Padmapriyadharshini

Dalit literature started its journey from 1960s particularly from the Marathi language and later extended its wings to Tamil, Telugu, Hindi and Kannada etc... the word Dalit is of a Sanskrit origin which means broken or scattered. Varna system, the classification of people based on their nature of occupation was the only responsibility of people suffering in the name of untouchability and denied basic human rights. The so called 'Dalits' were not even allowed to gain education. But some people strived hard top gain education and fight back with the awareness they had due to education. One such man is Dr B. R. Ambedkar. Being born in a Dalit family, being denied education, being ignored by fellow students, he gained education and now was appreciated and praised as the father of Indian constitution. Education has given such a glory to a man born in subaltern community. He strongly protested against all these odds in the society and tried his level best to bring out equality. His efforts are highly appreciable. There are still some crimes related to caste such as denial of hospital bed for a Dalit pregnant woman in Uttar Pradesh, honour-killing in Tamil Nadu, etc... are happening. However, the number of these crimes and its intensity was reduced by great leaders like Dr B. R. Ambedkar. He has spoken much about self-respect as he struggled a lot to attain it. Ambedkar strongly asserts that,

> It is disgraceful to live at the cost of one's self-respect. Self-respect is most vital in life. Without it man is chipper to live worthily with respect one has to overcome difficulties. It is out of hard and ceaseless struggle alone that one derives strength confidence and recognition. (1)

Feminism is a powerful movement that fights for the equality of women in education, research, employment and self-respect. It is the women belonging to Dalit community who experienced double marginalisation from the society. Dalit men faced discrimination in the society whereas the Dalit women faced suppression both in the society and in their family as well. In one of famous Tamil literary work *Periya Puranam*, Chekizhar presented the status of Dalit women in detail. He portrayed the image of Dalit women wearing only half dress and stood half naked. On meeting anyone belonging to upper caste, they are forced to remove the upper cloth which we call as 'Maarappu' in Tamil. There are so many inhuman things happened against Dalit people in ancient days. Now-a-days it is even difficult to identify one's caste as everyone to a greater extend has attained equality. People belonging to subaltern communities are found in powerful posts in the government and this is achieved only because of socially conscious leaders like Dr B. R. Ambedkar. Ambedkar defined Dalit-hood in his book *Ostracized Bharat* thus:

> Dalit-hood is a kind of life condition that characterises the exploitation, suppression and marginalisation of Dalit people by the social, economic, cultural and political domination of the upper castes Brahmanical ideology. (2)

India is a multi-cultural and multi-lingual country with a great unity in diversity. Classifying people based on the nature of their works was a crime but that was made with honour in the ancient days. People who indulged themselves in farming and sanitation works are heartlessly classified as Dalits by the so called 'Upper Caste'. They failed to understand that it is only because of them, they are leading a healthy happy life. If they were knowledged enough to understand this concept, the Dalit peoples must be the upper caste people now. But ironically, farming and cleaning shits made them 'untouchables' in the society. This is the real shame and deliberate injustice made to the people belonging to subaltern community.

There are many governmental and non-governmental organisations working ceaselessly for the upliftment of Dalit people in the society. The novel *The Elephant Chaser's Daughter* was the story of a Dalit young girl who was educated and uplifted by such a non-governmental organisation. There is a story behind every communal group. So, it is the fact that people living in any communal group is affected by the collective norms of the society. There are so many instances for understanding this particular concept. One such instance is this novel by Shilpa Raj.

The Elephant Chaser's Daughter is the debut novel by Shilpa Raj published in 2017 and it is purely autobiographical. This novel is adopted by Netflix and made as a web series with the title "Daughters of Destiny". This novel was appreciated and glorified by people across the world. Being born in a Dalit family, Shilpa acquired M.Sc graduation in Psychological counselling and became a young writer and social activist. All these achievements are due to Shanti Bhavan, a non-governmental organisation which works for the upliftment of tribal people. Shanti Bhavan offers free education to children living in the tribal areas and also in the unexplored villages of India. Shilpa shared her own life experiences and puts forth some questions to the readers to which the society struck unanswerable. She not only exposed the suppression and subalternity faced by those people, but also the poverty which leads them to even worse conditions. Some people courageously questions this but on the other side, there are people who are unaware of all these injustices and learnt to live with the flow.

Shilpa belongs to a remote tribal village called Thattaguppe in Karnataka. Her father worked as an elephant chaser in sugarcane fields. Her forefathers were indulged in illegal liquor selling and so their life was full of violence, poverty and hardships. She had a sister and a brother but they were not educated like Shilpa. Shilpa, at the age of four, attended an interview in Shanti Bhavan and was selected as the student there. People in her village never allowed their children to study in that school due to some prejudices. But Shilpa's parents took a brave step and allowed their daughter to get free education. Finally, Shilpa got her graduation and started working for the enlightenment of subaltern children living in remote villages of India. Now she was a full-time social activist who overcame poverty and suppression.

Shilpa courageously recorded all her life experiences in this novel. The problems and humiliations that she and her family faced due to casteism were exposed by her in this novel. Shilpa, though a young woman, she is filled with lot of responsibilities to bring up the children from tribal communities and help them to overcome poverty. She believed that the education was the only better way to transcend one's poverty and ignorance. Hence, she exposed all her sufferings in her work so that people could understand the sufferings that a Dalit woman faced to shine in the society. All she needs is the exposition to outer world and an access to basic education. Shilpa in an interview said a self-encouraging comment that, "I have chosen to favour my new world, and hope to change the one I left behind" (Interview).

Shilpa was emotionally attacked by the death of her sister Kavya at the very young age of fourteen. The reason for her death was not known to her but it hit her emotionally. Kavya's body was not allowed to be cremated in the common cremation ground by the village elders as they belonged to Dalit community. This was a deep blow to Shilpa where she personally faced the aggressiveness of casteism. The villagers forced her father to cremate her sister's body in a secluded place and not in the common place. Shilpa was deeply hurt by this incident. A few days after that incident, her father was arrested by police for making illegal liquor business. Unable to handle the family's economic crisis, Shilpa's mother was sent to a foreign land to work as a maid. Shilpa was left alone with her brother. After her father's release, he was given a chance to work as an elephant chaser in the sugarcane fields of the village. He stated working as the elephant chaser and sent Shilpa to the free boarding school. Even after joining the school, Shilpa longed for the love of her mother and sister. From then, the life of the elephant chaser's daughter took a drastic change. She says that,

> Looking through the window, I see a different world. My days are spent at Shanti Bhavan, a residential school named 'Heaven of Peace', where children from families who cannot afford even one proper meal a day are well cared for and given good education. Within its walls are orphans who otherwise would have been trafficked, and the children of construction workers and rag-pickers. I, Shilpa Anthony Raj, the daughter of an elephant chaser and a maid, have been one of these privileged few-children of poverty growing up in a world unrecognizable to those from the one we left behind. (11)

Though Shilpa's family followed Christianity, their family was marginalised and suppressed as her forefathers indulged in some menial jobs like skinning animals, making leather shoes, buying carcasses and some other works which were considered as the untouchable occupation in the society. Shilpa expresses this with a deep pain. She says thus:

> My family ancestors had played their part in reclaiming the land consecrating it to a Christian God. But though we are

> of a Christian family, we were once of low Hindu caste—part of a social order that has existed in India for over one thousand years. I discovered from my mother that my maternal great grand-father was considered below *Shudra*, the lowest position in the caste system that still divides Indian society. I am said to have inherited this Dalit or untouchable, status-far below the priestly, warrior, merchant and labour castes. (16)

Early marriages are one another spell made on women. Irrespective of caste or community or religion, young girls are forced to marry at their very young age. Shilpa, however, escaped this spell with the help of education she gained at Shanti Bhavan. The founder and organizer, Dr George advised his students as well as their parents to not to commit their children to child marriages and not destroy their life at a very young age. Shilpa's father gave his ears to Dr George's words. He further included that, it is his dream to enlighten the subaltern children and elevate their standards in the society and he has a dream to control caste discrimination. Whereas Shilpa's grandmother tried to force her to marry her uncle who was so much elder to her. But Shilpa rejected the proposal and believed in gaining proper education. She did not want to quit her education and lead a family life. On this aspect Shilpa's life was saved by awareness she gained due to education.

Shilpa's mentality on caste and casteism was expressed in an incident. When her father went into the forest, he encountered a dead elephant and informed it to the forest officers. The officers decided to cremate the elephant with proper rituals. Shilpa was along with her father throughout the ceremony. She listened to her father's pain. He says thus:

> When we die, no pujari comes near us, the elephant must have belonged to a high caste. Such rituals were done to receive blessings or deflect harm brought about by angry spirits. Unholy untouchables had no need for such rituals. They couldn't please the God in any case. (124)

Shilpa was affected by her father's words. She fell in to a deep well of thoughts that, even the animals are treated in a proper way by the people. Though they doesn't even know where it goes and what it eats, the respects animals and cremates it with proper respect but people born in lower caste are treated untouchables and are never allowed to cremate even in the common ground. She was deeply hurt by this incident but she never shared it even with her father.

Shilpa once escaped a sexual attack by her uncle Naresh, whom her grandmother wants her to marry. Though Shilpa escaped the harassment, she was totally in fear. She could not share this with anyone near her so she cried all by herself. This happened when her school was closed due to the terrorist attack happened in Dr George's New York Company. Soon when Dr George arrived, Shilpa took the incident to him and shared her mind with great pain. Dr George then spoke to her father and elders about the danger in close relative marriages and the evil outcomes of child marriage. He advices them thus:

> I don't want you to distract your children with talk of marriage at this age. We want them to be well educated and then they will go on to college for further studies. If I hear you are allowing men to make sexual advances towards your children, I will have you arrested. You are responsible for looking after your children, and these sorts of things can't go on. This has to stop. (147-148)

When Shilpa was taken to Gunna, the landlord's house, she was so much exeited to see the house as it was built with cement. She has seen only mud houses in her life so far. So, she wanted to see the house fully. But her father's reaction shocked her. He did not allow her to enter the house. He further said that the untouchables are not allowed to enter the house of the landlords even if they invited them to come in. She says that:

> We can't enter the kitchen, Appa whispered as I was about to cross the threshold. I knew what he meant, that lower

> castes were not allowed to set foot inside, but I ignored his warning. While my father waited on the doorstep, I walked through the entire house. I wanted to know everything about the landlord's lifestyle. My courage stemmed from what I had learnt at school that everyone is created equal. (227)

Shilpa's life is one fine example for what education does to casteism. The untouchability, subalternity and suppression prevailed only when the Dalits were uneducated. Education paved them a way to be in powerful places in the society. It was great that she wrote her story as an autobiography because it stays as an inspiration for many Dalit women to get accompanied by education and be a good example to the society. Though she was born in a Dalit family, she is now a writer, social activist, a psychiatrist and a great inspiration for many. Thus, her autobiography could be appreciated as one of the best Dalit feminist writings in Indian English literature.

Works Cited

Ambedkar, B. R. *Annihilation of Caste, with a Reply to Mahatma Gandhi*. Bombay: Bharat Bhusan Press, 1936. Print.

—. *Ostracized Bharat*. Book in Marathi.

Anthony Raj, Shilpa. *The Elephant Chaser's Daughter*. New Delhi: Rupa Publications, 2017. Print.

Rama Chandran, Indrani, *When Feminism Overpowers Caste Marginalisation: A Study of the Feminist Agenda of Female Paraiyar Writers*. Malaysia: Elseiver, 2014. PDF.

Thorat, Sukhadeo. *Caste Social Exclusion & Poverty*. New Delhi: Critical Quest, 2013. Print.

18

Re-reading Sujatha Gidla's *Ants among Elephants* as a Microcosm for the Indian Society

Devanshi Bhatnagar

Sujatha Gidla's *Ants among Elephants: An Untouchable Family and the Making of Modern India* is not simply a book recounting her family and her experiences. It is an attempt to bring to the forefront the political, cultural and social struggles of a country that is still fettered by caste and class conflicts. While being personal, the book is objectively political in its depiction of a newly independent India. Gidla raises several questions in the book but does not offer any answers or solutions. She simply shares her 'stories.'

Having being born a girl in an untouchable, middle-class family, Sujatha Gidla, discounted her stories as worthless; stories of shame... stories not worth telling. It was only when she went to a different land that she was able to share her experiences with her new found friends; friends who knew nothing of the abominable untouchability that still plagues certain parts of the country. It was probably because of this reason that Gidla found it easier to open up and give voice to all those feelings and thoughts that she had bottled up for so long. Distance gave her perspective and the support of her friends made her realise that she had nothing to be ashamed of; she was a victim, not a culprit.

Untouchability was not discussed in her family. It was not something that needed to be communicated. She could feel it from the disdain and contempt that people hurled her way. She was told that she was a Christian. For her, however, Christianity was synonymous with untouchability as she witnessed her family members turning servile in the presence of the Hindus. This made an indelible mark on her and she internalised that 'Christians are lowly. Hindus are superior. Christians are weak. Hindus are powerful' (Gidla 4). She understood and accepted this as 'the natural way of things' (Gidla 4). Her experiences in college and a Malyali film that she saw, challenged her belief system as in both she saw that Christians were given importance, were wealthy, fashionable and popular. This baffled her. A volley of questions pestered her; questions like, 'What is the relation between religion and caste? Between caste and social status? Between social status and wealth? Between wealth and caste?' (Gidla 7). It was then that she decided to ask her mother and her uncle about her family history.

Gidla discovers that her ancestors were not Hindus but were part of a nomadic clan that worshipped the tribal gods and goddesses and lived in the forests. It was when the British started clearing the forests for teak plantations that these people were driven out of the forests. They cultivated land and settled near a water body when the civilised people noticed them. They levied taxes on their produce and collected revenue from them. These tribals were forced to borrow money to make both ends meet. They could never pay back the loans due to the high rate of interest and were eventually forced to give up their lands. They 'were reduced to working on their old fields as labourers' (Gidla 14).

Originally, the castes were determined by the type of work done by the people. Since Gidla's ancestors were labourers, they belonged to the lowest of all castes and were referred to as the untouchables. Being ill-treated by the Hindus, the untouchables found favour with the Christians. The Christians often came to their aid and were kind to them. Thus, to express their gratitude, many of them started giving up their gods and goddesses and accepted baptism. They began sending their children to missionary schools, hoping that their children would not have to endure a similar fate. Their hopes, unfortunately, did not see the light of the day as the Hindus disliked the inclusion of the untouchable children in missionary schools and did not want their children to sit next to the untouchables. Therefore, the untouchable children were made to sit on the floor while all other children sat on the benches. Some missionary schools were called 'caste schools' and were reserved for the Hindus. It is noteworthy that a religion that preaches about offering equal status to all could not protect the lower caste people from untouchability and had to accommodate the whims of the dominating caste. It is also worth mentioning that hierarchy existed even among the untouchables. While growing up, Gidla's uncle, Satyam, was discouraged from visiting and befriending 'a young couple who lived on their own, even farther from the village than the other untouchables' (Gidla 21) because they were 'madigas.' Their job was to haul away dead animals and use the hides to make leather. They were considered 'filthy' even by the other untouchables and the 'malas' who were mostly labourers, did not associate with them.

This book not only showcases the experiences of Gidla's family but does so in the backdrop of the Indian Independence struggle, the trials and tribulations of a newly independent India trying to establish peace and order and the making of a modern India. Gidla depicts how the untouchables were divided even in their stance of India's independence. Satyam's own uncles were divided in their opinion about independence. 'Uncle Nathaniel was sceptical: "If we drive the white devil out, the Hindu devils will massacre us." Uncle John, who had earlier supported British rule, switched his allegiance to Congress: "Independence is the solution"' (Gidla 22). On one hand they wanted an independent India as it offered the hope of equality and better governance; on the other they had inhibitions about their treatment by the upper castes.

Satyam, always an advocate of equality, embraced the nationalist cause. He was voted treasurer of a regional Youth Congress when he was only fourteen years of age. Once he became politically inclined, there was no turning back. He identified with the oppressed and dedicated his entire life to the championing of the Communist cause. However, he faced betrayal several times and at many levels. To start with, independence which seemed to be the only solution widened the gap between the various strata of the social system. Satyam realised that 'Now that the common enemy was defeated, the differences between him and the other students came to the fore.' He was in college when India gained independence and 'He noticed that he was not included in any of the performances' (Gidla 28) that were a part of the celebrations. While he was observing and pondering on the same, he was approached by 'a short, chubby dark boy' who asked him a strange question, one to which Satyam had no answer: 'Do you think this independence is for people like you and me?' (Gidla 29).

It was Pitchayya, the 'short, chubby dark boy' who introduced Satyam to 'the red dragon', i.e. Communism. He introduced Satyam to Hanumayya and Manikya Rao, young lecturers at Satyam's college and informed them about the deplorable state of affairs in Telangana. He gave them several books and pamphlets on Communist. The trio charged with passion for Communism was eager to join the Communist party and followed the Telangana Armed Struggle closely. The Nizam of Telangana were not only contemptuous in their treatment of the lower castes but also outright cruel and merciless. The peasants, with the help of the Communists, revolted. The situation in Telangana got out of hand and the Indian army had to interfere. 'On September 13, 1948, the Indian army finally undertook a direct invasion of Hyderabad. In a shockingly short time... the Nizam had been deposed.' Unfortunately, 'the Indian army did not put down its guns. It immediately turned them on the peasants. This had been its real mission all along. The Nizam was annoying to India, but a popular uprising against landed property was intolerable' (Gidla 58).

To counter the ill effects of centuries of oppression and provide the low castes with the propulsion they needed, Dr B.R. Ambedkar, an untouchable himself, fought hard to 'include the right to reservations in the national constitution he drafted.'(Gidla 60) The right to reservation refers to the allotment of a proportion of government jobs and seats in government schools for untouchable candidates. 'But untouchable Christians were excluded from this policy.... The rationale was that when the untouchables convert to a religion that does not recognise caste, they are untouchables no longer and have no need of reservations.' (Gidla 60) Manikya Rao and Satyam fought for reservation for the untouchable Christians. Due to their consistent and persistent efforts the untouchable Christians were awarded 1% reservation in all institutions and agencies under the state government.

Sujatha Gidla, in this book, also talks about language politics. Hindi was declared as the national language. This also caused a lot of agitation in the southern part of the country as very few South Indians were fluent in Hindi. Most of the people living in the southern part of India could not even utter a word of Hindi. This action of the government further divided the country and a rift developed between the north Indians and south Indians. Gidla's mother, Manjula seeks admission in the prestigious Banaras Hindu University. From her arrival in the north Indian city of Varanasi till her departure from the same, Manjula struggled as she was neither proficient in Hindi nor English. Besides, the 'north Indian bullied south Indians and never mingled with them. There were separate messes for north and south' (Gidla 187). Manjula's roommates were mean to her. They bullied her for fun. One of her professors 'was revolted by the sight of Manjula. One look at her and he knew she was poor and untouchable' (Gidla 190). He gave her low marks on purpose due to which she got second division despite having scored top marks in all other papers. Her career suffered because of this. She faced discrimination not only on the basis of class, caste, gender, region but also language. This brings to mind the Feminist-Marxist approach of Gayatri Chakravorty Spivak. She iterates that Asian women are doubly marginalised. Their marginalisation is on the basis of their gender as well as their nationality as many countries in Asia are third world countries. In Manjula and Sujatha's case we witness triple marginalisation. Both of them are marginalised on the basis of their caste, class and gender as caste boys thought of untouchable girls as 'cheap and easy.'

Educational institutions and their work places are not the only places where Manjula or Sujatha experience discrimination and subordination on the basis of gender. They were exploited and subjugated by their family members as well. Trivial as well as important decisions of their lives were taken by their other family members without even consulting them. Manjula's father, grandmother and bothers decided when and what type of sarees should she wear. 'The decision about Manjula's dress had been made right in front of her, but no one asked her what she thought of it' (Gidla 124).

In this book we witness the process of 'girling'; a process in which a girl is taught how to be a girl. Manjula's brothers have different ways of doing this; one violent, the other subtle; nevertheless both of them, in their own ways, try to influence Manjula's behaviour. 'While Carey told her outright what to do and slapped her when he thought she was straying, Satyam never treated her that way. Instead, he and Nancharayya would make fun of bad girls in her presence so she would be led to think, "Oh, I should never do that thing' (Gidla 124).

Manjula's family's patriarchal approach is not just limited to her. When their grandmother, who takes care of them and does most of the household chores, falls, shatters her hip and becomes bedridden, they send her back to their uncle's place. Despite the fact that she raised them from a very young and tender age, they send her back when they feel that she would no longer be useful to them. Since they needed someone to replace their grandmother and do the household chores and look after them, they decided that 'It was time for Satyam to get married' (Gidla 144). The worth of women, unfortunately, is reduced to their functionality.

Satyam is attracted to Maniamma's beauty and decides to marry her. He then lists his demands. 'He had five. First, after marriage, Maniamma would have to take care of him in every way and see that he sat home and studied and passed his exams. Second, Maniamma must tend to all his sister's needs, cook her meals and wash her clothes, while she studied so she could pass her BA exams with first class.... Third, after exams, he and Maniamma would go to Parnasa and bring her back.... Fourth, when Parsanna Rao grew old, Maniamma would have to take care of him as well. And, finally, Satyam explained, Carey was a wild man. If Maniamma was going to be part of the family, she would have to put up with his temperament' (Gidla 147). Maniamma agrees to everything. What is baffling here is that Satyam does not even bother to ask Maniamma what her expectations from this matrimonial alliance were. He simply listed his demands and she simply accepted them. In this marriage, Maniamma mostly finds herself lonely as Satyam was always so involved in his Communist activities that he spends little time with her, and when he does, he impregnates her.

After finishing her post-graduation, Manjula stays with Satyam and Maniamma in Vijayawada. Manjula and Maniamma did not get along. 'The menfolk discussed the problem and decided to send Manjula away to get another masters'.... 'They needed peace in the house' (Gidla 184). So, Manjula was sent 'far, far away from home, to a place they had never been to, where people spoke a different language, ate different food, wore different clothes, and even lived under a different climate' (Gidla 184).

Soon after completing her education, Manjula was faced with the question of marriage. Having accepted patriarchy and resigning herself to several years of subjugation, Manjula 'left it to her brothers to find her husband' (Gidla 198). Her brother Satyam, through common friends, found a suitable match for Manjula. The prospective groom, Prabhakar Rao, asked Manjula if she knew how to cook. Manjula was offended but did not say anything. Later she discussed this episode with her friend O. Vijayalakshmi who like Manjula had internalised patriarchy as a way of life. She simply told Manjula that 'Any man would ask that question. It is a compulsory question' (Gidla 206). Women have, unfortunately, been objectified and oppressed for so long that they have not only come to terms with it but they also propagate it further.

A working woman, Manjula, has no freedom to spend her money as she pleases. Prior to her wedding, she had to spend all her money on Satyam and his friends and after her wedding, she had to give her entire salary to her husband, despite the fact that he squandered all her hard earned money and mismanaged their finances so much so that although both of them were working, they lived almost hand to mouth. As the book progresses, we witness that Prabhakar Rao's mother chides him for displaying affection to Manjula. She is not alone in doing so. Manjula's brother Carey tells Prabhakar Rao that 'Women should never be treated so kindly. You need to treat them sternly; otherwise they climb on your head and sit there' (Gidla 228). Prabhakar Rao adheres to this advice and hits Manjula whenever she tries to raise her voice against some injustice or wrong doing of her husband. He even hits Manjula when she is pregnant with their third child. Sujatha, a little girl then, witnesses this and it leaves an indelible mark on her. Although Manjula was unhappy in her marriage, 'she wanted to keep the marriage. She wanted social respect' (Gidla 235). Manjula, like many other women, was exploited physically, financially, emotionally and socially.

During the course of this book, a befuddling thing comes to light. In spite of Satyam's advocacy of equality, we witness his contempt and disdain for his own community. He does not invite his friend Rama Rao to his wedding as Rama Rao is 'a high kamma.' He tells his friend 'There will be pork, there will be tribal dancing. I wouldn't want you to see how my folks live' (Gidla 154). This scorn for their caste is not restricted to Satyam. On the last day of their graduation, all the girls of Manjula's class started for home together. After dropping off all the high caste girls, only Manjula and Chandra Leela remained. They walked on in silence. Taking leave of Manjula, Chandra Leela could no longer contain herself and lashed out at her with pent-up righteous fury. 'You know, Manjula, I've always wanted to be your friend but you only care to have caste friends, you don't care for your own kind!' (Gidla 162). Manjula did not react. On introspection, she realised that whatever Chandra Leela had said was true. Manjula likes high caste girls and values their friendship. She, like Satyam, is ashamed of her low caste. Whether they do this because several years of servitude and contempt have forced them to internalise that their low caste is something to be ashamed of or simply because they do not like their caste status and caste rituals, is something to delve on.

While growing up Sujatha Gidla had heard stories about Satyam's Communist activities from her mother. She was inspired by him. Satyam had devoted his entire life to Communism. He gave up his family, met several important leaders, organised strikes, revolted against authorities, helped collect volunteers for the Communist cause and was imprisoned a number of times. Gidla wanted to be a part of all this. She even became a Radical and joined the student-wing of her uncle's party. She was imprisoned once. Her family was socially ostracised. She fell ill soon after her release from the prison.

She became disillusioned when her uncle, after all that he had done, was expelled from the party he had helped build, on false grounds. This is one of the reasons why Gidla felt motivated to write this book. She wanted everyone to know that her uncle was not a traitor. He was expelled from the party because he was against the malpractices that had crept in the party. Although the party hailed itself as a Communist party, the high caste members ill-treated the lower caste people. The people, who held high positions in the party, demeaned those who did not; thereby proving that power corrupts. The very tenets of Communism, that had drawn Satyam towards it, were being challenged and disregarded. Satyam was expelled because he wanted reforms and if that was not possible, he wanted to create a new party that was free of these ill-practices. Till his last breath, he tried to fulfill this dream of his.

This book, is not just the story of Gidla's family, it is a microcosm for the macrocosm; an attempt to understand the growth and development of a society and nation through the prism of the experiences of an untouchable family. It brings to light the lust for power which eventually leads to corruption, the ill effects of discrimination on any basis, the adherence to hierarchal structures and the tendency of the oppressed to propagate the oppression further. It makes us ponder on our flaws as a human race. Gidla writes objectively, like a detached observer, however, the book is poignant and overwhelming.

Works Cited

Gidla, Sujatha. *Ants among Elephants: An Untouchable Family and the Making of Modern India.* Noida: Harper Collins, 2017.

Gottileb, Rogers. *An Anthology of Western Marxism: From Lukacs and Gramsci to Socialist-Feminism.* New York: Oxford, 1989.

Spivak, Gayatri Chakravorty. *Can the Subaltern Speak? Reflections on the History of an Idea.* Columbia University Press, 2010.

Warhol, Robyn R. Herndl, Diane Price. *Feminisms: An Anthology of Literary Theory and Criticism.* New Jersey: Rutgers, 1997.

19

The Weave of My Life: Urmila Pawar's Arduous and Harrowing Journey from Caste and Gender Discrimination to Resistance

Dr Vinod K. Chopra

Caste system is an age-old phenomenon in India, and what is worst and disgraceful is that it is still an integral part of the social life. On 4 December 2019, NDTV reported how a 28-year-old OBC groom was beaten by the members of Rajput community in Agar Malwa district of Madhya Pradesh only for riding horse during wedding process (www.ndtv.com). Not only this, the ghastly evil of casteism has spread overseas as well. Recently, on July 1, 2020, a piece of news accused Cisco—an American based multinational company—of job discrimination based on Indian employee's caste (gadgets.ndtv.com). Dalits, the so-called lower strata of caste hierarchy in Indian society, have been subject to mental and physical torture and countless atrocities are inflicted on them in the name of caste.

Caste prejudices, class discrimination and inhuman behaviour against Dalits find mention in the writings of many writers both from the lower and upper castes who have penned their sentiments in the form of poetry, novels, short stories and autobiographies. These writers aimed at bringing about change and revolution in society. Dr Jugal Kishore Mishra rightly avers that "Dalit is not a caste; it is a symbol of change and revolution" (Mishra n. pag.). They, through their writings, wish to raise their voice in resistance against the ill-treatment and cruelty wreaked on them. Meanwhile, they want to ensure equality and true independence to their brethren who, even today, fail to enjoy respectable place in society. As a Dalit writer, Urmila Pawar voices her resentment against the system that aims at trampling underfoot the pride and respect of Dalits. Besides, she also attacks the patriarchal system of Indian society that subjugates women.

Urmila Pawar has not ventured to write *The Weave of My Life* in passing with a casual bearing in her mind, rather the autobiography is an outcome of her deep sense of sensibility resulted from humiliation and discrimination that she suffered right from her childhood days to the days when she grew up. The pain, agony, humiliation and discrimination to which she had been subjected to resulted in a successful piece of writing that reflected the trauma and bitter experience of every Dalit woman. Urmila Pawar's autobiography, in the true sense, becomes an authentic document that archives the pain of every Dalit woman who becomes a victim in a caste-ridden society and where sufferings and dishonour become their fate, and where caste is used as an instrument to torture and disgrace them. Sir Henry rightly observes the caste system as "the most disastrous and blighting of human institution" (Mahajan 167). The urge that made Urmila Pawar write is clear in the following words, "I felt a terrible restlessness growing inside me, which refused to let me sit quiet. My own experiences, those of my friends and other women, that of living in the village, caste discrimination, being a woman built up a pressure inside me!" (Pawar 148). Through her writings, she fulfilled her responsibility and obligation towards Dalit women of her village, who showered their love and care on her. Besides, Urmila Pawar's *The Weave of My Life* manifests resistance against the wrongs done to women for being women and for being Dalits. Since Dalit women are victims of patriarchy and casteism, they are twice marginalised in society. This marginalisation and violence against them make them resist against the caste prejudices and gender discrimination through their gestures, silence, feelings and their rural language.

Pawar records how her ancestors were denied access to education as there was no school for Dalits in her village as "Just one *pantoji* used to teach only Brahmin kids, on the verandah of a Brahmin house" (Pawar 28). This was a strategy to close all possibilities for the Mahar children to get education. Pawar herself suffered caste discrimination right from her childhood days when she was in school. She was harassed by her school teacher. She remembers bitterly:

> One day Guruji asked me to clean the mess. It was not even the turn of our class. Still he told me to clean because I was late. It was so humiliating that I refused even to budge. Guruji ordered me to clean up once again. But I did not move from my place. My friends—more foes than friends really!—turned to look at me and laughed. Guruji got up. I could feel the heat waves of his anger. Aaye used to tell me that if one comes across a tiger or a python, one is paralyzed with fear. I felt just the same. Guruji came close and slapped me hard. Then he told me to get out. Howling, I ran home. (56)

This shows how even children became the victims of wrath resulting from caste-based hatred. This episode reminds us of Omprakash Valmiki who, too, was harassed in school and often was, shamelessly, made to sweep the school compound. How this culture of casteism is transmitted from one generation to other is very clear from the episode in school when Pawar is discriminated against by the children from upper castes. She remembers:

> One day my classmates decided to cook a meal. They were discussing what everyone must bring: rice, lentils, and so

> on. I went up to them, eager to participate in the cooking. I found this idea of cooking by ourselves very good. But they wanted to avoid asking me to bring something. I asked enthusiastically, "What should I bring?" "Nothing," they said. "You just bring some money." They were going to cook at the house of a girl called Tarulata Sawant, as her parents were away. Girls like Sushila Dhumak, Kamal Chavan, and Sunanda Bhosale cooked a simple but tasty meal of rice, dal, and vegetables. They did not allow me to touch anything.... (74)

Pawar has dealt with the issue of caste throughout the autobiography. It has engraved a very serious and traumatic impact on her psyche. The author recollects how a Muslim family who lived in their house as a tenant left as soon as the truth dawned upon them that Pawar's family belonged to Mahar caste. Owing to caste based biases amiable relationship gave place to bitterness and distanced them from one another. This pained Pawar so much so that it left lasting excruciating impression in her heart. Her traumatic self is laid bare in her words:

> Who knows what the fat woman in Rajiwada had told them about me, but somehow they stopped talking to me from that day on. They began to behave like strangers. Before this happened I would return eagerly from school to chat with them; now I began to feel guilty, as if I had committed some grave offense. At the time of going back to Mumbai at the end of their holidays, they just said bye and left. How this hurt me! I wept bitterly. .... The Hindi lesson that I prepared so well with their help now lost all its charm. The sentences turned to ashes in my mouth. The incident weighed heavy on my heart for a long, long time, like a suffocating dark evening in the rainy season. (76)

The Weave of My Life does not merely record anecdotes from Urmila Pawar's personal life. She adopts a wider perspective of the serious issue of caste and its repercussions. She agonisingly expresses how Dalit youth are used as slaves by the people of upper caste during festivals. During the spring festival of Holi, "Mahar youths are made to do the hard work of cutting down branches and trunks of trees and carrying them to the field where a fire will be lighted at dusk. But they are not allowed a place in the celebrations: it is the upper-caste men who carry the palanquin of the goddess, and the Mahars are forbidden to touch it" (16-17). What is more tragic is that in this festival, there are prayers for the well-being of the village and averting calamities. But, miserably, meanwhile prayers are made to divert calamities to the Mahars. The author remembers how "the ritual of howling and cursing began. Again terrible curses would target the Mahars. But the Mahars dared not lodge a protest against this" (45). And if Mahar boys ever tried to be the part of festival, they were thrashed like animals. Such humiliating treatment at the hands of upper caste people had a negative bearing on the psyche that devastated the Mahar youth so much so that they lost the sense of self-worth and develop a sense of triviality.

How even education and government job could not secure respect and honour for Dalits is clear from the fact that they were humiliated even in the suburbs and ghosts of caste also continued haunting her after she got married. When they shifted to Chiplun, the owner of the house, Kunbi—a non-Dalit, would not eat in their house. The hypocrisy of upper caste people can be understood by the fact that the landlady would often borrow sarees from the author but would never eat anything there. Once when the landlady returned the borrowed sari all soiled and stained and when Pawar grumbled about that, the lady spoke indecently, "Look for another room!" (137). The reason behind this impudence was not that sari but it was the disclosure of caste that made the landlady inflict humiliation on the author. Not only this, the house owners in Ratnagiri—where Harishchandra joined office after his transfer—were staunch practitioner of caste system and they humiliated and dominated the author and her husband whenever they got time. Keeping the intention to get the house vacated, the landlady made a story that the house had been haunted by the spirits of their ancestors who loved cleanliness most. In a way the lady hinted indirectly to make the author realise that they were now living among civilised and high caste people. The lady said, "You may not know it, but the spirit of our ancient ancestor guards this place. It moves everywhere and cannot stand any dirt. Otherwise it gets extremely wrathful. Many people have experienced this. I am telling this to you for your own good. Go find a room elsewhere!" (137). The incidence that humiliated the author for being a Mahar is an evidence that even after getting good education, learning manners and cultivating imposing disposition, Dalits will always be considered untouchables by the people from upper caste. Truly, in India still status of a person is determined rigidly through birth and "could not be altered by any talent he might show or wealth he might accumulate" (Ketkar 12).

It is really a great matter of grief that even in the twenty-first century, Dalits have to struggle for independence and honour in true sense. The notion of casteism is so deep-rooted that it keeps on tormenting Dalits wherever they go. Pawars were not free from the sting of casteism even when they shifted to metropolitan city, Mumbai. Urmila Pawar's colleague cheated her by taking the keys of the flat on the pretext of getting the wiring done, but by subletting the flat a clear-cut message was conveyed that they did not want to accommodate a Dalit there. However, when the house was vacated taking the legal help, the occupants expressed their wrath saying, "These are low-caste people! So what else can you expect from them? Look at their things! A tin cot and cheap pots and pans! The moment we saw their things, we knew what they were! Dirty, mean, uncivilised...!" (Pawar147). The humiliation meted out was so intense that Harishchandra had to quit the job. Once when his caste was disclosed, his officer served him food in the cattle shed during an official visit. Pawar remembers painfully how

Sawant, an upper caste person, humiliated her mother when he came to know that she had given birth to a baby boy. He said, "The bastards! They always had a son" (140). This was clear that he was jealous of the author's mother. Pawar's children were subject to the similar humiliation. Once her younger daughter celebrated her birthday at home and she had invited her friend there. When one of her friends described to her mother the presence of pictures of Lord Buddha and Ambedkar at Pawar's house, the woman told Pawar, "We did not know that you belonged to this particular caste! That is why I sent my children to you. From now on, don't you give my daughter anything to eat if she comes to your house. We are Marathas. We cannot eat with you" (156). This shows that the seeds of casteism are so deep-rooted that it is not easy to evade humiliation resulting from it.

Nothing can be more painful and harrowing for Urmila Pawar that she sacrificed her son, Mandar, at the altar of the politics based on casteism. Her son's sudden death was disastrous for her that severely changed her life. Though the reason for the accident of her son was not clearly known, it smelt of a conspiracy against him. Nobody could explain how he had fallen from the train. The college where he studied was against the reservation policy. Pawar suspected that there might have been some connection between ideology of the college and Mandar's death.

How Dalit women were also exploited by patriarchy is also manifested by Urmila Pawar in her autobiography. There is seen internalisation of patriarchy by Dalit women. Pawar candidly offers a forceful critique of feminist and Dalit politics. She links her mother's act of weaving baskets to her own act of writing. She openly writes about her familial and marital conflicts in her autobiography. Dalit women face the triple oppression and privation on the basis of caste, class and gender (Nubile 76-78). Dalit women are brutalised in order to subjugate and humiliate the whole community. In our male-dominated society, male values are always worshipped and a female does not exist at all. The writer herself thinks sadly that she is a 'downtrodden among the downtrodden.' It means she is a victim of class and gender. Right from the day Pawar was born, she was subjected to discrimination. In patriarchy girls are never welcomed. Their birth is lamented. She herself says in pain, "In fact, I was an unwanted child because I was a girl. When I was born, my cousin Govinda dada wanted to throw me away onto the dung heap. When I grew a little older, many would beat me" (Pawar 54). She herself mourns in her autobiography, "I was born in a backward region, that too a girl" (70). In her society uneducated girls were considered nothing more than cattle. Women were denied the access of good and nutritious food. Pawar records in her memoir that women served good food to the male members of the family and satisfied their hunger by the left over. Women had to satisfy themselves with *Kaat*—thick sauce like fish stock.

Customs and manners in patriarchy also manifest male supremacy. The institution of marriage is one of the customs used to subjugate women. Pawar records in her autobiography the games new brides used to play. "All these games were basically intended to control the bride and keep her in check" (16). Besides, these games aimed at imparting training to girls to behave submissively with their husbands. Pawar herself suffered such subordination. At the time of marriage her mother-in-law dictated her how to be submissive before her dirs—brothers-in-law. She narrates the incident:

> She was not very sure of me, because I was educated, and worried how I would cope with her family, people, and their customs. After Harishchandra left, she told me quite a few things to initiate me into their ways of life. Two points were always highlighted. One:
>
> "Always address your dirs with respect, in the plural. Never call them using the singular form, even though they are

> younger than you!" But I noticed that she had not included her daughter in this category! A man always has greatness thrust upon him, whereas a woman has to achieve it! (124)

In patriarchy women have no choice in the matter of giving birth to children. Pawar underlines the hypocrisy of the society towards men and women. It was Manu who assigned women a vital role for preserving the social order and simultaneously enabled men to achieve immortality through their sons. Uma Chakravarti has recorded Manu, ancient Hindu lawgiver, in the following lines, "The production of children, the nurture of those born, and the daily life of men, of those matters the wife is visibly the cause. Offspring, the due performance of religious rites, faithful service and heavenly bliss for the ancestors and for oneself depend on the wife alone" (Ramteke 7).

If ever a woman fails to give birth to a male child, she is held responsible for that and at the same time is looked down upon. The birth of a male child is worshipped in our patriarchal society. The birth of the baby son by Pawar was a cause of celebration for the family without caring for her health and the pain she underwent through the birth of the child. Her husband Harishchandra insisted her to have another son as two baby sons would be a matter of pride and joy for the family. So he said, "Let's take one more chance." But once again it was a girl. Pawar disappointedly writes "I thought how simple and easy it was to have a baby, like saying let's have one more cup of tea!" (Pawar 144). It is through her own bitter experiences that Urmila Pawar portrays the agonising state of every woman who is still subjected to male dominance and who suffers physical as well as psychological violence through patriarchy.

Urmila, as a woman, suffered discrimination and hostility not only from the society where she lived but also from her husband who otherwise should have been her protector. Her husband agreed at her doing graduation on the condition that she would do all the daily household chores and would also look after her children. She struggled hard to get education and pay attention to her children. This arduous life she led symbolises suppression of women's independence in patriarchy. Things took an ugly turn when she decided to get herself enrolled for master's degree. Her decision annoyed her husband causing bitterness in her marital relationship. Pawar, as a feminist writer and thinker, laments the societal norms where woman has to sacrifice her private space. Anyhow Pawar completed her post-graduation and Harishchandra started praising her in public, though not from the core of his heart. This reveals hypocrisy on his part and male chauvinism. The achievements of women are never seen with appreciation by the male members of society. She became a victim of secondary treatment not within the family but also in public places. She reminisces distressingly:

> The people from the Dalit movement, however, treated women in the same discriminatory manner, as if they were some inferior species, as they did the ones at home. Probably it was unconscious behaviour. Once I was invited to a programme organised by a group of Dalit activists in a printing press. They repeatedly called me on the phone and urged me to deliver a speech as a part of their programme. I accepted their invitation and reached the hall in time. But there was nobody to receive me there except the man whose loudspeaker was hired. So I quietly sat down on a bench outside. For a long time nobody came, and I was bored to death. Then a huge crowd of men arrived with some Member of Parliament, whom they ushered into the hall with great fanfare, with many garlands and flowers. Welcome speeches were broadcast from the loudspeaker. All the while I kept sitting on the bench. (153)

Such type of humiliating and belittling treatment was given for being a woman. It is really sad on her part that when she started attending public meetings and participating in writers' forum, she received harsh treatment and ill-will from none other than her husband. He hated the idea of his wife getting recognition as a public figure. His mindset was typically patriarchal as he wanted his wife to be servile like the village women whose mere duty was to do the daily household chores and serve their husbands devotedly. She reminds how he was at loggerheads over her work and association with Dalit Movement. She recalls one such occurrence:

> ....he immensely resented my being recognised as a writer, my speaking in public programmes, and my emerging as a figure in the public domain. Our arguments would invariably end in bitter quarrels. I would say, "Please, have a heart! I am a human being too. I too work like you. I too get tired. My work also has the same value as yours." But neither my words nor my work had any meaning for him! On the contrary, he would tell me, "Look at the village woman. The husband's wish is law for her. She does not dare to sit down or get up without his permission. Tell me, in that case, how is she able to run her home well?" Was not the answer implicit in the question itself? (159)

Not only this, Pawar also records some incidents of wife beating—a frequent form of physical violence which is not peculiar to any society but is "common to patriarchy all over" (Chopra 117). Pawar would remember about her cousin, Susheela who was victim of ill-treatment and beatings. Her drunkard husband and mother-in-law "beat her up mercilessly at the slightest pretext. They would drive her out of the house with her young children even on stormy dark nights. The poor woman would take her children and cross the hills and valleys at night, her face broken, body swollen, bleeding and aching all over..." (Pawar 37-38). Similarly, Shantaram—another character in the autobiography—used to give harsh thrashing to his wife just to release his frustration resulted from the failure of not allowed to marry the woman whom he loved. He attacked his wife with a big stone. Pawar records the callous and ghastly act of Shantaram:

> She lay unconscious in a pool of blood for a long time. No one demanded an explanation from him nor came forward to help her. People felt that he was her master and had the right to do anything to her. While she lay unconscious, her master, her savior, was shamelessly making a public announcement, "I have killed a sheep in our field. Anybody interested in getting the blood?" (102)

It really pains to note that society impudently justifies the cruel act of male members of society in patriarchy.

It is the literature—the mighty power of words—that empowers Dalits to articulate their pain. Words are used as weapon to attack that society which is full of dogmas, prejudice and injustice whether it is a Dalit or a woman. Literature, since time immemorial has tried its best to mirror the social evils prevalent in society. Meanwhile literature has also served as tool of resistance as against the heavy odds that do exist in the surrounding, in which these literary artist lived. Urmila Pawar, too, through her autobiography has attacked the prejudices based on caste and gender. She has overtly or covertly challenged the stereotypical society structured on the foundations of caste and patriarchy. It was Pawar's mother who resisted against the step-motherly attitude of the teacher who slapped Pawar in her childhood when she was asked to clean the school compound. She confronted the teacher saying, "Hey you Guruji wait a moment! My girl studies in your class, Guruji! ...And you treat my girl like this? How dare you? Let me see you laying even a finger on my girl again and I'll show you!" (56). This reminds us of Omprakash Valmiki's father who snubbed the teacher for making his son clean the school campus. The resistance that Pawar's mother displayed gave a lesson to Pawar to oppose any type of injustice and discrimination. Pawar exhibits such resistance within the household as well. When her husband forced Manini, their daughter, to get married to the boy of his choice, Pawar told her to assert herself and oppose her father against forcing her to do so. For this Harishchandra often intimidated her and asked her to leave the house but Pawar bore all the insults and remained there. Here, we observe that though religion provides an opportunity to woman to give or not to give her consent to marriage but the social practice has reduced it to meaningless ritual. In the grand scheme of patriarchy religion too is misrepresented to "circumvent the desires and rights of women" (Singh 55). Similarly, Manjula, her elder sister rejected the proposal of marriage from a person who wanted that she should look after the household chores and support the family so that he may dedicate himself to social work. Manjula's resistance and rejection of that man reveals that she could not sacrifice her freedom and ideals. When Pawar's husband died, she refused to perform the ritual of wiping vermillion mark from her forehead with the left toe of her deceased husband. This was an open challenge to the age-old customs that subjugated women and crushed their pride. After that many women also followed her move to challenge and resist the age-old customs because they inflicted insult on women. Not only this, she also challenged the practices of wearing *mangalsutra,* a sign of marital piety. It is, then, a fact that Dalit literary movement is not just a literary movement. It is also a cultural and social movement" (Valmiki 97). Pawar's association with the organisation called Maitrini began her journey as a feminist showing she would resist any patriarchal move to submerge women's freedom and identity. It was the exclusion of Dalit women in decision-making from the women's movement that gave rise to Dalit feminism and that was what Rege calls the 'Dalit feminist standpoint' (33-34).

Urmila Pawar started taking part in various Dalit and Women movements signifying a great change in her personality as she herself affirms:

> I had realised that I now had a new vision, a new perspective on looking at women. I had lost my fear. The women's movement had given me great strength to perceive every man and woman as an equal individual. It had taught me to

relate to them freely, without any prejudice whatsoever! (Pawar160)

Pawar started acting against the humiliation and injustices meted out to women by their husbands. She stopped people from beating their wives. She had awareness of the rights of women and she had a great desire to make every woman conscious of their rights. She also objected the practice of male supremacy at programmes organised in the Dalit movements. She raised her brows when she observed that in such programmes the chairs on the dais were occupied by the males. As a challenge to patriarchal strictures, she vowed to follow earnestly the slogan of Babasaheb—educate, unite and agitate—to improve the status of Dalit women.

It can be observed that Urmila Pawar's autobiography, *The Weaves of My Life* is different from those of Bama and Baby Kamble. The latter have concentrated on holding the mirror at their problems, whereas Pawar has shown the solution to those problems (Pavithra 421). Urmila has taken a bold step to fight for the liberation and justice for the Dalit women. She does not deal with her own life and success like others but she has motivated those who belong to her community to follow her footsteps to get their freedom and honour. By organising conferences and movements, she has ignited the dormant voice of all Dalit women to challenge the wrongs done to them and to fight tooth and nail for their rights and liberation.

Works Cited

Chopra, Vinod K. *Partition Stories: Mapping Community, Communalism and Gender.* New Delhi: Anamika Publishers and Distributers, 2009. Print.

Ketkar, S.V. *The History of Caste in India.* Ithaca: Taylor and Carpenter, 1909. Print.

Mahajan, V.D. *Ancient India* (1960). Rpt. New Delhi: S. Chand and Company Ltd, 2000.

Mishra, Jugal Kishore. "A Critical Study of Dalit Literature in India." www.sasnet.lu.se/panelabstract/4.html

Nubile, Clara. *The Danger of Gender: Caste, Class and gender in Contemporary Indian Women's Writing.* New Delhi: Sarup & Sons, 2003. Print.

Pavithra, N. "Portrayal of a Dalit Woman—A Study of Urmila Pawar's *The Weave of My Life*". *Language in India.* www.languageinindia.com > pdf 18:3 March 2018.25 February, 2020.

https://gadgets.ndtv.com/telecom/news/cisco-accused-of-job-discrimination-bases-on-indian-employees-caste-2254961

https://www.ndtv.com/india-news/obc-groom-beaten-up-for-riding-horse—during-wedding-procession-in-madhya-pradesh-police-2142932

Pawar, Urmila. *The Weave of my Life: A Dalit Woman's Memoir.* Trans. Maya Pandit. New York: Columbia University Press. E-Book. www.cup.columbia.edu

Ramteke, Sunil. "Baby Kamble's *The Prison We Broke* and Urmila Pawar's *The Weave of My Life*: Feminist Critique of Patriarchy". Vol. 1 Issue 5 Oct. 2015. Web. 20 February, 2020.

Rege, Sharmila. "Dalit Women Talk Differently: a Critique of 'Difference' and Towards a Dalit Feminist Standpoint Position". *Economic and Political Weekly.* 33.44 (1998): WS39-WS46.

Singh, Pankaj K. *Representing Woman: Tradition, Legend and Punjabi Drama.* Shimla: IIAS, 2000. Print.

Valmiki, Omprakash. *Dalit Sahitya ka Saundarya Shastra.* New Delhi: Radhakrishna, 2001. Print.

20

Analysing Bama's *Sangati* from a Dalit Perspective: A Discourse on Feminine Subalternity

Dr Avinash Kumar

Women are generally considered inferior to men even in the twentieth-first century. However, the government claims that women are equal to men but this statement will be half true because it may be possible through a constitutional law, but so far as the real condition of women in our rural society is considered, they still are at the backfoot of the hierarchy. If Dalit women's condition is to be discussed, it is really pitiable except few who are now working at good posts, otherwise the condition of a domestic woman is really pitiable.

Many social reformers, Dalit activists and political luminaries have worked for the Dalit consciousness and they have worked hard to make them aware towards their rights. Dalit literature is demarcated as unique because of this consciousness" (Limbale 32). In India the conflict over the ruler and the ruled, the exploiter and the exploited, the coloniser and the colonised, the oppressor and the oppressed has been for a long time. In Hindu religion also, there are different castes which are called upper and lower on the basis of their works. The upper caste people always try to suppress the lower caste people.

Among these lower castes, men also exploit the women of their family and this chain goes on. We should not look down upon anybody on the basis of caste becasue all people are equal in the eye of god. Dr Bijender Singh also opines in his book *Different Dimensions of Dalit Discourse*, "By the word "Dalit", I refer to include all those people who are poor, repressed, or oppressed belonging to any caste, class, creed, race, or religion" ("Introduction" xiii).

Dalit literature has produced some female writers who have broken all the boundaries of limitations in their literary career in depicting the pitiable life of their community. Though many such writers are those who have given enough description of the oppression and exploitation of their family and community, yet there are many who either could not dare to write or who were unable to write due to lack of their education.

In this context, there are several Dalit women writers who have directly or indirectly raised their voice against the tyranny and oppression. They wrote it through their autobiographies, memoirs, personal narratives, plays, novels, essays and short stories. Some women have been so frank in the depiction of their life that they have written even the personal moments of their life.

Many Dalit feminist writers depicted gender discrimination and Dalit exploitation in their works. Bama, Sivakami, Urmila Pawar, Baby Kamble, Phoolan Devi, Viramma, etc. Dalit writers have penned down the painful stories of their life. They have taken issues of caste, class and gender in their works.

If Bama's *Karukku* is called her personal autobiography, *Sangati* can be called a community autobiography in which she has described the trial and tribulation of her Dalit community. Bama has to face many problems in her childhood, youth and adulthood which narration can be easily read in *Karukku*. She was not satisfied with this work alone and she thought that there should be depiction of her community in her works and it could not be included in her personal autobiography, so she wrote everything about her community in *Sangati.*

Sangati can be called a piquant depiction of a South Indian Dalit community in which she has laid emphasis on the double oppression of women. This book was originally published in 1994 in Tamil Language but it was later translated into English by Laxmi Holmstrom. The book has been written in twelve parts. The word "sangati" means "events", and thus, it can be seen that the book has been written through different events which happened in her community. These events are mutually interconnected that's why it looks like the plot of a novel also.

The opening of this book has been with the description of Patti who is a midwife and all the deliveries of the lower caste women in the village are generally handled by her and she has got a wonderful experience of handling the most difficult cases of delivery. She can also handle the breech position cases also, "It didn't matter if the umbilical cord was twisted round the baby, if the baby lay in a breech position, if it was a premature birth, or a case of twins. She delivered the baby safely, separating mother and child, without harming either" (Bama 1-2). The upper caste people do not call her even in the worst condition just because "she was a Paraichi" (Bama 1). Bama has depicted the pain of many such low-caste women in this book. Patti was utterly unhappy with her life due to her poverty, gender and caste. Her words depict the life of these women, "If you are born into this world, it is best you are born a man. Born as women, what good do we get? We only toil in the fields and in the home until our very vaginas shrivel" (6). Bama thinks that women must be aware about their rights. She writes about the pains of Dalit women:

> My mind is crowded with many anecdotes: stories not only about the sorrows and tears of Dalit women, but also about their lively and rebellious culture, passion about life with

> vitality, truth, enjoyment and about their hard labour. I wanted to shout out these stories. (Bama 9)

As in her autobiography *Karukku*, she describes her childhood events in the early parts, likewise in *Sangati* also, Bama narrates the events through the first person narrative and the narrator is a young girl of about twelve-year-old. In the last three chapters of the book, the narrator is a young woman. Through this book, the joint struggle of women of the whole Paraiyya community has been depicted. Sharmila Rege observes:

> The Dalit Feminist standpoint is about reviewing how in different historical practices similarities between women have been ignored in an effort to underline caste-class identities, or at other times differences ignored for 'the feminist cause'. (*Sangati* xvii)

In this book, Bama voices out the grievances and pains of the Paraiyya women who are depicted in doing the household work, labour work, childcare and cattle rearing. They are burdened with the multiple responsibilities of the family. The men generally work as labourers in the agricultural fields, construction sites or do any other kind of manual labour. Bama has written that though women also work as labourers with their husbands for the equal hours, yet they are given less wages, "The women, in any case, whatever work they did, were paid less than men. Even when they did the very same work, they were paid less" (Bama 19). Women have to face this exploitation at the construction sites. The incidences of domestic violence are very common in these houses because even men are also uneducated and a good behaviour cannot be expected from those persons who are uneducated and those have done hard work throughout the day. Only few people have patience to that extent. Bama thought that she needs to write the pains of these Dalit women so that their voice may reach to the maximum people. Bama writes:

> My mind is crowded with many anecdotes: Stories not only about the sorrows and tears of Dalit women, but also about their lively and rebellious culture, their eagerness not let the life crush or shatter them, but rather to swim vigorously against the tide; their passion to live life with vitality, truth and enjoyment, about their hard labour. I wanted to shout out these stories. (Bama xvi)

The book opens with the narration of events from a child's perspective and the book describes all the humiliation and it criticizes the narrow-minded mentality of the upper caste people and the patriarchal hegemony. Thorough this text, the writer looks back at her past and the exploitation and disregard of women of her community. The objective of the writer is to shed light on these events through this book, "I wanted to shout out these stories" (Bama xvi).

Bama narrates that the little girls were expected to behave with maturity and the exploitation of a sixteen-year-old girl Mariamma depicts that Dalit women are not much better than animals. Mariamma feels so broken by her public insults that she thinks to commit suicide, "But Mariamma didn't sleep a wink that night. She even thought that it might be best to hang herself by a rope. She sat and wept all the night long" (Bama 27). This statement reminds one Simone de Beauvoir's statement in her seminal book *The Second Sex* (1949), "One is not born a woman rather becomes one" (Beauvoir 281).

Bama writes that the girls are given less importance in their house while the boys are given preference. The boys have rights on the property and girls are considered just other people's property. That's why even the parents also do discrimination with a girl. The girls are burdened with the responsibility of taking care of their younger siblings even in their young age. If the life of Dalit girls was worse and the life of Dalit women has been depicted worst in this book. Dalit girls also want their equal rights but nobody pays any attention to their words. Their pain has been depicted in the following words:

> Why can't we be the same as boys? We aren't allowed to talk loudly or laugh noisily; even when we sleep we can't stretch out on our backs nor lie face down on our bellies....We are allowed to eat only after the men in the family have finished and gone what Patti aren't we also human beings? (Bama 29)

The girls play games in which they have been depicted doing some household work and the domination of men has been depicted even in their games. Nobody cares for their rights. Bama writes, "People would say, 'Who does she think she is? She's just like a donkey, look. Look the way she plays boys' games" (Bama 7). These girls are generally seen cooking, getting married and doing other domestic chores even in their games. She writes:

> Even when we played 'mothers and fathers', we always had to serve the mud 'rice' to the boys first. They used to pull us by the hair and hit us says, 'what sort of food is this, di, without salt or anything!' In those days we used to accept those pretence blows, and think it was all good fun. Nowadays, for many of the girls those have become real blows and their entire lines are hell. (Bama 31)

Bama narrates how her grandmother would call the boys first to give any eatable she brought from market. Bama narrates that if her grandmother would bring mangoes, then the girls would get only the skin and stone only and the boys would enjoy its juice. She writes about this incidence, "If she brought mangoes, we would only get the skin, the stones and such; she gave the best pieces of fruits to the boys. Because we had no other way out, we picked up and ate the leftover skins" (Bama 8).

In *Sangati* Bama writes how Dalit women are lynched, slapped, canned, whipped and beaten by the men of their family. Bama has depicted it through the stories of Mariamma and Thayi in which marital discord and agony of married women has been depicted. The women have to do all the household chores and they have to eat what is left behind when all the members have eaten. Bama writes: "Even they lay down their bodies wracked with pain, they are not allowed to sleep, whether she dies or survived, she had to give pleasure and enjoyment to her husband" (Bama 59). These women face the tyranny of the caste discrimination throughout the day at the work places and the atrocity of gender discrimination at nights.

Sometimes the women would commit suicide leaving behind their small children and nobody would look after these children after their mother's death. These girls were deprived of their education. Bama gives the example of a girl Seyakkodi whose mother died when she was merely five or six-year-old. She had to do all the household chores. Bama writes, "She never went to school, but stayed at home and did the housework" (Bama 11). These girls' movements, thoughts and even freedom were governed by the whims of the men of their house. There were strict rules for them. Bama writes about it, "Young girls mustn't wander about here and there...They don't even allow us to go to the cinema that's right here. If we go out at all, it's only to the church, and even for that you have to try really hard" (Bama 13). Some girls like Maikkanni would have to work with their mothers in a tender age in order to support the family.

Bama advises the women of her community that they must be strong and they should gradually liberate themselves from the clutches of the patriarchy and Dalit discrimination. Bama writes that the women of the upper castes do not face the problems like this. Their honour is spoilt in their work places but Dalit women face such problems because they have to go to work places among strangers for their livelihood, "It is not the same for women of other castes and communities. Our women cannot bear the torment of upper-caste masters (mudalalis) in the fields, and home they cannot bear the violence of their husbands" (65). These women have to work under vulnerable conditions. Bama criticises some social evils of the Hinduism and calls that the women of her community are far better in some aspects. Dalit women remain financially independent and they are free to remarry while the upper caste women are not allowed to remarry. They had to confine their emotions only up to them.

Not only this, Dalit women who are converted to Christianity are also discriminated. Bama has depicted the discrimination with these women in the Indian Catholic Churches. Even the priests also did not behave nicely with the converted Dalit women. Bama writes:

> Everywhere you look, you see blows and beatings, shame and humiliation...Became we have not been to school or learnt anything, we go about like slaves all our lives, from the day we are born till the day we die, As if we are blind, even though we have eyes. (Bama 66)

Bama wants radical change in the life of the women of her community. She takes pride of her caste and wants that it is time for women empowerment. She thinks that the dalit girls should also get the equal opportunities, they will know the real power of being female. Bama writes:

> We must bring up our girls to think in these new ways from an early age. We should educate boys and girls alike, showing no difference between them as they grow into adults. We should give our girls the freedom we give our boys. If we rear our children like this from the time they are babies, women will reveal their strength.... 'women can make and women can break'. (Bama 123)

Bama has portrayed the sufferings of an eleven-year-old girl Maikkanni in the seventh chapter of the book. Bama calls her an unlucky girl just because after her birth, her father started having affair with another woman and now her mother was pregnant seventh time. It was her responsibility to earn something for her family. Her mother decides that "Maikkanni has grown up a bit and can go out to work" (69). She has to do all the household works when her mother would go to fields. Bama narrates, "From the time she woke up, scrubbed the cooking pots, collected water, washed clothes, gathered firewood, went to the shops, cooked the kanji. She did it all, one after the other" (70). The responsibility of the house was on her mother's shoulders and Maikkanni would take care of her five younger siblings when her mother was not at home. Bama writes, "It was Maikkanni who brought up all the five children who were born after her; her mother delivered them into the world and could do no more. Just as soon as one child began to walk, she was ready to deliver the next" (73).

Thus, through various incidences of the book, Bama has aptly narrated the problems of women of her community. Priti Sharma writes, "In *Sangati*, from beginning to the end, Bama has dealt with gender issues at large so the term 'gender' needs to be conferred" (Sharma 196). Thus, the Dalit discourse should be justified and free from any kind of lopsidedness" ("Introduction" viii). Adrienne Rich further writes about gender equality:

> We need to imagine a world in which every woman is the presiding genius of her own body. In such a world, women will truly create new life, bringing forth not only children (if and as we choose), but the vision, and thinking, necessary to sustain, console, and alter human existence .... This is where we have to begin. (Rich 85-286)

Works Cited

Bama. *Sangati (Events). Trans.* by Lakshmi Holmstrom. New Delhi: Oxford U P, 2005.

Beauvoir, Simone de. *The Second Sex*. Vintage Classics. UK. 1949.

Limbale, Sharankumar. *Towards An Aesthetic of Dalit Literature: History, Controversies, and Considerations*. Trans. by Alok Mukherjee. New Delhi: Orient Longman, 2004.

Rich, Adrienne. *Of Woman Born: Motherhood as Experience and Institution*. New York: W. W. Norton & Company, 1995.

Sharma, Priti. "Dichotomy and Dalit's Feministic Quest: An Insight into Bama's *Sangati.*" *Indian Dalit Autobiographies Marginalised Voices.* Ed. Bijender Singh. New Delhi: Authorspress, 2015, 186-98.

Singh, Bijender. *Different Dimensions of Dalit Discourse.* New Delhi: Atlantic Publishers & Distributors, 2019.

21

The Struggle of a Dalit Woman in Yashica Dutt's *Coming Out as Dalit: A Memoir*

Dr Tamanna

Dalit Literature is acquiring a radical new shape and it is growing rapidly as many new Dalit writers are emerging on the literary platform day by day. There was a time when Dalit girls were deprived of getting education but these days, time has been changed drastically and Dalit girls are also getting equal opportunities of education from India and abroad, and some of them settle there. Like this, Yashica Dutt is one of the contemporary Dalit women writers. Presently she lives in New York. She was born in a Valmiki family on 05 February, 1986. Her mother Shashi Dutt remained the main inspirational figure behind her success. Her mother told her that she needs to conceal her caste, and if she wants to get success in her life, she must learn and speak good English.

Yashica Dutt did her BSc from St. Stephen's College, Delhi in 2007. After that she went to the United State for her Master's degree in Arts and Culture, Journalism from Columbia University Graduate School of Journalism. She remained three years in Columbia. She is a good journalist who has worked with the *Brunch*, *Hindustan Times*, *LiveMint*, *Scroll.in*, *The Wire* and *HuffPost* and *The Asian Age*. She has written her articles on a wide range of subjects. She writes on Dalit issues and has been a correspondent for few countries such as India, Bhutan, Nepal, Hungary and Turkey.

In 2016, Rohith Vemula, a Dalit student from Hyderabad University committed suicide and her letter inspired her a lot and she decided to reveal her caste. Consequently, she wrote her memoir *Coming Out as Dalit: A Memoir*. She has written about it in the prologue of her book:

> So it wasn't unusual that when I first saw the Facebook post about a Dalit boy who had committed suicide in Hyderabad University, I didn't open the link. He was not the first Dalit boy who had died and he was not going to be the last. Dalit boys and girls, men and women, children and old people, have regularly died because of caste violence. It is among the most devastating but far from the only outcome of caste discrimination that endures through Indian societies in the subcontinent and across the world. (xiii)

Her memoir *Coming Out as Dalit* was published by Aleph Book Company and it was written and revised four times by her. She has a bit fair complexion that's why people ask her many times that you do not look like a Dalit woman. She replies Mahtab Alam in an interview:

> That was the most common response. It was also one of the reasons I was excited to see how people would react. The truth is that I *don't* 'look like a Dalit'—the kind of Dalit we are used to seeing in media, cinema, pop-culture (when we see them at all). But that doesn't change the fact that Dalits—around all 250 million of us—don't look the same. (*The Wire* n. pag.)

She has bitter experiences how people ask about her caste even in America and about her surname also. When she revealed her caste later, then also people told that she should not worry about it because she does not look like a Dalit. This kind of narrow-minded mentally would make her sad.

Yashica, like many other Dalit women, has to face many problems in getting education. Her mother's life remained much traumatic because she always tried her level best to provide the better educational opportunities to her children. She has written everything about her mother and that's why she has dedicated this book for her mother. Her book has been written as a non-fiction. Yashica Dutt's memoir has been written in twelve chapters, a prologue and an epilogue. She writes in the author's note of her book:

> In this book, I talk of the lives of a varied group of Dalits: those who live in the cities and in villages, those who read Ambedkar or don't, those who are out as Dalit or not and those who exist somewhere in between. Clearly, I don't speak for every Dalit in the world. There are thousands of stories I have yet to discover (ix)

In the first chapter of her memoir, she has written about the early years of her life. She narrates that India is unable to give a suitable platform for the Dalits and underprivileged people. Though the Indian Constitution gives an opportunity to Dalits to enter and survive in the government system but the poorest of the poor generally remain deprived of all facilities. The planning is done is such a way that Dalits remain outside the system. Yashica Dutt did not want to take the benefit of the reservation system but she was forced to it because she was unable to get scholarship in the general quota.

Yashica Dutt's relatives were at the good posts. Her paternal grandfather was the first Dalit Divisional Superintendent in the Rajasthan Police Service and her maternal grandfather was an inspector in the State Excise department in Uttar Pradesh. She narrates how her mother had misgivings about an arranged marriage and she had decided that she won't marry anyone who is an alcoholic. These are the opening lines of this book:

> UNTIL THREE GENERATIONS AGO, DALITS were denied access to learning. My great-grandfather defied this

> social order and learned to write by scrawling in the mud with a stick. His son, my grandfather, like many others of his generation, fought every step of the way to enter the civil services. (1)

Yashica's mother had four siblings and she was the oldest among them. At the time of her marriage, she was doing her master's degree in History from Gokuldas University in Moradabad. She told her father that she wants to join IPS before her marriage. She was given permission to appear for the exam and then she gave her consent for marriage also. Her husband was an Excise Inspector but he was fond of drinking.

Yashica's father would start drinking early in the evening and he would become intoxicated by the dinner time. He would also beat his wife. Her mother was fed up from this life and she tried to commit suicide but there was something else in her destiny, "...she decided to kill herself. Seven months pregnant, she jumped from the roof of the house and shattered her left ankle, damaging it permanently. The pregnancy was declared complicated and the doctors doubted the chances of my survival" (6). Yashica writes about the domestic violence in Indian families:

> Domestic violence against women is not limited to Dalit families. Women across the country face immense physical and emotional brutality from their families. But Dalit women—especially those from rural areas and those who are economically vulnerable, from urban or rural areas—are at the bottom of caste, class and gender hierarchies. (6)

Yashica Dutt could not forget her father's bad habit of drinking. Her father would sit hidden behind a curtain and drink McDowell's No. 1. Her grandfather did not drink and he tried several times to prevent his son from drinking but it could not be possible for him. Yashica's father has prepared for the recruitment examinations after his marriage and his father supported him during this time.

In the second chapter, Yashica describes how the caste system is prevalent in India and it has its firm roots since time immemorial. She writes about the *chaturvarna* system of the Hindu society and the social stratification of the Hindu society in four *varnas*—Brahmins, Kshatriyas, Vaishyas and Shudras.

She narrates that Ajmer was merely a small town in nineties but the essential commodities were available there. She remembers how her mother was not able to sleep till late night due to the pain of her injured ankle. Yashica writes that "Classmates who lived nearby, and other kids from the neighbourhood I hardly ever played with, would be invited, along with their families" (20).

Yashica could not get the opportunity to speak English in her school. She writes in her autobiography how many students have to rely on the various English speaking coaching institutes in their areas. Her parents would speak Hindi but Yashica grew up speaking Hindi and English really well. She started speaking sentences in bits when she was merely a child. She started reading English magazines and focused on her accent. She and her mother would rehearse to admit in the English medium school Sophia. She failed in her first attempt but she tried again and finally remained successful in getting admission next year.

Yashica's mother had to face much difficulty during her pregnancies both from Yashica's father and his family members. Yashica writes about the importance of the fair colour. She talks about the discrimination on the basis of their skin. She writes:

> These biases are blatantly manifest in educational institutions, workplaces and, inarguably, the arranged marriage market. The bias against dark skin affects both men and women, but in our patriarchal set-up, it is women who suffer its consequences the most. Hurtful and mean comments like 'black crow' and facetious concern regarding their inability to land a life partner are a big part of the lives of dark-skinned women. (27)

Yashica narrates how Dalits have to bear the curse of caste in the chapter "Humiliation in Mussoorie". When she was admitted in her new school, her mother tells her to conceal his caste and tell that she is a 'Parashar Brahmin'. Yashica feels that it is very difficult to hide the caste, "Hiding your identity becomes part of who you are. You internalise it" (*The First Post* n.pag.). She had to face humiliation due to her caste. Purnachandra Naik writes about her, "She was taunted, humiliated and suffered self-disgust in the hostel. After two years at Sophia, she had to move to a boarding school in Mussoorie. Things were never smooth in Mussoorie either as her internalised sense of inferiority always weighed on her psyche and selfworth" (20). Her parents could not afford the school fee on time. She writes about this experience:

> 'I don't want this!' Except, my screams never made it past my throat. As I sat there, watching the circus of their humiliation with mute horror and shame, I knew I did want the admission as much as Mum did. I knew this education would change my life, and I was willing to let my parents grovel for it. Eventually, Mr Katyal gave my parents six weeks to pay the rest of the fees and agreed to admit us. (36)

Yashica Dutt writes about the problem of untouchability in India. The writes about the bhangis and the manual scavengers who have to face humiliation publically. She narrates the Una Revolt how thousands of Dalits arrive in Una to show their protest. She writes:

> Mobs of upper-caste men attacked Dalit vehicles, particularly those with Ambedkar signage, 'Jai Bhim' or Bhim Blue stickers and assaulted the passengers. They forced Dalits to chant 'Jai Mata Di' and 'Gai Mata ki Jai' and hit anyone who said 'Jai Bhim'. The Dalits neither had warning nor protection from the police, who, according to reports, were present but did not stop the assault. (48)

Yashica's parents' separation and her father's court case also added problems in their family. Her mother has to take a job of teaching at the age of forty-eight at the salary of only one thousand rupees. Thus, Yashica's life remained much tumultuous and problematic.

She writes her experiences of St. Stephen's college. It is very difficult for a small city student to get admission in such a college. Yashica was worried there because she had fear that people would ask about her caste as her name was under SC/ST category. She depicts how the Dalit students face difficulties in approval of their application and getting scholarships or stipends on time. She gives the illustration of Rohith Vemula whose grant was extremely delayed in Hyderabad University and he had to remain dependent on his friends and well-wishers:

> In fearlessly announcing his Dalit identity and demanding justice for himself, Rohith possibly challenged a fundamental idea that many upper-caste professors hold—that Dalit students study in Indian colleges and universities on their largesse, so they should be grateful for whatever crumbs they are thrown instead of taunting them by demanding more. (70)

Yashica had published around fifteen articles during her graduation from St. Stephen's college. She was thinking that she can get a job of a reporter now, but unfortunately, she did not get guidance from her parents in this regard, "I didn't get any tips from my parents to help me find a job; their collective career expertise was limited to the 'civils'. But what I did have was the Stephen's stamp, which afforded me a different type of reservation" (92). She got a job but she was thinking to do her master's in Journalism, "After graduating from St. Stephen's, I was convinced that I didn't need a Master's degree to become a good journalist although Mum was keen that I do a postgraduate course" (99). She gets scholarship from Columbia University but she had to pay remaining fee and banks did not give her loan she needed. Her mother was ready to sell the house also but Yashica was thinking about some other way. She write to nearly every professor for help to provide her more scholarship but they either replied that only the scholarship department can help her out and some professors even did not reply her.

She would check her email daily and finally she got an email from Columbia University which has agreed to offer her full scholarship and she would have to meet the living expenses herself. She had spent very hard days in Delhi and her friends, supporters and colleagues had helped her a lot. She shows her gratitude to all of them, "I am so thankful to all of them. And I know how important a role my college networks played to help me get hold of opportunities that are not as easily available outside these spaces" (103).

Yashica Dutt writes that a Dalit woman remains doubly disadvantaged due to her gender and caste. She writes how a woman in the Indian society has to face many problems. She writes, "The bodies of women, which Indian societies consider the storehouse of their bloodline's honour, don't belong to them as much as they do to their families. But for Dalit women, their bodies are also where the upper-caste societies deliver abuse and caste violence" (142). She writes about the heinous practice how the upper caste people would sleep with a young Dalit bride on her wedding night. An upper caste person could rape her any time he wanted. The husband of the woman had to spend her night elsewhere if he sees the footwear of an upper caste man. Mahtab Alam asks her about the domestic violence Yashica's mother had experienced and why did she decide to write about it in her book. She replies about it in her interview:

> But I had to do it because my mother and her unwillingness to compromise with my education and freedoms allowed me to become the person who could grow up and write this book. Also, as I was discarding my shame around caste and even my lower class, I also gained pride in my mother's

> struggle, in her resilience and grit and her endless resolve to somehow never give up. (*The Wire* n. pag.)

Thus, Yashica's memoir is an authentic account of the hurdles she faced in her life. She has written all her experiences since her childhood to her adulthood in this memoir. This book has received many positive reviews and only a few negative reviews have been received. Some people try to attack her that is trying to win the sympathy of the people by narrating her personal life. However, this book is not a complete depiction but a glimpse of Dalit women's struggle in India. She writes in the "Epilogue" about this memoir:

> A memoir, it details my own experiences, those of my family and goes deep into the areas of Indian society I am familiar with, as well as those aspects of Dalit society and living that I have been interested in and studied. What it is not is a comprehensive history of Dalits in India and it should not be taken as such. There are many aspects of the Dalit experience that lie outside the scope of this book. (180)

Works Cited

Alam, Mahtab. Interview. "But You Don't Look like a Dalit: Yashica Dutt on *Coming Out as Dalit*." 24 Mar. 2019. https://thewire.in/caste/coming-out-as-dalit-yashica-dutt. Accessed 25 Sept., 2020.

Deodhar, Neerja. "Yashica Dutt on her decision to come out as Dalit: The truth was out, I didn't feel the need to hide". May 17, 2019. https://www.firstpost.com/living/yashica-dutt-on-her-decision-to-come-out-as-dalit-the-truth-was-out-i-didnt-feel-the-need-to-hide-6631961.html. Accessed 30 July, 2020.

Dutt, Yashica. *Coming Out as Dalit: A Memoir*. New Delhi: Aleph Book Company, 2019.

Naik, Purnachandra. "A New Note to the Polyphony." *Economic & Political Weekly*. 20 July, 2019, Vol. IV, No. 29. pp. 20-22. Accessed 20 July, 2020.

22

From Rejection to Resistance: Self-Assertion in Select Dalit Women's Testimonios

Dr S. R. Chaitra

Dalit Literature deals with the atrocities and inhuman subjugation afflicting the people born in the so-called 'low caste' according to the Hindu *varna* system. This compartmentalised rigid social structure in the Indian caste-based society is in existence from time immemorial thereby marginalising the non-Brahmanical notions. Dr Bijender Singh writes, "...the hegemony of the Brahminical literature was disrupted with the advent of Dalit writings" (15). Undeniably it is still prevalent in the prevailing era and has posed a difficult challenge for the socially segregated Dalits to claim their recognition in the mainstream culture. Their identity, existence, livelihood, chastity and dignity have been rejected. Thanks to the hardships and intelligence of Dr B. R. Ambedkar that Dalits have been legally recognised and liberated from the shackles of untouchability. Yet, the struggle to gain equal social respect and recognition is still persisting. As literature happens to be a powerful medium of expression to voice their experiences, Dalits have contributed to the emergence of a literature by voicing their plight in the form of various genres. Hence literature has served as a platform for the voiceless to articulate their difficult, disabled, depressed, degraded, dehumanised, depolarised, debased and demeaning existence of their downtrodden and underprivileged life. Ruman Sutradhar states that at a time when there were no means of communication with Dalits, pen was the only solution as Brahmins controlled the media and therefore Dalits began their own magazines and wrote about their pain, not with ink, but with their blood, they wrote from their own cuts—the cuts being basically mental, with instincts of physical in them. Hence "Dalit literature is a struggle of new life. It is a soul of humanity. It is a life story which faced the states of death" (Awad 4).

Among the various literary genres autobiography is one such genre where the Dalits have revealed their self-experience, insufferable sadness and indignation. Commenting on autobiographies, Devy states:

> It forces on question of otherness, difference, marginality, cannon and the categories of aesthetics. In order to voice the protest of the marginalised Dalit literature often follows the subversive historiographic paths of personalising history. It is, therefore, perhaps, that autobiography is the most potent and often exercised form of fiction produced in Dalit literature. (272)

Dalit men's autobiographies focused on social issues and never mentioned the pitiable condition and dark side of Dalit woman's life in the rigid religiously and culturally bound patriarchal structure. It is only in Dalit women's autobiographies that the trauma of women's very existence including the social, political and economic deprivation because of caste, gender and sex comes to light. Women are cornered and pushed to the lowest level to suffer the traditional atrocities by the male-dominated society and are compelled to endure domestic violence, physical and sexual abuse in her daily existence. Their struggle to assert their identity along with their desire for social and sexual equality is voiced in their testimonios. This paper concentrates on select Dalit women testimonios which trace their bold journey from social rejection to resistance. According to Shweta Singh, Dalit woman's personal narrator challenge their absence in Dalit men's narrative and voice the concerns shared by woman across all strata thereby criticising the patriarchal structure in their society by reflecting the woman specific problems that articulate the trauma faced by these woman under the patriarchal rule exposing all kinds of exploitation and oppression that woman had to endure both within and outside the society (42).

Urmila Pawar, a Maharashtrian, in her autobiography *Aaydan* (2003) translated by Maya Pandit as *The Weave of My Life: A Dalit Woman's Memoir* narrates several incidents of her life where she suffers humiliation at every step of her life. Literary writing is an endevour to assert the self and transcend caste by resisting the rejection. Urmila Pawar writes, "What the writer writes about is social reality and not his/her individual life" (342). As a Dalit she is allowed to stand outside and her touch is considered as a stigma to the upper caste people. The upper caste people buy the weaved baskets and sprinkle water to purify it. She notices the behaviour of the people in the society and realises, "We were aware, without anybody telling us, that we were born in a particular caste and in poverty, and that we had to live accordingly" (96). As Dalit women endure triple oppression of class, caste and gender, Pawar exposes the varied degrees of social rejection faced by the men and women in society and within community. She discloses that separate dishes were prepared for males and females. As female children she and her two nieces were deprived of food and were criticised and compelled not to eat to their satisfaction. She also depicts the fate of her elder sister who died because of misery and pain. Her brother's wife too had no voice. Pawar herself suffered harassment in school because of her weakness of English language. Her worse suffering as a woman was her sexual exploitation by her uncle. Her wedding night experience was not happy. Pawar describes the problem of domestic violence suffered by many women of her community. She too was rejected for being a Dalit. She was resisted to do her higher studies by her husband as she was a woman. She is expected by her husband just to focus on her domestic chores and kids. Maya Pandit writes in her "Preface", "A complex narrative of a gendered individual who looks at the world initially from her location within the caste but also goes on to transcend the caste identity" (xvii).

Even with no support, she takes part in school and college education and undergoes inner transformation by reading the books of Babasaheb Ambedkar and other women writers. As *Aaydan* implies weaving of baskets, weaves the memory of her life by detailed account of her community and suffering of woman. She concludes stating:

> Life has taught me many things, showed me so such. It has also lashed at me till I beld, I don't know how much longer I am going to live, nor do I know in what form life is going to confront me let it come in any form; I am ready to face it stoically. This is what my life has taught me. This is my life and that is me. (320)

Jina Amacha (1986) is an autobiography by Baby Kamble which is translated into English by Maya Pandit as *The Prisons We Broke* (2008). Maya Pandit claims in her introduction that "It is the first autobiography by a Dalit woman not only in Marathi but in any language" (3). It is not just the realistic story of Kamble's life but of the Mahars of Maharashtra. Kamble takes pride in herself and grieves:

> Today, our young educated people are ashamed of being called a Mahar. But what is there to be ashamed of? We are the great race of the Mahars of Maharashtra. We are the real original inhabitants, the sons of the soil. The name of this land is also derived from our name. I love our caste name,

Mahar—it flows in my veins, in my blood, and reminds me of our terrific struggle for truth. (3)

Kamble narrates the religious, social and economic life where women would be possessed especially during the month of Aashad. She narrates how on the special day of this month women would give their saris to their daughters to wash and how the daughters would clean the sari and kill the lice stuck in the sari. The women played a major role in managing the household. When men did nothing or just sat and chatted, these were always the women who managed the domestic sphere by collecting firewood and sell them in the village. They suffered due to their religion that Kamble says, "for the sake of Kumkum mark, we lay our lives at the feet of our husbands" (41). Marriage is no blessing for a female. The girls are married off at the tender age of eight or nine which is their age to play with dolls. Their married lives are filled with insults by enduring the beatings of their husbands and in-laws and bearing the accusations all the time. During childbirth the women had to suffer due to malnutrition. Kamble too has been a victim of patriarchy. She was married at the age of thirteen. Though she had written about her society, he doesn't dare to disclose as she says that she "used to be scared of both of my son and my husband, scared of their reaction" (147). Getting education too was a difficult task for Kamble. The Ambedkarite Movement changed her life and of the community. The people were so impressed and influenced by his words that they wished to claim their existence in the society. The women made up their mind to send their children to school, girls gathered strength to enter the temple, boys arranged rallies, the women participated in the unions and elder women would take care of the household in their absence. The upper caste people criticized Ambedkar saying, "That Ambedkar has educated himself, that's why these dirty Mahars are showing off!" (103) Kamble's autobiography asserts her resistance to social rejection due to strong influence of Ambedkar.

In the Dalit memoir *Viramma: Life of an Untouchable* the traumatic experiences of being a woman in Dalit community is depicted. When Josiane Racine had visited India for her project on ethnomusicology, she happened to meet the multi-talented Dalit woman, Viramma and she depicted Viramma's life in this memoir. Viramma belongs to a poor serf community living under the *jajmani* system. The auspicious day on which she is born, Viramma's father, Nadesan was found sitting next to the door with "his head in his hands" (3) very clearly indicating his frustration of begetting a girl child and men sharply uttered "Hey, here's another little bitch been born!"(3). Viramma is oppressed under Patriarchal society from her birth. She is married off at a very tender age though she sobbed day and night and begged her mother not to give her away in marriage. She realises it to be the 'fate of women'. When Viramma attains puberty three years after her marriage, she is horrified to see blood without any wound. Her marital life was not happy life with a dominant husband and sex being 'too crude', 'too brutal' and 'too awful' to her. Paraya men would go to drink every evening and the women had to work at home after their day long labour and fulfill the demands of their husbands. The husbands would demand delicacies without providing the monetary needs to the wives. Besides this, the upper-caste men would sexually exploit the poverty-ridden untouchable women for their sexual gratification. Hence Viramma comments:

> Those gentlemen of the *ur* talk a lot about the uncleanness of Untouchables, but our holes always turn them on. We're the ones they get up to all their dirty tricks with; it makes you think our juices taste better than their wives! (52)

Viramma is a mother of twelve children though only three survived. She narrates the status of women in the patriarchal world by giving an instance of how her sister went running to tell her sister's husband that his wife was pregnant and how his friends seems to congratulate him saying, "Hey! Manikkam, you have done your work well" (31). Viramma narrates how they are exploited even in the hospitals. The exploitation is both social and sexual. By the narration of Viramma's life the undignified life of Dalit women is exposed.

Mukta Sarvagod's *Closed Doors* too brings out the vicissitudes of Dalit women's life. It depicts the theme of social exclusion of Dalits. The narrator reveals the pathetic plight and the struggle for identity for a female, that too, of a Dalit community. She reveals how difficult it was to get educated in a school in the midst of partial and discriminating teachers. The hurdles made her realise her identity as an untouchable. She was troubled and tortured by people of her own caste and upper-caste. The women of her caste abused her too because of her audacity to go to school and they had mutely accepted their fate of being victimised. Dalit women were the worst sufferers of the brutal patriarchy. Their passivity and patience were never acknowledged by the men. The women suffered and pledge themselves to fulfill the hunger of their starving children with the rotten grains thrown towards them by the upper-caste people. The upper caste men used them sexually and the women used them physically to do work. Mukta makes an attempt to educate the girls. She involves in Mahila Mandal, makes containers for wholesale merchants and when a merchant sees the photo of Ambedkar hung on the wall, he declines to take them as he would not use the containers made by Mahar women to distribute the *prasada*. When no one agrees to buy them, all containers were forced to be thrown away. *Closed Doors* records her sufferings, her urge for liberation and her attempt to deconstruct the social identity of women. She concludes saying, "The closed doors cannot remain closed any longer!" (161).

Kausalya Baisantri's *Twice Accursed (Dohra Abhishaap)* exposes the 'gendered caste experience' where the narrator fights against the societal barriers of caste, class and sex. The Dalit woman is the 'other' in the Dalit man's world. Patriarchy is so deeply embedded in the lives that the oppressed becomes the oppressor. The autobiography is a disclosure of three generations of women: the grandmother, the mother and the writer, and subsequently the three periods of history such as the pre-independence, post-independence and the present era. Irrespective of the generations and the era, the trauma of being a woman and a Dalit persists. She narrates an incident where a woman, Sakharam's wife is being teased by a supervisor and in turn the society blames the women such that

> After sometime they all have brought Sakharam's wife out. Only the blouse was on her body and this woman has a small cloth to cover her body. On her forehead there was white *bindi* and in her neck the garland of footwear. She was sat on the back of donkey and held procession in whole colony. The people of the colony shouted at her. (72)

When the lady dies out of shame, the man marries again in a short time. Men are insensitive to the problems and feelings of women. Even being educated and getting married to an educated Dalit activist, Kaushalya is an unhappy women. Her husband who later turns traditional is not different from other men who ill-treat women. She was forced to seek divorce.

Bama is the pen name of Faustina Mary Fathima. In her autobiography, she narrates her experiences of being born as a Dalit Christian and her failed attempt to uplift her caste people by becoming a nun. She reveals the discriminatory behaviour of the nuns towards the poor Dalit children and their partial nature towards the wealthy students. She states:

> All those people who had taught us, had taught us only that God is loving, kind, gentle, one who forgives sinners, patient, tender, humble, obedient. Nobody had ever insisted that God is just, righteous, is angered by injustices, opposes falsehood, never countenances inequality. There is a great deal of difference between this Jesus and the Jesus who is made known through daily pieties. (104)

If Bama's *Karukku* is an autobiography of her self, *Sangati* happens to be the autobiography of the community wherein she portrays how women suffered under the hands of men of their community and outside. Most of the Dalit women's experiences of the community are narrated to the author by her grandmother. Every woman is the victim of male-ruled society that woman are forced to be submissive. The narrator questions this gender discrimination as:

> Why can't we be the same as boys? We aren't allowed to talk loudly or laugh noisily; even when we sleep we can't stretch out on our backs nor lie face down on our bellies. We always have to walk with our heads bow down, gazing at our toes even when our stomachs are screaming with hunger, we mustn't eat first. We are allowed to eat only after men in the family have finished and gone what Patti aren't we also human beings? (29)

The heart rendering life experiences of Dalit women are narrated in the form of multiple events in the novel. Hence the author acknowledges as:

> My mind is crowded with many anecdotes: stories not only about the sorrows and tears of dalit women, but also about their lively and rebellious culture, passion about life with vitality, truth, enjoyment and about their hard labour. I want to shout out these stories. (ix)

The women work hard at home and labour in the fields of the upper castes, get abused and become victimised both physically and sexually at their professional as well as domestic spaces. Hence the grandmother says, "It is not the same for women of other castes and communities. Our women cannot bear the torment of upper-caste masters in the fields, and at home they cannot bear the violence of their husbands." (65)

Hence Dalit women's testimonios not only reveal the sameness of their sufferings of pain and anguish but also celebrate the power of Dalit women to endure and rebel. Irrespective of the gender, all Dalits have faced problems in gaining their education and their fight for recognition and equal status is still persistent. Dalit literature has served as a tool to rebel against exploitation. Dalit autobiographies are the testimonies that have made people cognizant of the self-elevation and self-assertion. They have exposed the cruelties and prejudice of the caste-ridden society and have subsequently created social awakening by instilling cultural consciousness. These testimonios are life narratives which have resisted rejection. Hence Dr T. Deivasigamani in his book *Dalit Literature* says:

> Now the subaltern communities have found a new name by coming together with the perspective, "Dalit is dignified" thereby rejecting the sub-human status imposed on them by the Hindu social order.

Works Cited

Awad, Eknath. *Jeevnath Ghetlela Parivartnach Varsa*. Dainik Vishw: Savidhan Samrat. Ed. Nirmal, Friday: 2nd August, 2013.

Bisantri, Kausalya. *Dohra Abhishaap* (Hindi). Delhi: Parmeshwri, 2015. Print.

Bama. *Sangathi.* Trans. Lakshmi Holstrom. New Delhi: Oxford University Press, 2005, Print.

—. *Karukku.* Trans. Lakshmi Holstrom. New Delhi: Oxford University Press, 2015. Print.

Deivasigamani, T. *Dalit Literature.* New Delhi: Trinity Press, 2016. Print.

Devy, G. *The G. N. Devy Reader.* Hyderabad: Orient Longman, 1992. Print.

Janu, C. K. *Mother Forest: The Unfinished Story of C. K. Janu.* New Delhi: Kali for Women, 2004. Print.

Kamble, Baby. *The Prison We Broke.* Trans. Maya Pandit. Hyderabad: Orient Blackswan, 2009. Print.

Limbale, Sharankumar. *Towards an Aesthetic of Dalit Literature: History, Controversies and Considerations.* Trans. Alok Mukherjee. New Delhi: Orient Longman, 2004. Print.

Pawar, Urmila. *The Weave of My Life: A Dalit Woman's Memoir.* New Delhi: Columbia University Press. 2008, Print.

Pawde, Kumud. *Antaspot.* (Marathi). Aurangabad: Anand Prakashan, 1995. Print.

—. "The Life of Dalit Woman." *Dalit Women in India: Issues and Perspectives,* New Delhi, 1995. Print.

Sarvagod, Mukta. *MitleliKavaade* (Marathi). Amalner: Chetashri Prakashan, 1983. Print.

Singh, Bijender. (ed.) *Dalit Women's Autobiographies: A Critical Appraisal.* New Delhi: Kalpaz Publications, 2016. Print.

Singh, Shweta. "Representation of Dalit Women in Dalit Men's and Women's Autobiographies." *The Delhi University Journal of the Humanity and Social Sciences.* Vol. I, 2014, 39-47. Print.

Sutradhar, Ruman. "Dalit Movement in India: In the light of four Dalit Literature" *IOSR Journal of Dental and Medical Sciences.* Vol. 13, Issue 4, April, 2014.

Viramma; Racine, Josiane and Racine, Jean-Luc. *Viramma: Life of an untouchable.* London and New York: Verso, 1997. Print.

23

Cognitive Mind and Dalit Self in a Select Women's Personal Narratives

Dr B. Manivannan

Using cognitive science this article tries to explore the dalit consciousness in the personal narratives done by dalit women writers. Tracing this unique self in dalit autobiography in general and dalit woman autobiography in particular is based partly on Foulcautian concept of historicity of knowledge and partly of cognitive process involved in knowing about the acquisition of that knowledge 'nowing about the acquisition of that knowledge ular is based partly on Foalcautian transforming it to a document' or representation or text. And, the article comprises objectively three parts: (1) defining the role of cognition in the domain of creativity; (2) mapping the complex entity of dalit writing as life narrative emerging as against the mainstream literature; and (3) analysing a select dalit women autobiographies as personal narratives redefined from the point of view of epistemic cognitive perspective.

To know is the basic instinct of cognitive mind that is functionally related to verbal or non-verbal interaction with nature subjects and objects in any concrete or abstract contexts. Cognitive psychology is the recent development in the field of functional approach to study particularly human mind. "Neisser defined cognitive psychology as the study of how people learn, structure, store, and use knowledge" (qtd. in Sternberg 16). In the mid of the 20th century there happens an academic exploration in cognitive science and it has been redefined as:

> ...a shift in psychology from the behaviourist's stimulus-response relationships to an approach whose main thrust was to understand the operation of the mind. Chomsky's critique of Skinner's book was only one of many events in the 1950s that reintroduced the mind to psychology. These events provided a new way to study the mind, called 'the information-processing approach'—an approach that traces the sequence of mental operations involved in cognition (Goldstein 12).

'The information-processing' has a vital role leading to knowledge acquisition that cognitive psychology experiments to unravel the mystic relation between the function of language and the construct of various social contours and may also be considered a process, by which the transformation of ideas or thoughts is possibly created in any work of art.

Earlier the behaviourists have considerably contributed to the development of the behavioural psychology that tends to lead the researchers exploring the impact of environment on individuals. Skinner's (1957) observation is that men act upon the world, and change it, and are changed in turn by the consequences of their action. "Certain processes, which the human organism shares with other species, alter behaviour so that it achieves a safer and more useful interchange with a particular environment" (13). Eventually the creativity is an effect of cognitive task that relies on personal experiences and to Skinner (1971), "Those collections of personal experiences called history or with the distillations of experience to be found in folk wisdom" (10). In fact, history manipulated by human experiences is conditioned in terms of verbal cognition as representations and Richard Menary asserts:

> Humans manipulate their local environment with their bodies. They might directly manipulate the physical structure of the environment and they might use tools to do this. They create artefacts, such as tools and representational vehicles. Humans very often create and manipulate external representational vehicles to complete a cognitive task. In doing so, they are carrying out a cognitive practice which is governed by its own norms, which I call cognitive norms (6).

Also, states: "Cognition is simply defined as the processing of representations. This claim is usually coupled to an assumption about where the representations are located and I will call this assumption 'cognitive internalism'" (10). The process of representations is closely linked with creative tendency of an individual who is a unique part of a society. For, any creative work has its purpose that is measured by individual's social self or the collective selves of a mass. There is continuity in perceiving and knowing about new ideas derived from unusual circumstances or events which are rather political or cultural promoting the change in such knowledge construct that one in hundred shoulders the responsibility and the one is none but the creator emerging from the community. These creators are apparently strange enough to record the changes happened in their contemporary space and time. And, the three factors that determine the work of art are: the writer's racial memory, the present social milieu and the individualistic choice of the language used by the writer. In this regard, cognitive psychology supports to study the role of creative mind in representing the social issues in a creative text which is undoubtedly a culture text. To Csikszentmihalyi, "In psychology, creativity is usually defined as the production of an idea, action, or object that is new and valued, although what is considered creative at any point in time depends on the cultural context" (qtd. in Wissink 4).

Cognitive theorists believe that there is a kind of 'cognitive mechanism' explaining what happens in the mind during the course of creative process. Gabora insists the function of 'creative insight' while elucidating 'cognitive mechanism' and says: "The creative insight may take many forms: for example, an invention or scientific theory, story or myth, a way or moving, acting, or accomplishing something, or a way of portraying relationship and emotion artistically" (10). It is obvious that cognitive processes evolve and generate new knowledge from the existing one (Anwar and Khalil Ahmed 285). Thus, cognitive mind helps one to be creative and this is the cognitive process that involves in creative writing particularly any literary composition.

With this conceptual background of cognitive mind in creativity the next part of this article attempts to trace the emergence of dalit literature against mainstream literature. In general, any creative writer is consciously or unconsciously influenced by the knowledge he/she gained already forming, cognitively stating, the prime source domain from which the writer uses the elements for the making of writing. One of the providers of the knowledge source is reading which is also regarded as cognitive task and reading and writing are inseparable parts of creative writing. David Morely redrafts this concept as:

> Reading is a kind of rewriting but by many hands and eyes. Writing is only a more exacting form of reading, individual in its action and exactions. To become, and to remain, an original creative writer you must first become, and be, as original a reader, and pursue your individual taste with restlessness, competitiveness and trust in your intuition. Most writers agree that the best way to write well creatively is to write for yourself. It follows that the best way to read as a writer is to read for yourself. (25)

Moreover, the writer gains his knowledge not only through reading but also by interpreting the text using his/her personal exposure to critical thinking which one probably achieves by reading. And, no creative writer possibly exists without their efforts of transforming the information to knowledge of their own and so on to be wise enough to represent such knowledge system derived from the personal experiences that are encountered by the social events or culture politics. This is common either to mainstream writers or to alternative creative writers; but the latter voice for the marginalised community or suppressed social groups.

What makes the difference between these writers is that of resistance phenomenally experienced by such protesting creators against the traditional highbrow cult grand narratives. Primarily this is the experience of the author that matters: "Experience is not all about action and your physical reality, although it can be. It is also about your psychological reality; even your imagination and dreams. It is about your fears, uncertainties, failures, terrors, losses. Experience, for a writer, is an art of losing" (45). They are, no doubt, cognitive aspects that constitute the consciousness of a writer.

The subalternity is consciously attributed to the characters like Prometheus in Greek mythology and Jattayu, Ekalaivan and Karna in Indian legends, in sub-plots, only to strengthen the role of male protagonists of the core texts. Irrespective of languages, the popular classics of the world are mostly of male centered. The epic narrative of Homer or Valmeegi or Viyasar is one and the same in 'dealing with patriarchal and misogynistic ideologies which instruct that men were in charge and women were always subordinate to their male counterparts' (Meehan n. pag.). The ideological and hard-nosed discrimination between man and woman in terms of power becomes the knowledge source that in appropriate course of time has sharpened the creativity of woman writers proving not so inferior to male writers.

Thanks to post-structuralism as an intellectual movement, although absolutely against elitism, which has politically facilitated the post-colonial thinkers and writers who could tend to move from centre to tangential point giving importance to marginalised groups like subalterns, feminists, LGBT communities and thus born dalit writings. These writers are as Thalhammer *et al.*, define as "courageous resisters" and emphasise their stand:

> We define *courageous resisters* along three dimensions: First, they are those who voluntarily engage in other-oriented, largely selfless behaviour with a significantly high risk or cost to themselves or their associates. Second, their actions are the result of a conscious decision. Third, their efforts are sustained over time (4).

These traits are formative in their consciousness that strengthens the creative self to challenge against all socio-cultural-political environment which is not in their favour.

Autobiography or personal life narrative in the mainstream literary writing is composed as philosophical discourse. Because a note of philosophical insight blended with moralistic instruction is innate and unavoidable in the life stories of popular personalities. For instance, In *The Experiment with Truth*, Mahatma Gandhi asserts "... The experiments I am about to relate [in the Autobiography] are...spiritual, or rather moral..." (qtd. in Gangrade 1). 'Who I am' in an Autobiography of mainstream literature is a quest for self-realisation which is regarded as 'universality of Man', but in other it is social-realisation. Cavarero views this thus:

> We could define it as the confrontation between two discursive registers, which manifest opposite characteristics. One, that of philosophy, has the form of a definite knowledge which regards the universality of Man. The other, that of narration, has the form of a biographical knowledge which regards the unrepeatable identity of someone. The questions which sustain the two discursive styles are equally diverse.

> The first asks '*what* is Man?' The second asks instead of someone '*who* he or she is.' (13)

The translator's note for this book explains: "'who' someone is can be 'known' (although this is not epistemological knowledge) through the narration of the life-story of which that person is the protagonist (Introduction viii)". Thus, the subaltern self or dalit self or dalit woman self in personal narratives is exceptional as Gayatri Spivak construes subalternity with woman folk while reflecting on Mahasweta Devi's writings and critically enquires "can subaltern speak?" which has found an answer affirmatively that they can even write their life stories but in fragments. If the postcolonial study views that women are doubly colonised then dalit women would be colonised in multi-level. For, they too 'act or react on the world' with the knowledge of subaltern stories re-read or retold or politically motivated ideologies advocated by Indian social activist leaders like Phule, Ambedkar, in north and Ayothi Thas, Ayya Vaikundar and Periyar in south, diachronically forming their epistemic cognition, which in Moshman's diction:

> Epistemic cognition is knowledge about knowledge, especially knowledge about fundamental issues of justification and associated matters of objectivity, subjectivity, rationality, and truth. Research in developmental psychology since the 1960s has shown that adolescents and young adults often make progress from objectivist epistemologies, in which truth is deemed observable, provable, or known to the authorities; to subjectivist epistemologies, which see truth, if we even call it that, as constructed from, and thus determined by, one's point of view; to rationalist epistemologies, which, without any claim to absolute and final truths, maintain that ideas and viewpoints can be meaningfully evaluated, criticised, and justified. Epistemic development in adolescence is the potential outcome of active theorising about issues of knowledge rather than a

> universal and predictable result of increasing age. (*Encyclopedia of Adolescencee* n. pag.)

K.S. Kitchner also explains: "While cognitive and metacognitive processes appear to develop in childhood and are used throughout the life span, current research on adult reasoning suggests that epistemic cognitive monitoring develops in the late adolescent and adult years" (n. pag.).

Thus, the adulthood tapped by education and other social movements against Hindu caste system commonly in these dalit woman writers influences their self-consciousness to be aware of what the knowledge schema gained for their emancipation. These writers are rationalists whose knowledge acquisition is greatly analyzed by experimental psychologists working on epistemic cognition. Information about everything under the sky is now digitally available in every nook and corner of the world. Even Article 46 of Indian Constitution against Manu's law of the customary protocol in practicing caste system helps them develop their epistemic cognition socially. The social reformers cited have become iconic in their autobiographic writings representing the emergence of dalit self for social justice seeking caste equality in India. Article 46 reads thus: "The state shall promote with special care of the educational and economical interest of the weaker sections of the people, and in particular, of the scheduled castes and the scheduled tribes, and shall protect them from social injustice and all forms of exploitation" (qtd. in Parameswaran 157). Parameswaran justly points out:

> There are numerous articles that are made to protect equality among Indians. The articles that protect the lower caste people in the society are Article15, 16, 17, 19, 23, 25, 29, 38, 46, 164, 330, 335, 338, 341 and 366. The Parliament of India also passed an act called Untouchability Offence Act (UOA) to announce untouchability practice as an offensive practice. Government has taken many steps to eradicate the

> untouchability practice in India. Its efforts start from the textbooks of little children, saying, Untouchability is a sin, crime, and inhuman (157).

Even the godly figure of Lord Buddha has become core aspect of Dalit self defining the epistemic cognition. Most of the feminist writings or Dalit woman narratives are essentially autobiographical. The texture and structure of their personal stories are born out of their knowledge about the suppressed condition they undergo in their lives. Mostly these personal narratives are set against poverty by which the woman self has to endure the disability caused by the facets of economic, caste and gender. For instance, Urmila Pawar in her autobiographical writing, *The Weave of My Life: A Dalit Woman's Memoirs* (originally written in Marathi, title, *Aaydan*) describes an event happened in her childhood days:

> Kishore and her brother came, ate the cake, and went home after celebrating the birthday. Kishore's brother told his mother that he had seen photographs of Ambedkar and Buddha in our house. The next day, Kishore's mother came and stood at our door. Without even stepping inside, she started abusing us. "We did not know that you belonged to this particular caste! That is why I sent my children to you. From now on, don't you give my daughter anything to eat if she comes to your house. We are Marathas. We cannot eat with you." Before I could say anything, she had left! (202).

The episode of her life tale, on the one hand, elaborates the practice of caste hierarchy in society and on the other, the photographs of Ambedkar and Buddha are suggestive to deliberate the caste system as knowledge schema functioning differently in the minds of upper caste and outcaste. The personal note about Urmila Pawar, a prominent dalit activist and dalit writer in Marathi, is that at her 12th year with other people of her community including her family members adopted

Buddhism when B.R. Ambedkar addressed the dalit people to give up Hinduism. The 'Neo-Buddhist Community' is very serious about epistemic knowledge connecting the doctrines of Buddhism with the socio-reformist principles of B.R. Ambedkar.

On the other hand, Umadevi, an acclaimed Dalit woman poet in Tamil, reflects on Buddha's nirvana state realising through her personal experience as a protest against gender politics. The original Tamil title of the poem is "Buddha Nilai," rendered in English as "Nirvana's End" which reads in a surface level as a poem of a mystic state but it is metaphorical rather than philosophical; the poem leads thus:

> Even as it awakens to the bliss
> of the life beyond,
> the body struggles
> to free itself.
>
> A moment
> turn into an aeon
> devouring life in monstrous gulps
> till its very last breath
> takes the form
> of a disciple
> stammering in terror.
>
> Ascetic
> turns mystic
> in that half-second.
> The All-knowing Guru
> Enslaves the learner,
> injects him with
> *'knowledge'*.

> In the split second
> Being's
> Buddha's state
> comes to an end. (*The Oxford India Anthology of Tamil Dalit Writing* 31)

The "being's Buddha-state" in dalit woman's self is not of modernist concern for existentialist philosophy and it ironically subverts the absolute truth of *Nirvana* propagated by even the conservative disciples of Buddha whose path to truth becomes obsolete proving to be futile in 21st century. This needs to be re-questioned that how to delink the woman's body from the desire of man: "the body struggles/to free itself". Here, the body is the victim of gender discrimination which is socially constructed. This is the critical thinking of the dalit woman's self or her epistemic cognition which tries to prove through personal writing that all religion is dogmatic considering woman's body consumable. And, the traditionally contrived doctrines as teachings of "the all knowing Guru/enslaves the learner/injects him with/*'knowledge'* make the dalit women "courageous resisters" voicing not for women's liberty alone but for all human justice as Baburao Bagul, declared that 'Dalit Literature is but Human Literature'.

The body plays a vital role in the creative cognition of dalit woman. Sukirtharani, another dalit woman poet in Tamil reacts upon her individual self in the poem, "My Body" (original title, *Ennudal*) and the poem is a complete description of nature setting opening with the lines: "Through a mountain where small shrubs abound/flows a river" that symbolically mark the blend of nature's wilderness and her body. The speaker is independently in possession of her body and proclaims that man has no privilege over woman's body. Her body is inseparable from her 'self' as Chrisler opines:

> Without a body, there is no self. In the most basic sense, a living body provides a home for the self, and the brain creates

> the mind, which produces the sense of self. Experimental psychologists (e.g., Ferrè, Lopez, and Haggard,) consider sense of self to mean spatial unity between the self and its physical body ...even the basic understanding of body ownership (i.e., "This body is mine, or part of me.") is not a simple one; it requires complex cognitive interpretations of 'synchronous multisensory inputs from different modalities' (4).

The poem further expands the nature's wild outlook suggestively:

> ...
> Water spills over from the hollows
> in the rocks, and the cascade from the edge of cliffs.
> A tiger, replete from its hunt,
> wets its blood-smeared mouth
> at the swift water streams.
> As it climbs down, scarlet ash scatters
> From a volcano's gaping mouth.
> A vortex, whirling clockwise,
> agitates the earth. The day's heat
> dissolves itself into night's coolness,
> In the end. Nature becomes my body
> lying still. (*The Oxford India Anthology of Tamil Dalit Writing* 30)

In this context, it is just to quote the interrogation of Ortner: "Why is woman seen as closer to nature?" and answers thus:

> It all begins of course with the body and the natural procreative functions specific to women alone...this absolute physiological fact has significance: woman's body and its functions, more involved more of the time with "species life," seem to place her closer to nature, in contrast to man's physiology, which frees him more completely to take up the projects of culture (73).

Thus the poem figuratively speaks out that woman body and nature are procreative in nature and the poet's dalit self is cognitively aware of the fact that both are subject to exploitation.

In Bama's novel *Events*, (original title *Sangati*) the narrator of the life story recollects the bygone days in which the self of her girlhood represents all the girls of the street in the *cherri* where she lived and the cognitive self is no more of girls but of women discharging the responsibilities:

> In our streets the girls hardly ever enjoy a period of childhood. Before they can sprout three tender leaves, so to speak, they are required to behave like young women, looking after the house work, taking care of babies, going out to work for daily wages. (*The Oxford India Anthology of Tamil Dalit Writing* 160)

The protagonist's tale of her past is of sheer nostalgic depression of what she had lost and also of dalits' poverty state. As an adult she could transform her girlhood personal experiences into a cluster of knowledge and thus her epistemic cognition helps her record them in writing. Hence, these autobiographic notes occur in this narration of life 'events' are epistemic.

To sum up, critics are of the view that most of the women writings are based on their life stories and dalit women writings are not exceptional. In short, mostly dalit woman writings are autobiographic in tone. And, Brownley and Kimmich point out, "Autobiography...requires that the writer lay claim to subjectivity" (1). This subjectivity matters in constituting dalit self in a woman writer whose mind develops the cognitive task of knowing about the socio-cultural-economic-political environment which is creatively represented in her life story.

Works Cited

Anwar, Nida and Khalil Ahmed. "Creativity and Creative Innovation: Evidences of Cognitive Functions During Creativity with Reference to Machine Cognition". *IJCSNS International Journal of Computer Science and Network Security*. Vol. 17, No. 8, August 2017, pp. 285-289.

Brownley, Martine Watson and Allison B. Kimmich. *Women and Autobiography*. Wilmington, Delhi: Scholarly Resources, 1999, E-Book.

Cavarero, Adriana. *Relating Narratives: Storytelling and Selfhood*. Translated with an Introduction by Paul A. Kottman. London: Routledge, 2000. E-Book.

Chrisler, J. C., and Johnston-Robledo, I. "*Woman's Embodied Self: An Introduction.*" (eds.) *Psychology of Women Book Series. Woman's Embodied Self: Feminist Perspectives on Identity and Image*. pp. 3-14. American Psychological Association, 2018. <https://doi.org/10.1037/0000047-001> 10 July 2020.

Gabora, L. Cognitive Mechanisms underlying the Creative Process. T. Hewett & T. Kavanagh (eds.), *Proceedings of the Fourth International Conference on Creativity and Cognition*, 2002. pp. 126-133, E-Book.

Gangrade, K. D. *Gandhi's Autobiography: Moral Lessons*. New Delhi: Gandhi Smriti and Darshan Samiti Rajghat. <https://www.mkgandhi.org/ebks/GandhiAutobio_morallessons.pdf.> 10 July 2020.

Goldstein, E. Bruce. *Cognitive Psychology: Connecting Mind, Research, and Everyday Experience*. Third Edition. CA 94002-3098 USA: Wadsworth, 2011, E-Book.

Kitchner, K.S. "Cognition, Metacognition and Epistemic Cognition". *Human Development*. Vol. 26, No. 4, 1983.

Meehan, Dessa. "Containing the *Kalon Kakon*: The Portrayal of Women in Ancient Greek Mythology." *Journal of History* 7, No. 2, Bellingham, Western Washington University, Nov. 2017 <https://www.armstrong.edu/history-journal/history-journal-containing-the-kalon-kakon-the-portrayal-of-women-in-ancient> 09 July 2020.

Menary, Richard. *Cognitive Integration: Mind and Cognition Unbounded*. New York: Palgrave Macmillan, 2007, E-Book.

Morely, David. *The Cambridge Introduction to Creative Writing*. Cambridge: Cambridge University Press, 2007. E-Book.

Moshman, D. "Epistemic Cognition". R.J.R. Levesque (ed.). *Encyclopedia of Adolescence*. New York: Springer, 2012, pp. 847-853 <https://link.springer.com/referenceworkentry/10.1007%2F978-1-4419-1695-2_17>30 June 2020.

Ortner, Sherry B. Is Female to Male as Nature is to Culture? In M. Z. Rosaldo and L. Lamphere (eds.), *Woman, Culture, and Society.* Stanford, CA: Stanford University Press, 1974. pp. 68-87, E-Book.

Parameswaran, Pari S. "Dalit Consciousness in Society and Literature: An Overview." *Language in India.* 19.9. September 2019. S. Chelliah, editor. "Select Papers of the International Conference on *Paradigms of Marginality in Literature: Exploring the Nuances.*" pp. 155-158. <www.languageinindia.com> 11 July 2020

Pawar, Urmila. *The Weave of My Life: A Dalit Woman's Memoirs.* Trans. by Maya Pandit. New York: Colombia University Press, 2009. E-Book.

Skinner, B. F. *Verbal Behavior*. New York: Appleton-Century-Crofts Inc., 1957. Print.

—. *Beyond Freedom and Dignity*. England: Penguin Books, 1971. Print.

Sternberg, Robert J. and Karin Sternberg. *Cognitive Psychology*, Sixth Edition. CA, 94002-3098 USA: Wadsworth Belmont, 2012. E-Book.

Thalhammer, Kristina E. et al., *Courageous Resistance: The Power of Ordinary People*. New York: Palgrave Macmillan, 2007. E-Book.

The Oxford India Anthology of Tamil Dalit Writing. Ed. Ravikumar and R. Azhagarasan. New Delhi: Oxford University Press, 2012. Print.

Wissink, Geert. *Creativity and Cognition: A Study of Creativity within the Framework of Cognitive Science, Artificial Intelligence and the Dynamical System Theory*. Unpublished Thesis, Amsterdam, Department of Psychology, University of Amsterdam, July 10th2001. <https://pdfs.semanticscholar.org/d23c/f7922d25f58ea1f23eab8a7c57b6a3cd74e4.pdf1> 1 July 2020.

24

Convergences and Divergences of the Dalit Question in Literature: A Case Study of *The Bandit Queen of India: An Indian Woman's Amazing Journey from Peasant to International Legend*

Dr Aadil Amin Kak and Dr Deeba Sarmad

Caste in India is basic differentiation in society and as such, much has been written about caste in literature. Most of this literature now comes under the purview of Dalit Literature and is taught in Dalit Studies Centres or also under subcategory of Indian Literature. The current paper focuses on a major differentiation in these literatures, vis-à-vis the positionality of the writer. It tries to look at the convergence and divergence in literature about the Dalits written by Dalit women writers. Under the umbrella of this broader category, the paper also looks at the major divergences in the political ideologies vis-à-vis the Dalit question which is the Ambedkarite and the Gandhian attitude. The paper seeks to examine the question of Dalit lived experience via the radical feminist and subversive paradigm offered by bandit turned political Phoolan Devi.

Indian society is stratified not only economically and politically but more significantly socially also. The hierarchy of castes, which is a division of society into groups based on their traditional occupations, is both socially sanctioned and religiously followed. Etymologically, the word caste is of Spanish origin, derived from 'casta,' meaning 'lineage' or 'race' or a group with hereditary qualities. In loose terms, caste can be defined as hereditary endogamous group, having a common name, common traditional occupation, common culture, relatively rigid in matters of mobility, distinctiveness of status and forming a single homogeneous community. However, from the sociological point of view the social inequality and stratification caused by the institutionalisation of caste is the main concern. Dipankar Gupta (2000), one of the leading Indian sociologists, has defined social stratification as the ordering of social differences based on a set of criteria. Categories like caste, class, race, ethnicity, gender, among others, are markers of social hierarchy and differentiation in many societies.

Phoolan Devi's autobiography *I Phoolan Devi* has been written in 38 chapters preceded by a prologue and followed by an epilogue. Her life remains a series of pain. She narrates, "I had been crying calling, for my mother, and my father-in-law must have been afraid I would run away after I told him my husband has threatened to beat me" (*I, Phoolan Devi* 1).

Based on the nature of different situations, the meaning of the term "caste" keeps on changing. Its daily use, in the everyday life of social interactions, it is different from the one used in the traditional literature and its orthodox meaning. Caste can sometimes mean a small group of localised poor and ostracised people but can also refer to a collection of such groups. The term caste is used by sociologists and social-anthropologists in two different senses: it is used on the one hand to denote a type of class where stratification is sharply visible and the differences are rigidly foxed and on the other, it is used to define the traditional and regional social organisation found in the Hindu society in India. This is not to suggest that caste is a strictly Hindu phenomenon; it is prevalent in Muslim societies too but in the Hindu society it is more institutionalised and comes with a certain religious sanction. Max Weber, for example, stated categorically that "...caste is the fundamental institution of Hinduism" (qtd. in Leach 2). In the literature on caste and caste practices, there is a long debate to uncover whether the caste system is some unique social phenomenon or one of the manifestations of social stratification. Those who argue that it is a unique social phenomenon, almost entirely focus on the caste practices in Hindu society which is divided into four neatly defined categories based on their occupations. There are the Brahmins who are considered to be the purest of all, a priestly and academic class who don't do any physical activity. Then the second category is that of the Kshatriyas who are considered to be warriors. The third category in this hierarchy of castes is Vaishyas who include who form the agricultural and craftsman class. The fourth is called the Shudras who are at the bottom of this hierarchy and constitute the labour class profession. This classification called the *Varna* system in the Indian society is derived from the Hindu religious text the *Manusmriti*. However, this classification of the Hindu system in four *varnas* leaves out a significant chunk of the society. The people of the fourth category are called dalits or untouchables. This is here that the most striking feature of the caste system comes to fore.

There are those who argue that caste is one manifestation of the general theory of social stratification, comparable in many respects to hierarchical organizations elsewhere. In this vein, Berreman (1972) argues that "to define caste in terms of its uniquely Indian attributes eliminates or at least diminishes its use as a cross-culturally comparable phenomenon" (197). Berreman compared such practices of social stratification in other societies, majorly with the racial differentiation in the United States. However, here we focus on the caste system in the Hindu society in India and locate its origin and trace its history.

The Indian caste system is complex and follows an equally complex history. The social stratification is not restricted to the four categories explained above alone but within each category there are further divisions. These categories are called *jâtis*. Within a *jâti*, there exist exogamous groups known as *gotras*, the lineage or clan of an individual. The development of caste system does not seem to have one universally accepted trajectory of historical formation. However, there is this widely accepted notion that the earliest settlers on the land, the Indo-Aryans, might have actually established this system in India. As a result, they are placed at the highest ladder in this hierarchy. This constitutes the social-historical theory of the origin of caste system in India. The Aryans arrived in India in around 1500 BC. They disregarded the local cultures and began conquering and taking control over regions in north India and at the same time pushed the local people southwards or towards the jungles and mountains in north India. The Aryans organised themselves in three groups. The first group was of the warriors and they were called Rajanya. They changed its name to Kshatriyas later. The second group was of the priests and they were called Brahmins. These two groups struggled politically for the leadership among the Aryans. In this struggle the Brahmins emerged victorious. The third group was of the farmers and craftsmen and they were called Vaisyas. The Aryans who conquered and took control over parts of north India subdued the locals and made them their servants.

The religious theory of the origin of caste system states that the *Varnas* were created from the body of the Brahma, the creator of the world. The Brahmins were created from his naval; the Kshatriyas from his hands; the Vaishyas from his thighs and the Shudras from his feet. This is what sanctioned the role of priests, philosophers, and academics to Brahmins and the role of warriors to Kshatriyas. Hindu scriptures are also often taken as the source for the origin in caste system in India. These scriptures offer a clear and unambiguous sanction for the practice of caste. The first of the various Hindu scriptures, the Vedas, do not emphasise much on the caste and social hierarchy.

A similar line is taken in the Rig Veda. However, scriptures like the *Bhagvad Gita* and the *Manusmriti* essentially focus on social stratification based on caste and propound the establishment of four *varnas* as the creation of god. These texts are written in Sanskrit language and their origin dates back to as early as 1500 BC.

It is argued that the caste system was flexible in the beginning and people would shift from one caste to another merely by changing their professions. The famous Gupta Dynasty (320-550) was Vaishya and not Kshatriya. Many rulers in this period were also not from the castes who are supposed to be born to rule. Between 12th and 18th century much of what is known as India today was ruled by Muslims who sought to reduce the influence of the Brahmins, the priestly class.

However, this system was codified and further made rigid during the colonial times. The British, who were stratified on the basis of classes, tried to equate the Indian caste system with their own. When the British Raj began to take power in India in 1757, they exploited the caste system as a means of social control. The British allied themselves with the Brahmin caste, restoring some of its privileges that had been repealed by the Muslim rulers. However, many Indian customs concerning the lower castes seemed discriminatory to the British, so these were outlawed. During the 1930s and 1940s, the British government made laws to protect the "Scheduled Castes," untouchables and low-caste people. A movement toward the abolition of untouchability took place within Indian society in the 19th and early 20th centuries as well. In 1928, the first temple welcomed untouchables (Dalits) to worship with its upper-caste members. Mohandas Gandhi advocated emancipation for the Dalits, too, coining the term *harijan* or "the Children of God" to describe them.

The practice of caste and social stratification in India has been strengthened over the years. It manifests in almost every social aspect of life be it in education, public service, sports, or even armed forces. Discrimination based on caste has not waned even though many reformist movements tried to end caste practices. In the nineteenth century, Jyotirao Phule questioned the discriminatory social system which had rendered lakhs of people poor, ignorant and illiterate. He fought for equal rights and education for lower classes. In early twentieth century, Bhimrao Ramji Ambedkar catalysed political mobilisation of the oppressed. By then, the British had codified castes on the basis of occupation, and had placed the oppressed castes under a list called "Scheduled Castes," a term still in use today.

Most recently the focus on annihilation of caste returned after Arundhati Roy wrote a long introduction on the debate between Gandhi and Ambedkar, titled "The Doctor and the Saint". To understand the context of this very important book, it is useful to understand the caste system in the 1930s operated as the same way as race operated in the United States especially in the Jim Crow South. "Superior" castes (akin to whites in the Jim Crow South) were able to enforce an economic and social hierarchy through both oppressive social conventions and the threat of mob violence (when conventions were broken).

Gandhi wanted to do away with "untouchability", that is, the strict barrier between the people of the lowest caste (Dalits, or *avarnas*) and the remaining castes (*savarnas*). However, he did not want to mandate the abolition of caste entirely, as he himself was an orthodox Hindu. He believed that once untouchability was abolished, upper caste people should recognise that while people of all castes have equal standing in society, they are all suited for different tasks. This was largely in line with the "genetic thinking" prevalent throughout the Western world at the time.

Ambedkar's essay on the annihilation of caste was scheduled to be delivered to the Jaat-Paat Todak Mandal but was ultimately cancelled because it was deemed much provocative. The Jaat-

Paat Todak Mandal (which translates roughly to "the abolition of caste committee") was a group of Hindu reformers seeking to radically reform the religion to eliminate caste entirely. However, while they wanted to abolish caste, they were ultimately not willing to give up Hinduism, and some portions of Ambedkar's speech involved direct attacks on the *shastras*, to which there was significant objection. Throughout the essay, Ambedkar skillfully combines his attacks on the social evil of caste with an aspirational vision of what could come next. That is, as he argues forcefully against what is the "old India" (which his opponent, Gandhi, has idealised), he also begins to provide the material for the formation of a "new India". In one sense, Ambedkar can be seen as one of the first genuine nationalists—but one that argues for an inclusive nationalism of liberty, equality, and fraternity between all Indian people; which can only be achieved through the abolition of caste.

The caste system is still one of the central aspects of Indian politics, society and economy today. However, and thanks in large part to Ambedkar's articulation, there is most definitely a self-aware subaltern politics just as there is a broader sectarian/communal question that focuses on religion in general. However, both of these seem to prevent a conversation about gender rather than leading to liberal intersectionalities as they matter in 'the West'. The true liberation of India must involve the material freedom of women and girls. That is what it is to read Ambedkar now and learn from his example.

In the Dalit Pantheon, Phoolan Devi looms large as a mythic figure who provided a fitting paradigm of 'revolutionary' violence that has often been advocated as a means to emancipate Dalits. Her contribution brings to the mind that the untouchable Dalit's protests against caste violence that transcended the Gandhian consensual reformism marked by the passive 'harijan term'. Phoolan Devi's transition to violence points out that although anger is traditionally an emotion employed openly and demonstratively as an instrument to enact and enforce their domination, the Dalit can devise acts of 'emotion work' that subvert such mapping of social emotions. In her case, and all the proponents of Dalit revolutionary violence like 'Dalit Panthers' engage and confront the biased and sterile notions of 'axiological neutrality' of appropriating agency from Dalits. Rather, the adoption of revolutionary violence exhibits the experiential possibilities enabled by the Dalit revolutionary's personal and visceral exposure to emotion work enacted by social movements of Dalit upliftment.

Some excerpts from the book *The Bandit Queen of India: An Indian Woman's Amazing Journey from Peasant to International Legend*, show her transition from subaltern to Dalit revolutionary violence apparatus. The below excerpt provides an insight into the invisibility that comes allied with subalternity, and Phoolan as a woman becomes a double subaltern, objectified by male upper caste gaze:

> Phoolan was the daughter of a poor fisherman, born into one of the lowest castes so low, it was even beneath the Brahminical order. She didn't exist, unless it was to perform harsh or unpleasant chores or to satisfy the lusts of men belonging to wealthier castes. (Rambali's "Introduction" 9)

Religious scriptures are often used to justify subalternity, and as Marx said religion is the opium of mankind since it lulls the subaltern into complacently accepting the exploitative structures and strictures of society. The following excerpt demonstrate this employment of religion when Phoolan asks her father about God and His existence, "It was as if I wasn't allowed to exist in my village, as if my family was worse than the fleas on a dog. Was it just because we were mallahs, poor people? That was why I wanted to find God, to ask him" (*The Bandit Queen of India* 9). Her father would tell her the reality of her caste. She narrates it in her book, "That's the way it is, Phoolan. You have to bow down and touch the feet of those who are superior to you, because they protect you" (*The Bandit Queen of India* 21).

In her autobiographical account, Phoolan offers an insight into the repressed rage that finds little expression, as the subaltern struggle with meeting basic needs of life:

> I could climb trees better than other girls and I could run faster too. I could swim in the river and I could do all kinds of work. I could cut grass with my sickle and thresh it for the animals, I could carry heavy baskets and jars of water on my head. We didn't have very much to eat, so it must have been anger that gave me my strength. (*The Bandit Queen of India* 12)

Phoolan Devi acts upon her father's advice but she was born with a revolutionary zeal. She had never learn to succumb in life. She always fought for equality and justice. She writes in this context:

> It had always been so, according to my father. The poor must bow down and touch the feet of the rich. The poor eat a few grains of millet while the rich feast on mangoes. The pain of hunger in the belly of the poor produces fear and submission. I tried to submit, as my father said I should, but I was unable. I was like my mother. There was too much anger in me. (*The Bandit Queen of India* 21)

Some excerpts convey Devi's manifestation of anger perpetuated by enduring cruel poverty, constant humiliations, abusive marriage, few rights and fewer prospects. Submitting to the menace of child marriage and rampant toxic masculinity manifested in abusive marriages, and abandonment of women, is a common feature of the double subalternity that subaltern women have to suffer. An excerpt which proves the same is:

> But no one cared about the wishes of a girl, nor the wishes of her parents if they were poor and belonged to a lowly caste. The atmosphere changed in the village. I heard

> whispers as I passed. .... My grandmother had told me a girl ought to be married and should go to live with her in-laws before her periods started, so that there would be no doubt about her chastity. I had not yet had my first period, so I was still chaste in their eyes. (*The Bandit Queen of India* 141)

In a state of great class inequality, the bourgeoisie upper castes get to enjoy free and unpaid labour and benefit from the accruing of both cultural and material wealth. This system gradually becomes 'normative' and contributes to widening the gap between haves and have nots. Any attempt to alter this normative structure of exploitation is met with resistance and censure, as is proven by the following excerpt when she asks about the wages of her father and sister, when they worked for other people, and which the people did not want to pay:

> People threw me out, calling me insolent and saying I had been raised badly. They complained that I used bad language. But as far as I could see I was doing nothing wrong, simply requesting the money I was owed for my work. It wasn't bad language to ask for it loudly, with my head held high, and without fear. (*The Bandit Queen of India* 151)

Phoolan Devi was filled with pain when she peeped into the life of her family members. She wanted to get justice for the dalits by all means. She started this struggle when she was merely a child. She narrates, "I didn't think of what I was doing as rebellion; it was the only means I had of getting justice. But it was then that my rebellion began, when I was fourteen or fifteen years old and struggling to survive by any means I could. I was a woman who belonged to a lowly caste" (*The Bandit Queen of India* 154-155). When her father's neem tree was cut and sold by her cousin, she feels extremely broken, "I had been happy for a while, but this new pain, a crushing pain, the pain of being a slave, of being less than a dog, turned my stomach. I wanted to vomit. We were poor, and because of it we were powerless" (*The Bandit Queen of India* 61). Later she is kidnapped and raped repeatedly. In this way, Phoolan Devi was forced to become a bandit queen. Her vengeance by killing thakurs at Behmai village proves that even a weak person can retaliate if time is favourable for him/her.

Contrasted to Gandhi's participatory reformism, Phoolan Devi presents another paradigm of Dalit upliftment by seeking emancipation through symbolic appropriation of violence. Basing their political idiom in the revolutionary potential and agency of the Dalit proletariat, the response of Devi didn't just stand in confrontation with the Gandhian notion of the sterile 'harijan', but also illustrated the Dalit appropriation of democratic idioms of outrage and injustice. The peculiar type of emotion work performed by Devi and framing their anger as an outrage to moral values of 'established' hierarchies of society, highlights that the paradigm of the 'revolutionary violence' offers an intersection of outrage and the language of democratic rights.

The public display of anger by Phoolan Devi and her supporters entails a conflictual emotion—one the Mallahs were largely inclined to avoid in order to co-exist and avoid repression and further hardships. The open manifestation of anger and massacres perpetuated by Devi is an appropriation of upper class male prerogative that relies on coercion to cement its authority. Her actions, therefore, provide a key to map out emotive structures that form the bed rock of social structures and observe how vectors of domination flow into each other, in order to understand the counter-narratives offered by social movements. By inciting and motivating the powerless Mallahs to publicly demonstrate their sense of deep-rooted injustice felt, Devi offers a paradigm of Dalit subalternity that allows an emotive reframing of reality. This emotive reframing subverts traditionally received notions of reality, and disrupts the flows of legitimacy that legitimize narratives of oppression and subjugation.

Works Cited

Berreman, G. D. *Hindus of the Himalayas: Ethnography and Change*. Berkeley: University of California Press, 1972.

Devi, Phoolan Marie-Therese Cuny and Paul Rambali. *I, Phoolan Devi: The Autobiography of India's Bandit Queen*. Little and Bown Publishers, 1996. London: Sphere, 2014.

—. *The Bandit Queen of India: An Indian Woman's Amazing Journey from Peasant to International Legend*. Connecticut: Lyons Press, 2003.

Gupta, Dipankar. *Interrogating Caste: Understanding Hierarchy and Difference in Indian Society*. New Delhi: Penguin Books, 2000.

Leach, E. R. "Introduction: What Should We Mean by Caste?" In E.R. Leach, (ed.) *Aspects of Castes in South India, Ceylon and North-west Pakistan*, pp. 2-10. Cambridge: Cambridge University Press, 1960.

25

Celebrating Women: Gogu Shyamala Relives Her Childhood in *Father May Be an Elephant and Mother Only a Small Basket, But ...*

Dr Suchitra Gupta

Gogu Shyamala, an established name in the literary circles, is a dalit feminist writer, a philosopher, a poet who has written captivating stories on the dalit rural life in Telangana. She was the first dalit girl of her village to go to school and the only one amongst her siblings to receive education. Her firm determination not only led her to complete her higher education but also inspired her to write and to expose the incongruities of the life of the marginalised and earned her the title "Raichaitri" from the prominent Telugu author Gorusu Jagadishwar Reddy. He wrote, "She has built her childhood like a nest in her heart. What else might be there, waiting to come out?" (Ravindran n. pag.)

This paper is structured in three sections. The first section gives an introduction of Gogu Shyamala, her ideologies as an activist and as an author; the second section brings out the stoicism and resilience of a woman while traversing through the childhood of Gogu Shyamala in *Father May Be an Elephant and Mother Only a Small Basket, But ...* and the third section forms the conclusion which reinforces the superiority of a woman over man thereby celebrating her relentless struggle.

A highly respected activist and Telugu writer Gogu Shyamala was born in Peddemul village in Ranga Reddy district outside of Hyderabad in 1969. In search of social and gender equality, she joined left movement but soon abandoned it in utter dismay as the movement itself was not free from caste and gender discrimination.

A senior fellow at the Anveshi Research Centre for Women's Studies, Hyderabad, Gogu Shyamala, is a self proclaimed feminist. Her contribution to feminist Telangana Dalit literature is remarkable and impressive. Her writings focus on the women in Madiga household. Following the less trodden path she restrains from delineating her characters in either extremes—as metaphors of oppression and exploitation on the one hand and models of heroism on the other. To quote her, "There are two types of dalit narratives that you will read and hear about. Either the person is a hero who fought all odds or a victim. With my writing I try to present them as normal people like anyone else, who try and battle with the mainstream stereotype" (Nitin n. pag.). She projects them as outspoken, courageous, assertive with an indomitable fighting spirit. This defiance in Gogu Shyamala's writings can be traced in the works and ideologies of Bheem Rao Ambedkar, Maxim Gorky, Galima Nikolyava, who inspired her to raise voice against discrimination and exploitation.

Delineated in Telangana rural backdrop, Shyamala's writings furnish new perspectives towards understanding life, to emphathise with life in all its variations. Moreover, the free use of colloquialism and songs lend authenticity and regional element to her works.

Father May Be an Elephant and Mother Only a Small Basket, But ... a collection of twelve short stories by individual translators, is a landmark in Telangana dalit literature in translations. All the twelve stories portray the travails of the simple women of the Madiga community. Of this collection of short narratives, this paper takes for its study the first narrative titled *Father May Be an Elephant and Mother Only a Small Basket, But* ... translated into English by Diia Rajan.

Remarkable for its regional and universal appeal the work gives a panoramic view of her childhood days, of the life of Madiga women, Madiga community, its culture, the commradrie of dalit people, the layout of the village without any sugar coating. The regional effect is further augmented by the deft use of local vocabulary, beliefs and customs. The realistic depiction of the socio-cultural ethos in the text piques the reader to contemplate over the suffering of the protagonist.

Shyamala's childhood village is inhabited by Mala and Madiga community who are "untouchable village servants and agricultural labourers" (Shyamala 215). They lived in their separate 'Keri' away from the upper caste settlement. Shyamala herself belonged to Madiga community though says "I never realised that there was any discrimination as a kid. It was after growing up that I discovered" (Nitin n. pag.).

The narrative has a pastoral beginning with a wonderful description of the delighted children engrossed in playing their fill in the rains on the bunds outside the village. "We were lost in our game and nothing in the world could distract us" (Shyamala 1).

They sing and play "Kotlapeta market on your head a blanket, Sayalu, you run, I run Sayalu" (Shyamala 2). Shyamala recalls how they would play on the 'bunds' till it was time for their mothers to return. They would wait anxiously for their mothers to return from the fields not wary of the gathering clouds. We get a picturesque description of the gathering clouds, of the women returning from the fields walking one behind the other over the ridges of the fields and the children trying to identify their mother from the row. Elaborating on the scene, Shyamala says that despite the downpour the pace of these women remains the same. The stable pace of their walk speaks volumes of the resilience and stoicism which perhaps is the aftermath of their continuous struggle for survival. Shyamala in an interview has said, "I remember (women) agricultural labourers who would gather together, make sure that all the work was done and ensure that the landlords gave them every rupee they earned. I always saw them being bold and courageous. But that does not deny the difficulties that they face living in a patriarchal society." (Nitin n. pag.) As protection from the rain and the chill, the women cover their heads with home-made "Kulla". A necessity gradually transforms into a culture—Madiga culture. Young Shyamala loved wearing 'Kulla' as it made her feel like a princess: "I would drape my head with it and pretend I was a princess" (Shyamala 3).

We have tender moments of the child meeting her mother half way, mother chiding her child for getting drenched in the rain for no purpose and neglecting the young siblings at home. "She was not at all pleased to see me drenched in the rain. I rushed to her and clung to her waist" (Shyamala 3).

It is a universal and perennial truth that there are no working boundaries for a woman irrespective of her caste, her class or her nationality. No sooner the mother reaches home her domesticity overtakes her and she instantly starts heeding to her youngest son who had remained unattended the entire day. She gives some green gram as chewy to her children to momentarily gratify their pangs of hunger till the time dinner is cooked. She then tends to the water seeping through the roof and hastily puts vessels under the leaking areas. A sorrowful and pathetic picture. But Shymala infuses symphony to the water falling in the vessels, "Tapa tapa tan tan tin tin ..." (Shyamala 4). This "inventive oral quality" irrepressibly uplifts the grey atmosphere. There is little complaining inside the house where the focus is on action, on survival. Shyamala celebrates 'karma', the elasticised used of limited resources, the joy in work and the feeling of kinship in the terrible oppressed community.

The eldest son Ramchandra contributes to the family sustenance by tending to the cattle of a Reddy. Old Sangava does tit bit job at dorasani's house. For cleaning jowar she is given some roti of day before, some watery daal and some paddy. They survive on their daily earning, living life in the present and for the present.

The mother is shown struggling and battling to give her children a life of sustenance. The uncertain monsoon makes her anxious and she bursts out "This famine has come like Yama. People like us will survive only if the rains are good this year, otherwise a time may come when all of us will starve to death" (Shyamala 6).

The father has not been home for almost a year. He is falsely accused of theft and the fear of the wrath of Venkat Reddy Patel has forced him to leave his family and village. He is intensely missed by the family but the mother infuses hope in the family. "Next year your father will come back from the town. He will pay back the debts." (Shyamala 6) With unquestioning allegiance to her husband the mother curses the 'Patels' for their oppressiveness, "We devote our labour to the Patel and we have always trusted them. How can we steal from them?" (Shyamala 6).

One fine day the father returns. The mother was just about to cross the threshold with a basket on her head when the father comes. All are happy and jubilant. There is weeping, there is comfort, there are questions and there are answers. Neighbours join in the happiness of the family. They also advise the mother against putting down the basket without crossing the threshold as it is inauspicious "... walk a few steps ahead, empty it out and come" (Shyamala 6).

Jowar that is kept aside as seeds is grinded and roties made. As the old mother indulges her son, the neighbours too show relief at his arrival and concern for his welfare "Ningampalli Sayavana of the neighbouring Keri came asking "How are you

Balappa? ... If a person is alive we will meet him some day; only if he is buried, will we never see him again" (Shyamala 7). The old mother and the neighbours refresh him with the struggles and the survival of the family in his absence "These are the true mother and daughter-in-law .... your people! They looked after your piece of land, they brought up your three children" (Shyamala 7).

Carrying the celebrations forward and hopeful of better times with the coming of her son, the old mother expresses the desire to eat meat as all these days they been eating nothing but gruel "Today we have gathered a few more neem seeds .... We can buy salt, chilli, broken rice. Why not go to the butcher Ismail a buy a kilo of meat and make a curry!" (Shyamala 8). All are excited—the mother to feed the family and others to feast. Father, too, excited at the prospect of meat asks for money to buy toddy. When the mother tries to reason with him "My father pounced on my mother, you say, it's not fair? You have learnt to talk. What? Have I seen everything? How do I know what you have done? He kicked her hard on her back ... Father beat her like cattle (Shyamala 9) and continues to beat her black and blue. The marginalised have no voice even in their homes. Basically Madiga is a productive community where the work is not defined following the gender norms. Earlier, it was alright for a man to do the washing and for a woman to rear the sheep and vice versa. But as the civilisation progressed gender based division of labour took place robbing women of their freedom to assert. Caste and gender intertwine in a dalit woman's life. The entire family had waited eagerly for the return of the father. But what happens is that soon after his arrival he unleashes his anger on his wife who had sustained the family in his absence.

Children hide fearing their own safety. Neighbouring women try to rescue the mother. The old mother laments her son's behaviour "When you left us to wander around the country, she looked after your children and me. Anyone else would have left us at our fate. She kept all those who cast their eyes on her at distance and looked after this house, you jack ass" (Shyamala 10).

At this high point of tension, there is news of premature delivery of the eldest daughter. The tradition has it that the mother should help in the first delivery of a daughter. The mother has to go. There is no alternative. So now the wounds have to be taken care of immediately, "New mother needs her mother to wash her soiled clothes" (Shyamala 10). A mother can take care of the family in entirety. She is the epicenter of every household. Despite all patriarchy the father is incompetent to most of the needs of a family therefore the old saying "an elephant like father may go but the small basket like mother should stay" (Shyamala 10). With all social, political and cultural superiority man is inefficient as compared to women, who has the expertise of managing both inside and outside house activity. A woman is half the society and raises the other half. Her love for her family, children and her allegiance for her family surpasses all human limits. A woman, a mother is the noblest creation on earth.

Works Cited

Nitin, B. "For Gogu Shyamala, being Dalit and Women in Survival, Beyond Victimhood and Outside of It." *Dalit History Month*. www.thenewsminute.com. April 09, 2016.

Ravindran, Shruti. "The Subaltern Sings". www.openthemagzine.com. 7 April, 2012.

Shyamala, Gogu. *Father May Be an Elephant and Mother a Small Basket But* ... Navayana, 2012.

26

Pangs of Patriarchy and Casteism in Shantabai Kamble's *Amchya Jalmachi Chittarkatha: The Kaleidoscopic Story of My Life*

Dr S. Chelliah

Dalit Literature has brought out the voice of the suppressed and the untouchables since long time. Only a Dalit can understand the pain of a Dalit; that's why the upper caste people generally fail to think from their perspectives. In this context, Dalit women have to face many difficulties in their life because their problems start even from home. The men of the home do keep them under so many restrictions.

Human society has been divided into many parts and it is based on the nature of their works and religions. Religion shapes the life of a person to great extent. In ancient time, Chaturvarnya System of the society was prevalent in Hindu society. This system was based to bring balance in human life but some selfish people used it for their selfish motives. M. S. Rajpankhe also writes about the Varna system:

> Hindu is a typical religion based upon *Varna system*. It has gradation of four *Varnas* such as *Brahmin, Kshatriya, Vaishya* and *Shudra.* For every grade, Manu—the maker of this

> system—maintains different rule and regulations of the ways of life. (Rajpankhe 2007:132)

The fourth varna remained the mostly rejected and exploited one. Dalit literature emerged due to this fourth varna. Many dalit writers have written their autobiographies to bring out their pains in front of other people. Dalit women also did not lag behind and in this context, Shantabai Krushnaji Kamble is a well-known name from Maharashtra who was born in 1923 in a Mahar family. Her birthplace Mahud is in Sholapur district in Maharashtra. It is no doubt, that being a Dalit, she was born in a poor family where there was no any chance that Dalit girls may get education and live their life with respect. Their family belonged to a socially and economically weak community.

In her family also, there was no chance that Dalit girls may get education but Shantabai Kamble was an intelligent girl and that's why she gets a scholarship also in her school. At that time Dalit children were not allowed to sit on the benches with the upper caste children as Omprakash Valmiki and Laxman Gaikwad also write in their respective autobiographies. Urmila Pawar also writers that the women of her community were forced to do manual labour and the children were depended on their fate. In her time, Dalit children were forced to sit either in a corner or they have to learn everything only by sitting outside or away from other children.

Shantabai Kamble's autobiography *Majya Jalmachi Chittarkatha* (in English: *The Kaleidoscopic Story of My Life*) was published in Marathi in 1986. Earlier it was presented to reading audience in *Purva Magazine* in 1983. This autobiography was telecasted by the Mumbai Doordarshan in 1990 as "Najuka". This autobiography has been translated into English and French. Shantabai started writing it after her retirement. This autobiography has been prescribed in the syllabus of the University of Mumbai.

Dalit women have been depicted as helpless creatures in this autobiography and the low caste people are also suppressed, oppressed and tyrannised by the upper caste people. Everything has been described in this autobiography. Shailaja Paik writes that, "She emphasised that women have to manage everything, and work hard to get out of the mundane rut" (43).

Shantabai got never 'Shanti' or 'peace' in her life. Her life remained a constant struggle. She dedicates this autobiography to her parents who worked in the hot sun to feed their children. They had to work without water and food many times. But they were determined that they would try to save their children from this hellish life. That's why they decide to admit Shantabai in a school so that they may save her life from spoiling like them.

This autobiography opened the window for writing for other Dalit women writers. It is considered that it was the first Dalit woman's autobiography. In this autobiography, she calls herself Naja (full name Najabai Sakharam Babar, later changed as Shantabai Krishnaji Kamble due to her marriage). She has to bear the stigma of class, caste and gender. Thus, the triple marginalisation remains the main theme in this autobiography. She belongs to Mahar caste which was one of the biggest Dalit communities in Maharashtra.

Not only this, she was the first Dalit woman teacher in Solapur district. She joined as a teacher in 1942 and after two years training, she becomes an education extension officer in the Jat taluka of Sangli district and she retired from her service in 1981.

Dalit women have to face maximum problems in their lives just because they live in the community of the uneducated people. Education can make human beings sensitive for others and without education, there is not much difference between human being and animals.

Kancha Illaiah writes in his autobiography *Why I am Not a Hindu* that Dalit women are better also in some cases because they do not have to follow the rules made by the upper caste people. There are some social evils also in the Hindu society. Women are not allowed to remarry after the death of their respective husbands. In ancient time, Hindu women had to burn in the pyre with their dead husbands. Urmila Pawar also writes in this context:

> The Dalit woman in contrast to the Brahman woman was not bound by customs such as sati, child marriage, etc. The Dalit woman was not confined to the four walls as the upper caste woman. [...] She did not address her husband or elders with imposed veneration. (Pawar 1994: 84-85)

In this autobiography, Shantabai (Naja) describes her school experience how her school headmaster calls her one day and tells her that she will get a scholarship. The school headmaster tells her to bring her father so the official formalities may be completed. Naja goes to her house and brings her father. The headmaster tells his father Sukharam that the government will give Naja three rupees a month so that she may not face any difficulty in her studies.

The headmaster further instructs him that the girl should come to school regularly. He tells her that she should study well and if she gets failed, she will not get this scholarship. She was in sixth class at that time and she was to get scholarship up to seventh class.

Naja was the only girl in her class up to fifth class. In sixth class, there was another girl Shaku who was a Brahmin. One day she does not come to school and the headmaster sends her to Shaku's house to fetch her. When she reaches at Shaku's house, Shaku's mother yells at her because she was a Mahar girl, she shouts, "You daughter of a Mahar; stay there. You will trample the *rangolis*. (20). She tells her daughter to go with the daughter of Mahar. The words of Shaku's mother were piercing her heart.

Shantabai tells in her autobiography that her friend failed in the annual examination. Naja solved two sums out of three. When she tells her parents that she has been promoted to the seventh class, they become happy.

The issue of gender emerges as a strong motif in this autobiography. Naja had already three elder sisters and her parents wanted a boy for them. His father's reaction at her birth is totally disheartening and this conversation is itself a strong belief that the parents discriminate between boys and girls. Her father gets angry at her birth:

> Appa said, "All bloody girls. Granny, hand over that girl. And give me the pick and the shovel. I will go bury her.... she is a good girl. Two sons came after her. She is a fortunate girl." (21)

Thus, a female child is considered a burden in our society and in Dalit community, it becomes a double problem because the parents have to spend money on the marriage of a girl and then on dowry. Still they remain worried about her because she remains depended on her in-laws' family now. In this context, Naja was considered an unwanted girl at her birth but her actions and arrival brings some happy news in the family. Two boys are born after her and the family becomes happy to hear it.

Now Naja was doing well in her studies. She had proved it that the Dalit girls can excel the upper caste girls in their studies and they also have rights to get education. Naja used to go with her nephew Jalinder and all was going very smoothly.

After some time, the headmaster Patil was transferred from the school and new headmaster Kadam joined the school. He calls Naja and says that she must apply for migration in the nearby girls' school in Pandharpur. It is not good for her to study in this school because there must be other girls in her class.

Though, headmaster was perhaps saying keeping in view the better future prospects but literally, it was not easy for Naja because it was not possible for her to go to a remote school. It was very difficult for her give money for the fare on daily basis or to buy a bicycle. She tells about it to her father:

> 'Headmaster Hadam says to me you won't be able to study in the agricultural school. Go with your application to the girls' school in Pandharpur.' Appa said to me, 'Naja, we have no food to eat. We are the poorest of the poor. We know nobody in Pandharpur. How can you go to school in Pandharpur? Forget school now.' (22)

It was her journey of school life. If her headmaster had allowed her to study in the same school, she would have studied well but now she was helpless because her parents also did not have any money. She had to remain home. She would feel very bad when she would see other children going to school. Her father was also feeling bad that he is unable to help her. He says, "Naja, I too feel very bad that you have to stop school halfway" (22).

Not only this, gender discrimination also remains as a main theme of this autobiography. Shantabai tells the story of Akka's daughter Gomi who returns her parental home unexpectedly one day. When Akka asks her who has come with her, she tells her mother that she has come alone because her mother-in-law is harassing her. She was feeling much desperate and says that she will not return there because her husband does work if he gets, otherwise he remains idle in the home.

Deva's mother tells him that his wife might have gone to her parental home at Mahud. He comes there to see whether she has gone there or not. When he notices his mother-in-law in the home, he complaints that Gomi has come without telling his family members.

When Gomi is asked the reason of it, she tells that he has been entrapped in this marriage. Gomi reveals her problems to her family members. Akka says to Deva, "You are making Gomi work like an animal and your mother doesn't give her enough to eat. We don't want to send her back" (22).

Finally, he returns and he brings four men from his village so that they may help him. They sit in the square and discuss with Gomi's family. But keeping in view Gomi's problems, Akka does not listen to these people. All the men who had come to take Gomi back return glumly.

From this, it is clear that Dalit women's position was very bad at that time because they had to remain depended on the family of their in-laws. They had to do lot of work in the home and they could not get proper meals on time. There was nobody to listen to them except their parents. That's why the married girls would return to their parental home many times. But in the present time, there has been much change in their condition.

If a survey is done in this context, it is found that there is dearth of education in most of the Dalit families and it is the reason that most of the dalit families are depended on the wages. The earning heads of these families are drunkards, and the children and women have to work to run the family. Dalit men also have to take some risky jobs in which they lose their life and their widows are forced to become a labourer.

Shantabai Kamble's autobiography beautifully narrates the pictorial description of her childhood, her school experiences and the problems in getting education, but she keeps on struggling and finally becomes the first Dalit woman teacher in Sholapur district. Education has helped many Dalit people come out of their degraded life. Balbir Madhopuri also writes in his autobiography:

> I realised that life was a struggle and there was no escape from it. If I wanted to expand my horizons, I needed to put all the tumult within me into my writings ...(209)

Shantabai also faces many problems even after getting job due to her low caste. She joins the Ambedkarite Movement and actively takes part with her husband. She embraces Buddhism and she finds that her life has been changed drastically. Thus, Shantabai Kamble's autobiography *Majya Jalmachi Chittarkatha* vividly and realistically portrays the problems of dalit women.

Works Cited

Dangle, Arjun, (ed.). *A Corpse in the Well: Translations from Modern Dalit Autobiographies* (1992). Hyderabad: Disha Books, 1994.

Kamble, Shantabai. *Majya Jalmachi Chittarkatha.* Bombay: Popular Prakashan, 1986.

Madhopuri, Balbir. *Changiya Rukh: Against the Night.* Tripti Jain, translator. New Delhi: Oxford UP, 2010.

Paik, Shailaja. "*Amchya Jalmachi Chittarkatha* (The Bioscope of Our Lives): Who is My Ally?" *Economic & Political Weekly.* October 3, 2009. Vol. 44, No. 40, pp. 39-47.

Pawar, Urmila. "What Has the Dalit Movement Offered to Women?" *At Crossroads Today, Dalit Movement.* Sandeep Pendse, editor. Vikas Adhyayan Kendra, 1994. Print.

Rajpankhe, M. S. *Impact of Dr Babasaheb Ambedkar's Philosophy on Indian Writing in English With Special Reference to Subaltern Autobiographies,* V. U. Bhatkar and Ingole M. Z., editors. SRT College, 2007.

Index

D

E

F

G

U

V

W

Y